ICT Based Library and Information Services

6.6 Reader Collision

The signal from one reader can interfere with the signal from another where coverage overlaps. This is called reader collision. One way to avoid the problem is to use a technique called time division multiple access, or TDMA. In simple terms, the readers are instructed to read at different times, rather than both trying to read at the same time. This ensures that they don't interfere with each other. But it means any RFID tag in an area where two readers overlap will be read twice.

6.7 Tag Collision

Another problem readers have is reading a lot of chips in the same field. Tag clash occurs when more than one chip reflects back a signal at the same time, confusing the reader. Different vendors have developed different systems for having the tags respond to the reader one at a time. Since they can be read in milliseconds, it appears that all the tags are being read simultaneously.

6.8 Lack of Standard

The digital ID tags by RFID vendors are not compatible even when they conform to the same standards because the current standards only seek electronic compatibility between tags and readers. The pattern of encoding information and the software that manipulates the information differs from vendor to vendor, therefore, a change from one vendor's system to the other would require retagging all items or modifying the software.

7. [illegible] CENTERS

Today's [illegible] to increase [illegible] automation and self-service [illegible] their operations [illegible] all kinds of media easily [illegible] system.

ICT Based Library and Information Services

Akhtar Hussain

Ess Ess Publications
New Delhi

ICT Based Library and Information Services

ISBN: 978-81-7000-694-7

₹ 875/-

First Published 2013

Published by:
Ess Ess Publications
4831/24, Ansari Road,
Darya Ganj,
New Delhi-110 002.
INDIA
Phones: 23260807, 41563444
Fax: 41563334
E-mail: info@essessreference.com
www.essessreference.com

Cover Design by *Patch Creative Unit*

Printed and bound in India at Salasar Imaging Systems.

Contents

Preface

This book describes *usage of Information and Communication Technology in library and information centers*. This work would be found useful by students and research scholars in humanities and social science disciplines particularly B.L. & I. Sc., M.L. & I. Sc., & Ph.D. scholars and information professionals who aim to carry out a study in library and information science. This book would be highly useful to fulfill the research needs of scholars in others disciplines of social sciences as well.

The book has been broadly divided into nine chapters. Chapter-1 deals with use of Information and Communication Technology (ICT) in libraries and information canters. The application of ICT technologies have provided one of the best innovations in the history of libraries and it is changing the shape of libraries and role of librarians at unique way. The user information seeking behavior is also changing at fast rate. Use of ICT allows easy integration of various library activities, increases efficiency in acquisitions, access to data, cataloguing, classification, information retrieval and dissemination

Chapter-2 focuses the library automation software packages in India as well as developed countries. The impact of ICT in libraries and information centers, one of the greatest challenges before the library managers is the selections of good library automation software package which can be cater to the need of particular libraries. The study of the five software packages namely Alice for Windows, LibSys, SOUL, SLIM++ and Virtua emphases that each package has got its own capabilities and limitation. Virtua supports Unicode Standards. It allows for switching of keyboards. It is also facilitates entry of the Arabic, Persian, Hebrew, and Urdu records preserving their original scripts. Significantly these records can be viewed by the users in OPAC in the natural scripts. LibSys has got its uniqueness to run on any platforms which provides options to import data in MARC and non-MARC formats from established bibliographic databases. AfW and SOUL has a unique feature of tracing a document at a particular location in the library. SLIM++ has the capability of putting your library information on the www / Intranet. This module allows the users to login as a library member and view his/her loans and reservations.

Chapter-3 highlights that the Database Management Systems (DBMS).It requires a query language, a structured way for expressing search requests. Relational DBMS alone have a standard query language called SQL (structured query language). My SQL Server is a Relational Database Management System (RDBMS) that runs as a server providing multi-user access to a number of databases. In this chapter also discusses about CDS/ISIS & WINISIS software packages. Unlike Dbase or MS-Access, CDS/ISIS is not a relational database system, although it provides some relational facilities.

Chapter- 4 contains open-source software (OSS) tools for digital library management .OSS is available free of charge, and includes both the source code and the compiled version. Developers who accept the open-source concept believe that software is a common good that should be shared rather than sold for profit, and that it can best be adapted, improved and de-bugged by its users. To make this possible the users need access to the source code. DSpace and E-print are institutional repository software package. Koha is the first open source Integrated Library System (ILS), used world-wide by library and information centers. It is a one of the digital library open source programs for acquiring, organizing, storing and distributing the documents in digital format. It is also discusses about Greenstone, Fedora, WEBLIS etc. OSS packages for management of digital library system.

Chapter-5 RFID systems consists of three components (1) RFID tags that are electronically programmed with unique information (2) readers or sensors to interrogate the tags and (3) a servers or docking station on which the software that interfaces with the automated library system is loaded. This RFID technology may eventually replace the bar code and optical technology in library circulation systems. Tags are available in various shapes and sizes for use in a wide range of applications, with read/write capability for interactive application. The fact that high frequency radio waves can be used to track moving objects at a distance has raised concerns about privacy.

Chapter-6 in this chapter paper describes background, concepts, impact, features; development of social networking, various application domain of social networking and key applications of Web 2.0 services in libraries. The web was widely embraced by academia and librarians recognized a great information delivery system. The term Web 2.0 indicates the development of online services that encourage collaboration, communication and information sharing. It also represents a shift from the passive experience or read only web pages to the participatory experience or read write web pages. Web 2.0 services as forums, wikis, RSS, blogs, podcasting, video sharing, social networking, instant messaging; tagging and social bookmarking, etc. are increasingly embedded in many areas of life. Similarly, it is also used in all over the world to promote information services by librarians. Chapter-7 deals with the innovative technology based online library services. This chapter describes background, concepts, features, function, types of online search services; barrier of online services in academic libraries, and online libraries services in India and abroad and challenges to libraries.

Chapter-8 this paper describes background, e-resource management systems, need of E-Resources, types of e-resources, and features of ERM systems. The chapters presented are Digital Library federation (DLF) ERM initiatives, life cycle of e-resources, standard of ERM systems, organization of electronic resources, and challenges faced with ERM systems. It gives a reference framework for describing the electronic and web resources on the capacity building of libraries and information centers as well as the users. This work will function as underpinnings to the concerned aspects and setting up and utilization of e-resources in libraries and information centers.

Chapter-9 discusses digital preservation; it is the umbrella terms now apply to a wide variety of collection management responsibilities intended to preserve collections of print and non-print materials for future generations. This paper describes background, concept; objectives of the digital preservation. It also focuses the preservation requirement and strategy for the long-term preservation of digital objects.

(Akhtar Hussain)

List of Tables

List of Figures

[illegible]

[illegible] Open Source Software (OSS) [illegible]

[illegible]

[illegible] such as Libsys, SOUL, Alice for Windows [illegible] This chapter describes Koha, DSpace, E-Prints and Greenstone Digital Library software which is [illegible] digital libraries.

List of Abbreviations

AACR	Anglo-American Cataloging Rules
ACS	American Chemical Society
AGRIS	International Information System for the Agricultural Sciences and Technology
AIM	AOL Instant Messenger
AIP	American Institute of Physics Journal
ALA	American Library Association
AOL	America Online, Inc.
API	Application Programming Interface
APS	American Physical Society
ASCII	American Standard Code for Information Interchange
ASI	Archeological Survey of India
ASME	American Society of Mechanical Engineers
AV	Audio Visual
BUBL	Bulletin Board for Libraries
CAD	Computer-Aided Design
CALIBER	Convention on Automation of Libraries in Education and Research
CAS	Current Awareness Service
CCF	Common Communication Format

CD	Compact Disk
CDROM	Compact Disc-Read Only Memory
CDRS	Library of Congress Collaborative Digital Reference Service
CDS/ISIS	Computerized Documentation System - Integrated Set for Information Systems
CERN	Central European Research Network
COBOL	Common Business-Oriented Language
CORC	Cooperative Online Resource Catalog
CUP	Cambridge University Press
CUSAT	Cochin University of Science and Technology
DBAs	Database Administrators
DBMS	Database Management System
DDC	Dewey Decimal Classification
DELMS	Defense Library Management System
DELNET	Developing Library Network
DESIDOC	Defence Scientific Information and Documentation Centre
DLF	Digital Library Foundation
DMV	Dynamic Management Views
DOAJ	Directory of Open Access Journals
DOI	Digital Object Identifier
DSRC	Dedicated Short Range Communications
DTP	distributed transaction processing
DVD	Digital Versatile Disc
EAS	Electronic Article Surveillance
EBSCO	Elton B. Stephens Company
EDINA	Edinburgh Data and Information Access
EM	Electromagnetic
ERM	Electronic Resource Management

ERMI	Electronic Resource Management Initiative
ERNET	Education and Research Network
ESN	External Social Networking
FRBR	Functional Requirements for Bibliographic Records
FSF	Free Software Foundation
FST	Field Selection Table
GHz	GigaHertZ
GIST	Global Information Systems Technology
GNOME	GNU Network Object Model Environment
GNU	Gnu's Not Unix
GOI	Government of India
GPL	General Public License
GSDL	Greenstone Digital Library
HTTP	Hypertext Transfer Protocol
IASLIC	Indian Association of Special Libraries and Information Centres
IBM	International Business Machines
ICE	Interactive Connectivity Establishment
ICQ	Internet Chat Query
ICT	Information & Communication Technology
IEL	IEEE/IEE Electronic Library
IFF	Identify Friend or Foe (Radar)
IFLA	International Federation of Library Associations and Institutions
IGCAR	Indira Gandhi Center for Atomic Research
IGI	Instrument Ground Instructor
IGNOU	Indira Gandhi National Open University
IIITM	Indian Institute of Information Technology Management

IIM	Indian institute of Management
IIT	Indian Institute of Technology
ILL	Inter Library Loan / Lending
IM	instant messaging
INFLIBNET	Information and Library Network
INIS	International Nuclear Information System
INSPEC	Information Services for the Physics and Engineering Communities
IRC	Internet Relay Chat
ISBN	International Standard Book Number
ISDN	Integrated Services Digital Network
ISI	Institute for Scientific Information
ISN	Internal Social Networking
ISSN	International Standard Serial Number
IT	Information Technology
KDE	K Desktop Environment
KHz	KiloHertZ
LAMP	Linux, Apache; MySQL, PHP/Python/Perl
LAN	Local Area Network
LC	Library of Congress
LIS	Library and Information Science
LSDIS	Large Scale Digital Preservation Initiatives
MAN	Metropolitan Area Network
MARC	Machine-Readable Cataloguing
MBP	Million Book Project
MEDLARS	Medical Literature Analysis & Retrieval System
MEDLINE	Medical Literature Analysis and Retrieval System Online
MHz	MegaHertZ
MIMAS	Manchester Information & Associated Services

MIT	Massachusetts Institute of Technology
NACIDS	National Access Centers to International Database Services
NASA	National Aeronautics and Space Administration
NIC	National Informatics Centre
NICNET	National Informatics Centre Network
NINCH	National Initiative for a Networked Cultural Heritage
NISCAIR	National Institute of Science Communication and Information Resources
NISO	National Information Standards Organization
NISSAT	National Information System for Science and Technology
NUCSSI	National Union Catalogues of Scientific Serials (NUCSSI)
OA	Open Access
OAIS	Open Archival Information System
OCA	Open Content Alliance
OCLC	Ohio College Library Centre; Online Computer Library Centre
OCR	Optical Character Reader or Recognition
OECD	Office of Exchange Coordination and Designation
OLAP	Online Analytical Processing
ONIX	ONline Information eXchange
OODBMS	Object-oriented database management system
OPAC	Online Public Access Catalogues
OSD	Open Source Definition
OSI	Open Source Initiative
OSS	Open Source Software
OUP	Oxford University Press
PC	Planning Commission

PC	Personal Computer
PLoS	Public Library of Science
PURL	Persistent Uniform Resource Locators
RDBMS	Relational Database Management System
RDMS	Relational Database Management System
RF	Radio Frequency
RFID	Radio Frequency IDentification
RLIN	Research Libraries Information Network
SAARC	South Asian Association for Regional Cooperation
SDI	Selective Dissemination and Information
SGML	Standard Generalized Markup Language
SLIM	System for Library and Information Management
SMIT	System Management Interface Tool
SMS	Short Message Service
SNS	social networking sites
SOAP	Simple Object Access Protocol
SOFTNET	Software Technology Network
SOUL	Software for University Libraries
SUSHI	Standardized Usage Statistics Harvesting Initiative
TCP/IP	Transmission Control Protocol/Internet Protocol
TDMA	Time Division Multiple Access
TDO	Trustworthy Digital Objects
TLC	Technology Learning Center
UDC	Universal Decimal Classification
UGC	University Grant Commission
UK	United Kingdom
UNESCO	United Nations Educational, Scientific, and Cultural Organization

UNIX	Uniplexed Information and Computing System
UPC	Universal Product Code: another name for bar code
UPF	Universal Preservation Format
URL	Uniform Resource Locator
USA	United States of America
VHP	Very High Frequency
VSAT	Very Small Aperture Transmission
VSNL	Videsh Sanchar Nigam Limited
VTLS	Virginia Tech Library Systems
WAIS	Wide Area Information Servers
WAN	Wide Area Network
WLAN	Wireless Local Area Network
WORM	Write-Once-Read-Many
WWW	World Wide Web
WYSIWYG	what you see is what you get
XML	Extensible Markup Language

XML Extensible Markup Language

1

Application of ICT in Library and Information Centers

0. INTRODUCTION

Information and communications technology or information and communication technology, usually abbreviated as ICT, is often used as an extended synonym for information technology (IT), but is usually a more general term that stresses the role of unified communications and the integration of telecommunications (telephone lines and wireless signals), computers, middleware as well as necessary software, storage- and audio-visual systems, which enable users to create, access, store, transmit, and manipulate information. In other words, ICT consists of IT as well as telecommunication, broadcast media, all types of audio and video processing and transmission and network based control and monitoring functions. The expression was first used in 1997 in a report by Dennis Stevenson to the UK government and promoted by the new National Curriculum documents for the UK in 2000 (Wikipedia, 2012).

Information and communication technology (ICT) plays a vital role in bringing about changes in our society. As technology is getting more sophisticated and more affordable every day, the range of services that are provided also increases accordingly. Electronic technologies for collecting, storing, processing and communicating information are divided into two main categories: those that process information, such as computer systems, and those that disseminate information, such as telecommunication systems. The term Information and Communication Technology (ICT) is more commonly used. Whilst Information Technology (IT) has been the accepted term in the UK and USA, it is not the universal term: telematics is widely used in France, and Information is also used elsewhere in this sense (International Encyclopedia of Information and Library Science, 2003). In India the term IT and ICT are simultaneously used.

ICT has been one of the major factors causing changes in the way people communicate, locate, retrieve, and use information. Libraries and information centers have embraced the ICT more profoundly than many other fields, and most of them are currently using electronic products and services. It is evident that ICT has created a division in the modern society: information poor and information rich. The countries that had the ability to utilize ICT for information resource development have generated information-rich societies while those countries which were weak in utilization of ICT have created information-poor societies. As information is directly related to knowledge and skills which influence socio-economic development, one could hypothesize the relationship between information and development. This has speculated the assumption that information-rich countries have developed economies and information while poor countries have less developed economies (Yapa, 2003).

Because economy and information are closely related and information resource development leads to economic development, policy makers pay special attention to the development of information resources. It is recognized that ICT is a tool which could be manipulated effectively for information resource development. This explains why economists in the Developed World are interested in ICT. Library systems were re-structured to accommodate ICT in library operations, because of the belief that the success of a library can be measured by the extent of ICT use by the library (Yapa, 2003).

1. INFORMATION TECHNOLOGY

Information technology; a generic term that covers the acquisition, processing, storage and dissemination of information of all types textual, numerical, graphical and sound - and in all application areas e.g. banking, business, science and technology - not just librarianship and information science. The term is restricted to systems dependent on a microelectronics-based combination of computing and telecommunications technology. Has largely been replaced by 'ICT', Information and Communications Technology. Some of the modern and emerging fields of Information technology are next generation web technologies, bioinformatics, cloud computing, global information systems, large scale knowledge bases, etc. Advancements are mainly driven in the field of computer science (Wikipedia, 2012).

UNESCO defines Information Technology as "scientific, technological and engineering disciplines and the management techniques used in information handling and processing information, their applications; computers and their interaction with man and machine and associated social, economic and cultural matters" (Stokes,1985).

According to Online Dictionary of Library and Information Science define, "Information Technology is a very broad term encompassing all aspects of the management and processing of information by computer, including the hardware and software required to access it".(Joan M. Reitz).

The McGraw-Hill Encyclopedia of Science and Technology (2002) defines information technology as "the field of engineering involving computer-based hardware and software systems, and communication systems to enable the acquisition, representation, storage, transmission, and use of information." According to the Webster's New Encyclopedia, "Information Technology is the collective term for various technologies involved in the processing and transmission of Information they include computing telecommunications and microelectronics". A.L.A. Glossary defines "Information Technology as the application of computers and technologies to the acquisition, organization, storage, retrieval and dissemination of information".

The British Department of Industry, it defines Information Technology as "The acquisition, processing, storage and dissemination of vocal, pictorial, textual and numerical information by microelectronics based combination of computing and telecommunication".

Thus, IT allows easy integration of various library activities, increases efficiency in acquisitions, access to data, cataloguing, classification, information retrieval and dissemination. It eliminates uninteresting and repetitive work, helps to avoid duplications of efforts, increase the range of services, provides marketing opportunities, facilitates cooperation and the formulation of networks and resources sharing in libraries. These technologies enable users to have remote access to information and data from a variety of places, provide more up-to-date information and speedy, easy, around the clock access to information.

1.1 Growth of Information Technology

Automation in libraries first began in the 1960s and in the 1970s, libraries started adopting software applications and machine readable cataloguing. In the 1980s, networking technologies, optical discs, CD-ROMs and communications technologies were introduced. The primary objective of the early technology applications was to automate circulation, acquisitions and the catalogue to bring efficiency and effectiveness in library operations and services. The 1990s witnessed revolutionary changes in the application of ICT in libraries such as the internet, World Wide Web protocols, information retrieval standards, integrated library systems and online databases. The 2000s are an era of digital libraries, virtual collections, paperless environment and round the clock instant remote access to unlimited resources. The rapid advancements in computers and telecommunications, exponential growth of information and media, availability of online databases, reduction in hardware and software costs, passion of using the internet, provision of cost effective communication mechanism and growing user demands are the major factors responsible for the increasing use of IT in libraries around the world (McCallum, 2003; Moyo, 2004; Jain and Babbar, 2006; El-Sherbini and Wilson, 2007).

1.2 Information Technology For Library

The ICTs that are relevant to libraries include (Murthy, 1999): *Computer technologies:* its function and activities include database organization and management, library management and operation; *Telecommunication technologies*: its function and activities include library networks and information networks, etc.; *Reprographic technologies*: its function and activities include photocopy, microfilms, optical and digital reprographic technology, audiovisual, etc.; *Library technologies:* its function and activities include classification, cataloguing, indexing, abstracting, database creation, CAS/SDI, etc.; *Technical communication:* its function and activities include technical writings, editing, publishing, etc.

On the other hand Veena Saraf in her paper mentioned the following as part of ICT given by Siddiqui (Saraf, 1998,): Automation; telecommunications (networks);electronic mail, electronic bulletin and electronic conferencing; online searching; compact disk (CDROMs); telefaxsimile (fax); and personal computer applications.

2. INFORMATION AND COMMUNICATION TECHNOLOGY

ICT has transformed the way of collection, storage, processing, dissemination and access to information. Recent technological developments such as explosive growth of Internet and WWW, sophisticated search engines, fast processing power and reducing cost of the computers, high bandwidth networks and increasing number of electronic publications assist the libraries in providing extensive access to the variety of information sources and provide a way to enrich the teaching and learning environment. Accessibility to the required information at a fast rate as well as quick response to the query is the expectations of users. These factors are responsible for the changes in library environment.

ICT have transformed Library and Information services globally. It has changed the traditional practices of library and information centers in distribution of services to the end users. Now users can access to a variety of information and scholarly journals through online. ICT literacy is the ability to use digital technology, communication tools, problems including the ability to use technology as a tool to research, organize, evaluate, and communicate information and the possession of a fundamental understanding of the ethical/legal issues surrounding the access and use of information more easily than ever.

In ICT environment, every library grows in terms of reading material, equipment, space, staff, readers, etc. The library and information scenario is changing at a dynamic pace there is a paradigm shift from print media to web media; from ownership of documents to access to information, intermediary to end-user model of services, and from location of specific libraries to digital/virtual/ hybrid libraries. Similarly, there is a change in the needs and interests of the readers. Hence, the role of library and information professionals has also changed dramatically. To meet the current requirements, library professionals must be able to perform various tasks coping up with the changes in technological environment. However, the ICT has nowadays become an important technology in libraries and information centers as it plays a very important role in meeting information needs of the researchers and institution as a whole.

The term ICT is now also used to refer to the merging (convergence) of audio-visual and telephone networks with computer networks through a single cabling or link system. There are large economic incentives (huge cost savings due to elimination of the telephone network) to merge the audio-visual, building management and telephone network with the computer network system using a single unified system of cabling, signal distribution and management. This in turn has encouraged the growth of organizations with the term ICT in their names to indicate their specialization in the process of merging the different network systems.

Adeyoyin (2005) cites *Bayode* who defines ICT as "the acquisition, processing, storage, and dissemination of information by means of computers and other telecommunication equipment."

The Wikipedia free Internet encyclopedia defines "information technology (IT) or information and communication(s) technology (ICT)" as the" technology required for information processing. In particular the use of electronic computers and computer software to convert, store, protect, process, transmit, and retrieve information".

In keeping with their complex nature and multiple applications, information and communication technologies (ICTs) may be viewed in different ways. The World Bank defines ICTs as "the set of activities which facilitate by electronic means the processing, transmission and display of information" (Rodriguez and Wilson, 2000). ICTs "refer to technologies people use to share, distribute, gather information and to communicate, through computers and computer networks" (ESCAP, 2001). "ICTs are a complex and varied set of goods, applications and services used for producing, distributing, processing, transforming information - [including] telecoms, TV and radio broadcasting, hardware and software, computer services and electronic media" (Marcelle, 2000). ICTs represent a cluster of associated technologies defined by their functional usage in information access and communication, of which one embodiment is the Internet. Hargittai (1999) defines the Internet technically and functionally as follows: "the Internet is a worldwide network of computers, but sociologically it is also important to consider it as a network of people using computers that make vast amounts of information available. Given the two [basic] services of the system - communication and information retrieval - the multitude of services allowed...is unprecedented". ICTs, represented by the Internet, deliver "at once a worldwide broadcasting capability, a mechanism for information dissemination, a medium for interaction between individuals and a marketplace for goods and services" (Kiiski and Pohjola, 2001).

"ICT is an umbrella term that includes any communication device or application, encompassing: radio, television, cellular phones, computer and network hardware and software, satellite systems and so on, as well as the various services and applications associated with them, such as videoconferencing and distance learning".

From these definitions, some of the applications of ICT have become clear such as video conferencing and distance learning, both of which can be facilitated by the academic library. Other applications of the ITC specific to libraries could include: access to online resources on the internet such as e-journals, e-books and e-magazines, e-publishing; using CD-ROM for literature searches, access to local or network data bases on LAN (Local Area Network) or WAN (Wide Area Network), the opportunities for the application of the ICT in library and information centre especially in a developing nations.

3. COMPONENT OF ICTS

ICT is a broad term that covers wide range of technologies. It is the convergence of computers, communication and microelectronic-based techniques. The technologies and devices like Radio, Telephone, Telegraph, Fax, TV, Telephone, Mobile phone, Internet, WWW, Email, LAN, ISDN, Videoconference and Satellite communication Techniques are major part of the ICT. With the help of LAN, Library and Information centre users community easily shares the information. Telephone and another device play important role in library services like SDI, Inter library loan, reference services, and online information retrieval. ISDN has increased the capacity for data transmission which facilitated introduction of new services such as E-mail, Fax etc. Cheaper data storage media has increased the storage capacity of libraries (Antherjanam and Sheeja 2008).

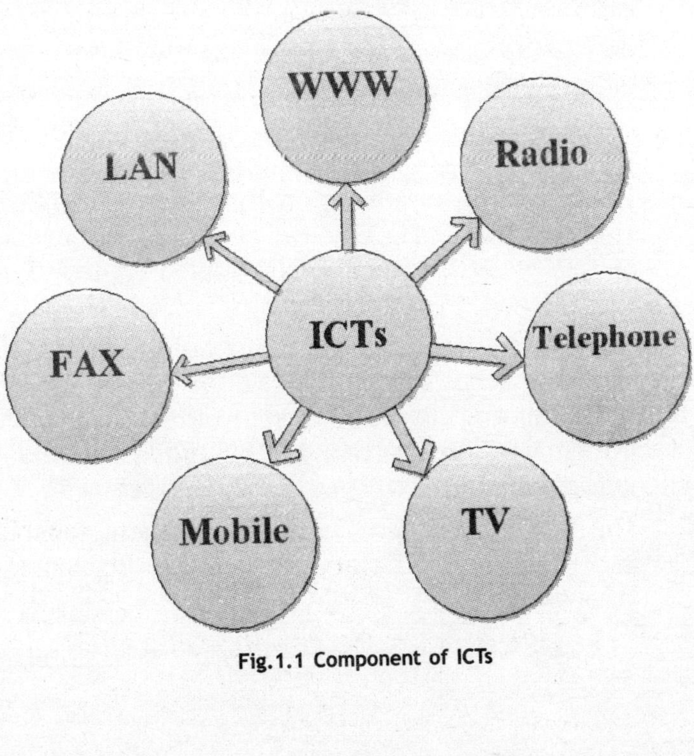

Fig.1.1 Component of ICTs

4. NEED FOR ICTS IN LIBRARIES

The application of ICT in libraries and information centers are very importance, committed to providing better library services to the users. Kanakachary (2002) stated the necessities of ICT in libraries, some of these are:

1. There are many advantages like speed, accuracy, and reliability in the process of information.
2. In the future there is also a danger of no availability of hard copies of documents, particularly the secondary sources that are available only on CD-ROM. Knowing this, continuing education about ICT for librarians is essential.
3. Due to the escalation in prices of periodicals and books, no library can afford to acquire all the publications, requiring active resource sharing through networking. To participate in the network, computerization of libraries is a prerequisite.
4. Many international databases like DIALOG, MEDLARS, INIS, AGRIS, etc. are delivering the information electronically. Unless the libraries are automated, there is no possibility for accessing the information from these global level databases.
5. The literature in almost all the fields is increasing tremendously and in a multidimensional way. Because of this growth, manual bibliographic control is not feasible and ICT is needed.
6. The information seeking behaviour of the users is also changing according to their varied needs. To meet these changing needs, storage capacities of information and retrieval techniques should be improved.
7. The quality, user friendliness, effectiveness, reliability and regularity of library services can be improved through ICT.
8. To be able to utilize the growing world of electronic

information, application of ICT is a must.

9. With the help of ICT it is possible to gain local, national, regional and international reputation.
10. To be able to provide round the clock access and service to users.

5. ADVANTAGES OF ICT

ICT helps in growth and development of libraries in different directions. Veena Saraf in her paper mentioned some of the advantages of ICT given by Cochrane (Saraf, 1998)

a. allows easy integration of various library activities
b. facilitates cooperation and the formation of library networks
c. helps to avoid duplication of efforts within a library and between libraries in a network
d. eliminates some uninteresting and repetitive work of librarians, i.e. a database created with bibliographical information can be updated easily and unnecessary information can be deleted with much less labour than in manual operation
e. helps to increase the range of services offered
f. provides marketing opportunity to its services
g. ultimately may save/generate money
h. increases efficiency.

Further, use of ICT in libraries enhances users' satisfaction. It provides numerous benefits and advantages to library users. Veena Saraf also mentioned some of the other advantages given by Hendersson: (Saraf,1998)

6. APPLICATION OF INTERNET AS AN ICT TOOL FOR LIBRARIES

The global network of networks called 'Internet' is an information superhighway that allows information to flow to unimaginable distances at an incredible speed. Internet has made all the information resources available through connectivity tools. These connectivity tools described in brief are as follows:

6.1. Electronic Mail (E-mail)

E-mail, meant for exchange of electronic information, is the most popular feature of the Net. It is cost effective and fastest mode of communication wherein one can correspond electronically with anyone anywhere in the world. Message can be sent or received in the form of texts graphics, images, photos and sounds. There are various possible usages of e-mail like communication, exchange of documents, entertainment, email discussion forum, collaboration and many more.

6.2. File Transfer Protocol (FTP)

It allows users to access and retrieve files at remote sites. This is both a program and a method used to transfer files between computers on the Internet. FTP sites may contain any type of files (binary or text). The files may contain books, articles, software, games, images, sounds, multimedia, course work, databases or any other thing.

6.3. Listservs/Mailing Lists

As well as sending e-mails to individuals it is possible to send them to groups using mailing lists, which are also called discussion lists. There are thousands of mail lists available on the Internet, and each is devoted to a particular topic and aimed at a specific audience. Mail lists can be used in a variety of ways. In general they provide a forum for requests for factual information; requests for advice and opinions or experiences; information about new websites, products and publications; information about job vacancies, etc. A mail server may be hosted by a public library to send up-to-date information to the user via e-mail regarding new arrivals, news release and so on.

6.4. Telnet (Remote login)

Telnet is a program that allows one to log into computers on the Internet. Once you are connected to another system, the same keyboard will be become the keyboard of the remote computer and you can use their resources or download the information available on the other side. To utilize this service, a telnet client is to log on to host computer on the Internet then provide the services of a terminal. It uses online databases, library catalogues, chat services etc.

6.5. Newsgroups or Usenet

Newsgroups or Usenet are similar to discussion lists in that they provide an opportunity to share with like-minded people, and libraries should introduce them to users.

It is a global electronic bulletin board, in which millions of people exchange public information on every conceivable topic. It is also called "Net news". It consists of thousands of news groups covering vast range of topics. The newsreader software allows you to post an article to any group for others to read.

6.6. Wide Area Information System (WAIS)

Wide Area Information Servers or WAIS is a client-server text searching system that uses the ANSI Standard Z39.50 Information Retrieval Service Definition and Protocol Specifications for Library Applications" (Z39.50:1988) to search index databases on remote computers. It was developed in the late 1980s as a project of Thinking Machines, Apple Computer, Dow Jones, and KPMG Peat Marwick. WAIS allows the users to search text, sound, or images from a single interface located anywhere on the network.

6.7. World Wide Web (WWW)

The WWW is the most powerful navigation tool on the Internet. It is based on a concept and technique called 'hypertext'. The Web is a client or server system used to access all kinds of information to anyone on the net provides access to information in the form of text, graphics, pictures and even sound.

WWW is an important tool for librarians, as it provides and extremely powerful method of organizing and providing access to information. It presents a wide variety of information resources to library users and all Internet users in efficiently and effectively.

6.8. Internet Relay Chat (IRC)

IRC is a service where user can talk on different channels by typing to people around the world. It is a public talk facility which can be used by anyone on the Internet at any time. Within IRC, there are many conversations on a particular topic or idea going on at any time. To use a client program connects to an IRC server, then enter IRC commands. Using IRC commands anyone can join a group of people and whenever wants move from one group to another (Rathinasabapathi, 2000; Khan, 2003; Panwar & Murthy, 2004).

7. APPLICATION OF ICT IN LIBRARIES

Information and Communications Technology (ICT) have transformed Library and Information services worldwide. The Internet has provided worldwide access to information. Technological innovation has dramatically increased the rate of conversion of knowledge, information and data into electronic format. Developments in the software arena has generated powerful knowledge management software which has transformed the way knowledge is organized, stored, accessed and retrieved (Tam & Robertson, 2002).

7.1. Collection Development

Information and communications technology has had a fundamental impact on library collection development policies. Collection development can be defined as the selection and acquisition of library materials based on current and potential user needs. It is concerned with managing the utilization, storage and accessibility of a collection.

Collection of reading material plays a vital role for the user of any library. Large numbers of documents are accessible on net; few of them are available fee and rest against payment. Libraries can access on-line the electronic journals via Internet. A number of electronic books, including encyclopedias are available on the Net. Acquisition of documents in e-form is becoming the order of the day as now-a-days there is a remarkable shift from the concept of ownership to accessibility. Collections of material through Internet save the space of the library. Postage stamp, binding, transportation cost are not required. Multiple copies of documents are not required, as any number of users can access them anytime from anywhere in the world.

One of the benefits of ICT is enhanced access to library services and resources. The academic library can expose its users to a much larger collection than it can house physically because users can access information remotely. With online access it is possible to accurately measure utilization of e-resources and that is invaluable in determining which resources to purchase. It is easier to search e-resources and access speed is greatly enhanced. Other advantages are that users can simultaneously access the same resource, and there are no incidences of lost copies or mutilated issues (Moahi, 2002).

7.2. Acquisition

With the advent of Internet, the job of acquisition librarian has become much faster and easier and has substantially reduced the paper work. The library is integrating electronic and Internet based information sources in its collection. The library has been keeping non-book materials like floppy disks, CD-ROMs and multimedia reference books in the collection. With the help of web, acquisition work has become very much simplified. Order placing, duplication checking, price checking etc are done very effectively using ICT technique. Online bookshops and publisher's websites save the time of the librarians. For the procurement of journals, order is placed in the prescribed format to the publishers through Internet. Invoices can be downloaded from the Websites that makes service faster and avoids postal delay. Through e-mail correspondence with book sellers and publishers become very easy and speedy. E-mail also helps in sending the reminders to the users and booksellers etc. Foreign publications can be acquired in a few days whereas earlier they used to take several months to reach the libraries. IT also helps in the process of the serial control in the university library. It helps in preparing union list of serials and helps in circulating via e-mail to the branch libraries.

7.3. Technical Processing

Reading material can be classified and catalogued with the help of on-line classification schemes and Online Public Access Catalogues (OPACs). There are many classification systems available on the Internet e.g. BUBL-user DDC, Cyber Dewey, Engineering Electronics Library Classification, Internet public Library and Gateways users Classification System etc. Internet sources like LC and OCLC or the publishers' catalogues are available on the Internet. Other cataloguing systems are interact, CORC and MARC adds 856 fields etc. Standardization and uniformity in classifying and cataloguing of the documents can be achieved as these are in conformity with international standards such as MARC format.

7.4. Circulation

With the computerization of libraries, the world wide OPACs can be accessed online to see the collection of their libraries. The users can see the particular book by subject/

author/title. Documents can be reserved are requested online using Internet facility. All the work of circulation can be done through computer except the delivery of the document physically.

6.5. Resource sharing

Resource sharing has become an important facility where Internet is being used heavily due to high cost of documents. Under this programme all networked libraries make their resources available on the Net to be used by other libraries. Union catalogues can be accessed, added and downloaded. Access to databases over networks e.g. Ohionet, WLN, OCLC and full text journals, ILL became very economical.

7.6. Consortia collaboration

Library consortia are a means to achieve more users for a lesser price and are finally beginning to become established in India. For the library it is more-for-less bargain strategy. Another initially libraries got involved in consortia in order to reduce costs particularly with regard to the acquisition of e-resources (Hirshon, 1999). Consortia development is thus an attempt to maximize limited resources through co-operation and resource sharing. In the consortia scenario the emphasis is on access to information rather than ownership (Darch, Rapp & Underwood, 1999). Consortia collaboration provides more power when it comes to negotiating contracts. It also provides a platform for libraries to co-operate in terms of services (Hooper, 2001).

Nowadays libraries also turn to consortia to provide advice and guidance in complex decision-making. The input of consortia is also valuable in terms of evaluating e-resources in terms of quality, different options e.g. whether to subscribe to journals or pay article-by-article (Hirshon, 1999).

7.7. User Education

User education is required for all library and information services and facilities, and far retrieving information precisely, exhaustively and expeditiously. In user education, instruction has been given to readers to help them make best use of a library. All the guides like know, your library policies, library rules, instruction can be put on the Web, particularly using Internet solutions.

7.7.1. Changes in Educational Environment

ICT have changed every fiber of society including education. Lifelong learning has become essential. A very competitive working environment has influenced this. Even educational methodologies have changed. Greater interaction between learner, educator and material is becoming the norm. Learners have greater choices in terms of curricula. The 24 hour networked classroom became reality leading to the birth of the virtual library. Network technologies and new educational methodologies have empowered learners, given them a greater measure of control and participation in the learning process and enabled network interaction with both fellow students and lecturers (Tam & Robertson, 2002).

7.7.2. Distance Education

In distance education, ICT can be used in preparing and presenting lectures. A distance education provider can create and use a portal to provide technical and methodological help for academic staff for developing ICT based courses and provide video conferencing facility for distance learners. New technologies driven by ICT innovation have enhanced the virtual delivery of academic programs and stimulated unparalleled growth of distance education at institutions of higher learning (Moyo & Cahoy, 2003). The phenomenal growth in distance education technologies has led to an escalation in the availability of online academic programs and a tremendous increase in remote users (Moyo,

2002). In order to support these programs academic librarians have developed excellent portfolios and programs for remote students.

7.8. Electronic Resources

ICT has fundamentally changed academic library collections. Forever gone is the era when an academic library's physical collection determined its stature. In the modern networked technological era the emphasis has shifted from ownership of physical resources to access to electronic resources that are globally accessible. There are huge amounts of unedited information on the Internet. There are countless Web sites and no single listing of them all. There is also the phenomenon of Web sites disappearing overnight that create problems in terms of access. There are huge amounts of unedited information on the Internet. There are countless Web sites and no single listing of them all. There is also the phenomenon of Web sites disappearing overnight that create problems in terms of access (Singh, 2004).

These days a single search can yield hundreds of thousands of items. The unfiltered nature of Web resources has made evaluation of these resources essential. One often finds that unlike in traditional printed media, e-resources found on the Web often lack important criteria such as author or date. Web pages because of its non-linear textual nature has added new effects to the search process such as sound, videos and access to thousands of items by clicking a mouse. These new elements imply that new sets of skills are required on the part of the researcher (Stapleton, 2003).

7.8.1. E-Books

E-books have numerous advantages. There are no printing, storage, warehousing and shipping costs. Consequently e-books can be published at costs much lower than conventional books. Additional advantages are online availability, keyword-searching capability, cross-referencing, adjustable fonts, electronic bookmarks and imbedded audio. Updating e-books will be easier than re-editing conventional books. From an academic library point of view benefits would include cost savings in terms of shelving, binding, circulation, overdue notices and management of fines. All needed would be a person to maintain the collection and a person to manage user accounts (Grant, 2002).

Print collections in academic libraries are very expensive to acquire and maintain. E-books are also environmentally friendly in the sense that no tree pulping is necessary to for its production. The flaws in current e-book technology will be overcome. When that day dawns e-books being much cheaper to produce and publish than printed books as well as economies of scale will tip the balance in favour of e-books (Grant, 2002).

7.9. Open Access Journals

The open access initiative is aimed at making scholarly research freely available via the Internet (Correia & Teixeira, 2005). Open access journals are journals available on the Internet for academics, researchers and the general public. The open access journal philosophy received a tremendous stimulus with the birth of the Public Library of Science (PLoS).

The first open access journal to emerge was PLoS Biology in the year 2003 which was received with great enthusiasm. In the publishing arena the Biomed Central publishing house embarked on free access to peer-reviewed journals. Recently the Directory of Open Access Journals (DOAJ) made open access journals available covering different languages and subjects (Falk, 2004).

7.10. Open Access Archives

Many leading universities are setting up electronic archives as depositories for their research output and are granting access to it. There are plans in progress to use theses archives as a platform to provide open access journals. The Massachusetts Institute of Technology (MIT) has made software (Dspace) freely available for managing electronic archives. Currently there are approximately 140 universities that have established open access archives. the development of publishing of Open Access journals from 1993 - 2009 published in 2011 suggests that, measured both by the number of journals as well as by the increases in total article output, OA journal publishing has seen rapid growth particularly between the years 2000 and 2009. It was estimated that there were around 19,500 articles published OA in 2000, while the number has grown to 191,850 articles in 2009. The journal count for the year 2000 is estimated to have been 740, and 4769 for 2009; numbers which show considerable growth, though at a more moderate step than the article-level growth. These findings support the notion that OA journals have increased both.

In Europe the Open Archives Forum was established. The goal of this forum is to establish electronic archives and make it globally available (Falk, 2004).

7.11. Online Database Searching Facilities

Libraries and information centers in developing countries like India, Bangladesh, Pakistan, South Africa etc. should introduce online database services to their users. As online information is growing very fast, it is necessary to introduce online database services as soon as possible so that users of variant interests can fulfill their information needs quickly.

7.12. CD-ROM Services

CD-ROM (Compact Disc-Read Only Memory), a remarkable breakthrough in IT, has been increasingly used since 1985, when it was commercially introduced in various fields, especially in libraries and information services (Siddiqui, 1991). Some benefits of CD-ROM are (i) access through personal computer,(ii)searching and retrieval of information rapidly,(iii) multimedia information can easily be stored, and searched in CD-ROM,(iv) user friendly,(v) permanent storage,(vi) durability,(vii) low cost and so on.

CD-ROM services should be introduced in libraries of all types. It opens the door to search a huge volume of information rapidly. Most of the reputed organizations in the world are producing CD-ROM databases, encyclopedias, and books for the sake of the users. So, it is an important service that can meet the users' needs to a large extent.

7.13. Information Services

Internet is playing a very significant role in providing personalized services such as Current Awareness Service (CAS) and Selective Dissemination of Information (SDI) at a minimal cost and time. Internet is very useful in reference service because it links the useful sites, directing the right sources, answering short range and long range questions. Important references sources like encyclopedias, dictionaries, directories, bibliographies, abstracts, indexes, current contents etc. are readily available on the Internet.

7.14. Current Awareness Service (CAS)

In the age of ICT most of the services in developed countries have become automated including CAS. Electronic methods make CAS easier to access and to offer to users. However, many of them are still very expensive and therefore out of reach for some libraries. The Internet, on the other hand, has not only reinforced the need to have access to information and to keep track of new developments, but has also introduced a number of interesting, affordable, easily accessible and user friendly CAS to keep track of developments. (Fourie, 2001). Some newer methods of CAS are :(i) book alerting services (ii) news alerts(iii) notification systems(iv) push services, etc.

Examples of these services include the Mining Company (http://www.minigco.com), Directory of Scholarly and professional E-Conferences (http://www.n2h2.com/KOVACS.htm) and the International Federation of Library

Associations and Institution's Internet Mailing Lists Guides and Resource (http: / /www.ifla.org/ifla/l/training/listserv/ lists.htm).

7.15.Selective Dissemination of Information (SDI)

In the age of IT SDI services involve the automatic notification of users when new records are added to the database. The records are matched against a search strategy reflecting the user's interest profile. In the case of SDI services, the search strategy is often referred to as the search profile (Fourie, 2001). These services are predominately used in special libraries, but public libraries can also offer these services to its community scholars.

7.16.Virtual Reference Service

Virtual reference service does not mean 24 h a day, 7 days a week (24/7 service) availability by default. Rather it means real time, synchronous service for users, available remotely and/or within the library. The library sets the hours and service levels it is willing and able to support. What hours to offer the service may be based on staff availability, peak traffic times on the library website, or the times questions are posed via e-mail (Ronan, 2001). Once a library begins investigating and offering digital reference (either real time or e-mail), the door opens for collaborative 24/7 access. Examples of collaborative services include the joint OCLC/Library of Congress Collaborative Digital Reference Service (CDRS) and Alliance Library System 'Ready for Reference System'. Advantages of virtual or digital reference service include the opportunities for the librarian to know what page a user is looking at, by viewing the browser remotely using the software to send a specific Webpage to the browser. Many programs allow one to walk through a process or search with the user via co-browsing or escorting, and most of the available packages provide the ability to e-mail the chat transcript and URLs visited to the user at the end of the session, either automatically or through a saved file that the librarian then passes along via e-mail. (Epps, 2002).

Not all modern information services and technological tools are discussed here, but some of the most prominent and essential services and tools are discussed briefly. No doubt to keep pace of IT and to satisfy the users it is inevitable to introduce ICT facilities in libraries in developing countries

7.17. Scholarly Communication

The rising of the Internet and subsequent Web during the 1990's has resulted in the decline of the printed journal as the principal medium of scholarly publication (Correia & Teixeira, 2005). The costs of journals have increased dramatically driven by commercial publishers trying to control research content. This resulted in depriving many researchers of access to needed resources. The Web has also made fast and easy electronic publication possible and has increased direct communication between researchers (Tam & Robertson, 2002:3).

Publishers immediately started making electronic versions of printed journals available on the Web. This was however seen as perpetuating the status quo in a new medium. Scholars started seeing in the new technology the potential to develop a new model for publishing research and an opportunity to return ownership of scholarly output to the rightful owners of the research. These sentiments were driven by shortcomings in existing scholarly journal publishing which were:

- The time to publish an article was to too long.
- The existing model demanded transfer of copyright to the publishers.
- A too rigid peer review system that tends to favour publication of authors from the more prestigious institutions.
- Journal prices had become unaffordable.

One of the outcomes of this dissatisfaction was the birth of the e-print which is essentially an electronic version of a research paper. E-prints lead to the development of e-print repositories that are an archive of e-prints accessible to the public. Some of the advantages of e-print repositories are the reduction of publishing barriers, increased visibility of research and rapid dissemination of research results to a wide audience (Correia & Teixeira, 2005).

8. CHALLENGES FOR LIS PROFESSIONALS

Rapid revolutionary advances in ICT have now transformed the way information is gathered, processed, organized, accessed and disseminated to the user community. Today, the libraries are increasingly viewed as outdated and under rated with the use of modern web based services. The pressure on libraries to modernize the way of delivering their services is now intense and more demanding. The user expectations on libraries to deliver high quality, comprehensive, user-friendly new generation services have grown tremendously in recent years. The survival demands change, updation and modernization. Libraries need to change quite dramatically to modernize almost every aspect of their operations, information resources and services in order to meet the rising users' expectations of the modern world. As the world advances, the library must also evolve and redesign their activities in order to deliver highly quality, need based value added services according to the expectations of today's library users (Chad & Miller, 2005).

In the Modern World, the role of the LIS professionals is adapting to changing technologies, information environment and customers' expectations. Library professionals are increasingly responsible not only to provide traditional library information services but also to deliver ICT enabled online information services according to the actual user needs. Librarians need to keep up with their users' expectations to survive and service them. Librarians need to become information knowledge navigators who condense data into usable information.

In the 21st century, everyone is going through many occupational changes to face the future challenges. Information and Communication Technology has transformed the role of not only libraries but also library professionals in the changing environment in which they now work. Library professionals are functioning under great pressure to become more efficient to deliver more effective services to the users. As the role of LIS professionals is changing to face the new challenges posed by ICT, they must be keen to stay at the forefront of innovation in the library world. LIS professionals need to be confident and competent that they can prepare for new challenges, deal with emerging technologies, manage change effectively and claim new professional roles. A well-informed competent and creative LIS professional shall play multiple evolving roles in the 21st century.

Today, Librarians have to play multiple evolving and expanding roles to face many new challenges in the dynamic technological environment. A librarian must be a professional expert, techno literate, web usability expert, knowledge manager, navigator, trainer, educator, marketer, service provider and many more (Ramana, 2006).

8.1. Future Strategies

There are a number of specific problems and issues facing library and information science professionals in India. Regarding financial aspects, stagnating budgets, increased prices of journals and inflation are the prominent problems among LIS professionals. In the area of human resources, due to the organizational policy of not filling positions, Indian libraries are facing the problem of inadequate and limited staff. The Indian government lacks finance for recruiting library and information science teachers having IT skills and for procuring the necessary IT infrastructure (Gulati, 2004).

The Government of India, recognizing that the remarkable growth the country has achieved since the mid-eighties in information and communication technology is still a small proportion of the potential to achieve, has resolved to make India a Global IT. Superpower and a front-runner in the age of information revolution. The Government of India considers IT as an agent of transformation of every facet of human life which will bring about knowledge based society in the twenty-first century. The brightest spot in the available superstructure for library and information services is the "Information technology action plan" submitted to the government of India on 4 July 1998 by the National Task Force on Information Technology and Software Development. One of the 108 action plans, number 73, deals with setting up of digital library projects at national and state level (Times of India, 1998).

Library professionals face complex challenges posed by rapid revolutionary advances in ICT. Libraries have to redesign their positions to meet evolving needs. Librarians need to implement new practices and new technologies, manage change, and improve performance and competencies to face future challenges of knowledge society. In its Five-Year Plan (2002-2007), The Government of India proposes that: Museums should be directed to place more emphasis on digitization and documentation of works of art as part of their planned activities. In the area of museums, the Archeological Survey of India (ASI) will initiate the process of modernization of galleries; digital documentation of antiquities, rare manuscripts, historical document/painting; and the publication of catalogues, museum guides, picture postcards etc. (PC,GOI, 2002-2007).

A national bibliographic database in electronic format would be developed to encourage resource sharing, networking and to improve reader services. The retrospective conversion of existing records in electronic format would be taken up in the National Library, the Central Library and the Delhi Public Library. Upgrading takes place of the conservation laboratory in the National Library as well as the oriental libraries such as Rampur Raza Library,

Rampur, U.P., and Khuda Baksh Oriental Public Library, Patna, Bihar.

9. COCLUSION

Today is an information age and a tremendous flow of information is emerging in all fields throughout the world. As such, it has become very difficult to manage the information manually due to the exponential growth of literature. The problem of providing timely information is not due to lack of information, but the way in which it is handled to enable the user to fulfill his needs. The traditional way of information handling methods have become almost ineffective in providing the specific information of an individual's interest. To overcome this problem, the Libraries, Information and Documentation Centers ought to change their attitude towards information handling. The user community is also expected to change their methodology, attitude and approach to information searching. ICT-based information handling is a viable solution in this direction. ICTs have enhanced the variety and accessibility to library collections and services to break the barriers of location and time (Shuva, 2005).

The library and information science professionals of these libraries should be made aware of recent advances in IT and how they can jump on the ICT bandwagon in order to reduce the prominent problem of the "digital divide". It is need of the day that every library should go in for computerization/Internet speedily to provide efficient and effective service despite of the difficulties coming in the way. It is also necessary to rebuilds; redefine the objective of libraries and the functions of the information professionals. The librarians have to develop skills to cope up with the changing scenario.

REFERENCES

1. Adeyoyin, S. O. (2005). Information and communication technology (ICT) literacy among the staff of Nigerian university libraries.

Library Review, 54(4), 257 - 266.

2. Antherjanam, S.D. & Sheeja, N. K. (2008). *Impact of ICT on Library and Information Science: Major Shifts and Practices in CUSAT Central Library.* Paper presented at the 6th International CALIBER-2008, University of Allahabad, Allahabad. February 28-29 & March1, 2008.
3. Commission, P. (2002-2007). Tenth Five Year Plan (2002-2007). New Delhi: Planning Commission, Government of India.
4. Correia, A.M.R. & Teixeira, J.C. (2005). Reforming scholarly publishing and knowledge communication: from the advent of the scholarly journal to the challenges of open access. *Online Information Review, 29*(4), 488-495.
5. Correia, A.M.R. & Teixeira, J.C. (2005). Reforming scholarly publishing and knowledge communication: from the advent of the scholarly journal to the challenges of open access. *Online Information Review*, 29(4), 349-364.
6. Darch, Collin *et al.* (1999). Dirt road or yellow brick superhighway? Information and communication technology in academic libraries of South Africa. *Library Hi Tech*, *17*(3), 285 - 298.
7. El-Sherbini, M. & W., A.J. (2007). New strategies for delivering library resources to users: rethinking the mechanisms in which libraries are processing and delivering bibliographic records. *The Journal of Academic Librarianship*, *33*(2), 228-242.
8. Epps, A. S. V. (2002). Virtual reference-the way of the future? Available at: http://caliban.emeraldinsight.com/vl=8058844/cl=31/nw=1/rpsv/librarylink/technology/july02.htm#article.
9. ESCAP. (2000). Are ICT Policies Addressing Gender Equality? , from http//www.unescaporg/wid/04/wideresources/11wideactivities/01cctegm/backgoundpaper.Pdf.
10. Falk, H. (2004). The revolt against journal publishers. *The Electronic Library,* 22(2), 184-187.
11. Fourie, I. (2001). Current awareness services in an electronic age: The whole picture. Retrieved May 8, 2012 from http://www.aslib.co.uk/pubs/2001/09/05/1.html
12. Grant, S. (2002). Ebooks: Friend or Foe? Book Report, 21(1), 50 Retrieved from http://tpsskbmt.wordpress.com/2010/10/08/research-article-ebooks-friend-or-foe/
13. Gulati, A. (2004). Use of information and communication technology in libraries and information centers: an Indian scenario. *The Electronic Library,* 22(4), 335-350.
14. Hargittai, E. (1999). Weaving the Western Web: Explaining difference in Internet connectivity among OECD countries.

Telecommunications Policy, 23, 701-718.

15. Hirshon, A. (1999). Libraries, consortia and change management. *Journal of Academic Librarianship, 25*(2), 124-126.
16. Hooper, T. (2001). Management issues for the virtual library. *The Electronic Library, 19*(2), 71-72.
17. Information Technology. (1986). In J. G. Allee (Ed.), *Webster's New Encyclopedia of Dictionaries*. USA: Ottenheimer Publishers Inc.
18. Information Technology. (2002) *McGraw-Hill Encyclopedia of Science and Technology* (9 ed.). New York: McGraw-Hil.
19. Information Technology. In M. L.-C. & T. M. Carter (Ed.), *ALA Glossary of Library and Information Science* (4 ed.). New York: ALA Editions.
20. Jain, P. K. & B., P. (2006). Digital libraries initiatives in India. *The International Information & Library Review, 38*, 161-169.
21. Kanakachary, M. (2002). *Information technology vis-a-vis the libraries*. In A. A. N. Raju, et al. (Eds.), New vistas in library and information science. Hakkani Publishers: New Delhi.
22. Khan, K. M. (2003). *Internet: An Indispensable Tool to Access Information in Libraries in the Age of Globalization*. Paper presented at the New Challenges in Information Management and E-learning in the Globalization: Issues and opportunities, Roorkee.
23. Kiiski, S., & M. Pohjola. (2002). Cross-Country Diffusion of the Internet. *Information Economics and Policy, 14*(2), 297-310.
24. Marcelle, G. (2000). Gender Justice and ICTs, from http://www.un.org/womenwatch_daw/csw/marcello.htm.
25. McCallum, S. (2003). 40 years of technology in libraries: a brief history of IFLA section on information technology. From: http://archive.ifla.org/VII/s21/publications/40YearsOfSIT.pdf
26. Moahi, K. H. (2002). Issues of just-in-time (access) v. just-in-case (ownership) for libraries in developing countries: lessons to be learnt from developed countries. *Library Review, 51*(7), 341 - 349.
27. Moyo, L. M. (2004). Electronic libraries and the emergence of new service paradigms. *The Electronic Library, 22*(3), 220-230.
28. Moyo, L.M. & Cahoy, E.S. (2003). Meeting the needs of remote library users. *Library Management*, 24(6/7), 281 - 290.
29. Moyo, L.M. (2002). Reference anytime anywhere: towards virtual reference services at Penn State. *The Electronic Library*, 20(1), 22-28.
30. Murthy, T. A. V., & Cholin, V. S. (2003). Library automation. Paper

presented at the First international CALIBER—2003, Ahmedabad, India.13-15 Feb.2003.

31. Panwar, S. & M., T.A.V. (2004). *Librarian's Guide to WWW*. New Delhi: Ess Ess Publications

32. Rathinasabapathi, R. (2000). *Internet: A Briefing for Layman* Paper presented at the 7th National Convention for Automation of Libraries in Education and Research (CALIBER-2000), Ahmedabad.

33. Reitz, J. M. (Ed.) Online Dictionary for Library and Information Science. From www.abc-clio.com/ODLIS/odlis_A.aspx

34. Rodriguez, F. & W., E. . (2000). *Are Poor Countries Losing the Information Revolution? mfoDev Working Paper*. Washington D.C.: World Bank.

35. Ronan, J. (2001). Chat reference: an exciting new facet of digital. Retrieved June 08, 2012 from http://www.arl.org/newsltr/219/chat.html.

36. Saraf, V. (1998). Dynamics of the information technology and its implications for library and information education in the millennium. *Bangladesh Journal of Library and Information Science*, 1(1), 5-14.

37. Saraf, V. (1998). Dynamics of the information technology and its implications for library and information education in the millennium. *Bangladesh Journal of Library and Information Science*, 1(1), 5-14.

38. Shuva, N. Z. (2005). Implementing information and communication technology in public libraries of Bangladesh. *The International Information & Library Review, 37*, 159-168.

39. Siddiqui, M. A. (1991). Can CD-ROM replace online? *INICAE*, 10(1), 40-47.

40. Singh, S.P. (2004). Collection management in the electronic environment. *The Bottom Line: Managing Library Finances, 17*(2), 55-60.

41. Stapleton, P. (2003). Assessing the quality and bias of Web-based sources: implications for academic writing. *Journal of English for Academic Purposes*, 2(3). 229-245.

42. Stokes, A. V. (1985) *Concise Encyclopaedia of Information Technology* (2 ed.). London: Gower. pp.114-115.

43. Tam, L. W. H. R., A.C. (2002). Managing change: libraries and information services in the digital age. *Library Management, 23*(8/9),369 - 377.

44. TOI Correspondence (1998). Information Technology Action Plan. *The Times of India*.9 July 2012, Retrieved from http://itt.nissat.tripod.com/itt9803/itap.htm

45. Wersig, G. (2003). Information Technology In J. F. a. P. Sturges (Ed.), International Encyclopedia of Information and Library Science (pp. 310). London: Routledge.

46. Wikipedia. (2012). Information and communications technology. Retrieved 6 May, 2012, from http://en.wikipedia.org/wiki/Information_and_communications_technology.

47. Yapa, N. U. (2003). Utilization of ICT for LIS with special reference to Sri Lanka. Paper presented at the First international CALIBER–2003, Ahmedabad, India.13-15 Feb.2003.

2

Application of Library Automation Software in Library and Information Centers

0. INTRODUCTION

We live in an information age, and libraries and information centers are expected to use Information and Communication Technologies (ICT) to provide information more expeditiously and exhaustively than before. Computerization of library "housekeeping" operations is an important activity in this context. "Automation," when used in a library or similar environment, refers to the computerization or mechanization of activities (Kumar, 1987; Harinarayana, 1991)

1. LIBRARY AUTOMATION

Automation is the use of control systems and information technologies to reduce the need for human work in the production of goods and services. In the scope of industrialization, automation is a step beyond mechanization. Whereas mechanization provided human operators with machinery to assist them with the muscular requirements of work, automation greatly decreases the need for human sensory and mental requirements as well.

Automation plays an increasingly important role in the world economy and in daily experience. (Wikipedia, 2011).

Library automation which started in late 70s in few special libraries has now reached most of the university libraries. The library automation is used to refer to the use of computers, either stand-alone or in a shared manner, to increase the productivity of library personnel and to provide new and/or improved library services to patrons. Library automation is an integrated library system (ILS), also known as a library management system (LMS), is an enterprise resource planning system for a library, used to track items owned, orders made, bills paid, and patrons who have borrowed. An ILS usually comprises a relational database, software to interact with that database, and two graphical user interfaces (one for patrons, one for staff). Most ILSes separate software functions into discrete programs called modules, each of them integrated with a unified interface. Examples of modules might include:

1. Online Public Access Catalogues (OPAC) (public interface for users)
2. Circulation (lending materials to patrons and receiving them back)
3. Cataloging (classifying and indexing materials)
4. Acquisitions (ordering, receiving, and invoicing materials)
5. Serials Control (tracking magazine and newspaper holdings)

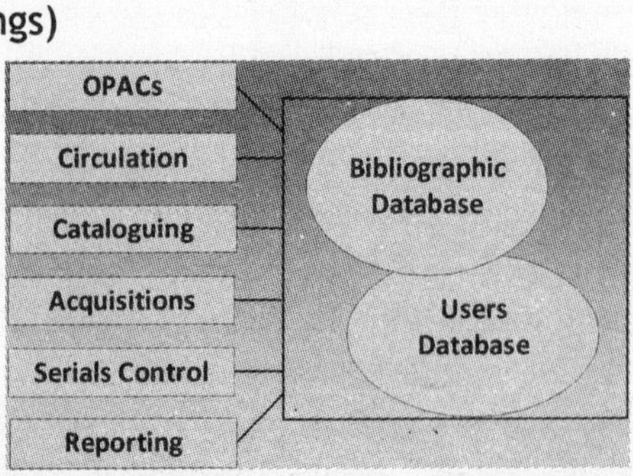

Fig. 2.1. Modules of Library Automation Software

Each patron and item has a unique ID in the database that allows the ILS to track its activity. Larger libraries use an ILS to order and acquire, receive and invoice, catalog, circulate, track and shelve materials. Smaller libraries, such as those in private homes or non-profit organizations (like churches or synagogues, for instance), often forgo the expense and maintenance required to run an ILS, and instead use a library computer system. (Wikipedia, 2012)

The factors necessitating automation of libraries and information centers are the subsequent: explosion of knowledge resulting in numerous specializations and flow of almost non-stop information; inability of users to explore unlimited literature; wastage of enormous precious time in handling routine and repetitive library operations; even the largest of the libraries cannot acquire and make available the entire published materials; and to facilitate easy, fast, and reliable sharing of resources between libraries, cutting across space and time.

The design and implementation of ever more sophisticated computer systems to accomplish tasks originally done by hand in libraries. Beginning in the 1960s with the development of the machine-readable catalog record (MARC), the process of automation has expanded to include the core functions of acquisitions, cataloging and authority control, serials control, circulation and inventory, and interlibrary loan and document delivery. The library automation field is currently dominated by a handful of systems vendors (Auto-Graphics, EOS International, Ex Libris, Follett, Innovative Interfaces, Polaris Library Systems, SirsiDynix, TLC, and VTLS).

Recent trends in library automation include the growing importance of "add-ons" mostly related to the delivery of digital content (link resolvers, portal and meta-search interfaces, and e-resource management modules often provided by third-party vendors), better integration with the Web environment (rewriting fat PC clients as browser applications, using XML and style sheets for display, and developing XML import and export capabilities) and for academic libraries, closer integration of library systems with learning management systems.

2. ANTIQUITY OF LIBRARY AUTOMATION

Punched cards were invented by Hollerith in 1880 and used in tabulating the US census data. The library at the University of Texas was perhaps the first to use punched cards in 1936 for circulation control. The Library of congress used the unit record machines for the production of catalogues in 1950. Many libraries in the US followed the system for automating their activities.

Library automation entered into its second era in 1960s with the advent of computers. The notable ventures were MEDLARS, MARC, etc. Until the early 1990s, "automating the library" involved generally the same features as those in place since the advent of machine readable cataloguing record in the late 1960s.Libraries created integrated text based systems using micro/mini computers in which traditional library housekeeping operations were computerized using the library's database as the foundation.

In the last decade, library automation has undergone a transformation that reflects changing definitions of library service in general and access to resources in particular. The introduction of global networking such as internet, cheap availability of technology and new media technologies made information more accessible.

Librarians often referred to ILSs as *library automation systems* or *automated systems* in the 1970s and early 1980s. Before the advent of computers, libraries usually used a card catalog to index their holdings. Computers came into use to automate the card catalogue, thus the term *automation system*. Automation of the catalog saves the labor involved in resorting the card catalogue, keeping it up-to-date with respect to the collection, etc. Other tasks automated include checking-out and checking-in books, generating statistics and reports, acquisitions and subscriptions, indexing journal articles and linking to them, as well as tracking interlibrary loans.

Since the late 1980s, window systems and multi-task have allowed the integration of business functions. Instead of having to open up separate applications, library staff could now use a single application with multiple functional modules.

As the Internet grew, ILS vendors offered more functionality related to computer networks. As of 2009[update] major ILS systems offer web-based portals where library users can log in to view their account, renew their books, and authenticate themselves for access to online databases. In recent years some libraries have turned to major open source ILSs such as Koha and Evergreen. Common reasons noted were to avoid vendor lock in, avoid license fees, and participate in software development.

3. GROWTH OF LIBRARY AUTOMATION SOFTWARE

While the software industry is a well-organized sector, library software is largely confined to some premier institutions and their libraries. Many of the library automation efforts use in-house expertise. Initially, only simple and important functions such as acquisitions, circulation and cataloguing were automated; integrated packages were implemented at a later date. These efforts generally led to the development of a total integrated system, or were used to convince the authorities to purchase library automation software from the market. In some cases, the vendor of the library automation software helped to convert the automated data into a compatible form for use with the new software. Both the machine-readable cataloging and common communication formats are used now to develop bibliographic databases. After the introduction of the CDS/ISIS software package from UNESCO in Indian libraries in the mid-1980s, National Information

System for Science and Technology, the Indian Institute of Science and National Institute of Science Communication and Information Resources organized a number of training programs on the application of CDS/ISIS to library activities. These courses, besides training professionals in using the software, have made them aware of the benefits of library automation. Another benefit of the courses was that they introduced computer culture among the library and information science (LIS) professionals. This also gave impetus to many institutions to develop their own library software while putting special emphasis on the routines and services important to those institutions. Thus, began indigenous efforts towards developing integrated library software packages in the country.

4. LIBRARY AUTOMATION SOFTWARE IN INDIA

With the exponential growth of digital information, libraries have to play vital roles in the community. India is experiencing the impact of new technology in every facet of information handling. There is a strong need to computerize library housekeeping activities and user services in the information age. In computerizing the library, it is essential to implement good library software that is user friendly. There are a number of library automation software packages in India. Some of the well-known library softwares of foreign origin are Alice for Windows, Techlib Plus, Virtua. Among the indigenous library software packages, LibSys (LibSys Corporation, New Delhi) is the widely used software. Other library software packages developed in India are DELPLUS(DELNET, New Delhi), I-Lib (Infobank, Nagpur), Libman (Master Software, Nagpur), Libtech (Libtech Software Developers, Wardha), SLIM 21 & SLIM++ (Algorhythems Consultants Pvt. Ltd, Pune), Softlib (Synchronic Library Software, Nagpur), SOUL(INFLIBNET, Ahmadabad), Wolk Soft Tech (Wolk Soft Technology, Pvt. Ltd, Hyderabad), Granthalaya (NISCAIR, New Delhi), Maitreyi (CMC, Calcutta (for the CALIBNET Project)), Sanjay

(DESIDOC, Delhi), DELMS (Defense Library Management System), Librarian (Soft-Aid, Pune), WYLYSYS (Wipro Library System), DELDOS, TLMS, Libsuite ASP+ etc. Few of them have been developed by the Government organizations, while others by private software companies.

In the present library scenario, a number of foreign as well as indigenous library software packages are being used in India. On the other hand, for the present study, various library software packages have been highlighted:

4.1. Alice for Windows (AfW)

Alice for Windows (AfW), an integrated library automation software package is the product of Softlink, a Brisbane based Australian company. Since its foundation in 1983 in Brisbane and as Softlink Asia (New Delhi) in 1996. "Softlink Asia" is a leading software company with diversified business activity. This includes the software development, complete library automation, web portal development etc. The company is associated with "Softlink International" the world leader in library software and having own establishment for more than Ten years with the goal to capture the Asian region of the globe. At present it has around 250 installations in India. Considering the global growth and the steadily growing clients, the company started its operation in Sri lanka as "Softlink Sri Lanka". To keep pace, it has ventures to start various business activities in other SAARC Countries. Softlink Asia has installations in country like Sri Lanka, Bangladesh, Maldiev, Nepal and Pakistan. Its International association has around 17,000 installations all around the world and more than 80 Offices around the Globe.

Alice for Windows (AfW) has the following modules:

(a) Acquisition

(b) Management

(c) Circulation

(d) Periodicals

(e) Journal Indexing

(f) Multimedia
(g) Subject Authority
(h) Web enquiry
(i) Book hire
(j) Multilingual
(k) Patron self-checking

(a) Acquisition

Maintenance of budget information, the Wish List, On Approvals, ordering, receipt of resources and non-book expenses. The Acquisitions module is designed to assist the librarian with: Budgetary control of purchases (resource and general library expenses). Production of orders. Processing of items received. Recording of suggestions and requests onto a "wish list", Orders and requests to suppliers, lists of resources purchased from a budget dissection, claims for late orders, budget reports, and wish list reports and "on approval" reports are all available.

(b) Management

This module deals with the entry of new books, and accordingly updates in the concerned database. During the entry of books, this module first checks the existing book database to see if a copy of the book is already exists. If yes, then the no need to make a new entry for book only we enter the new accession no. for this book, and the database is updated. If no other copy of the book exists, then the book is first assigned accession no. and then the other details of the book are entered and the database is updated.

(c) Circulation

The circulation module of AFW is the area in which you record resource transactions. Circulation allows resources to be loaned out to borrowers and returned to the library. Circulation also maintains and follows your library policies regarding who can loan out what resource type and for how many days. When selecting Loans, this is the window that appears. The cursor is automatically positioned in the Enter barcode field and awaits a barcode or command.

To loan out a resource, scan the borrower's barcode or find the borrower by name. Here you can see the image of borrower. When the name or barcode is entered, the Loan tab will turn green indicating resources may now be scanned. Scan the resource barcode on each resource the borrower wishes to have and the transaction is complete.

(d) Periodicals

Details for each journal subscription are entered, a list of expected issues is generated and the expected arrival date of each issue is calculated. As each issue is received, it is accessioned and may be circulated. Any missing or overdue issues are displayed and a claim may be printed automatically for the supplier. A circulation list is maintained for each journal and may be printed automatically for circulating newly arrived issues to users.

Each journal or each issue becomes part of the main catalogue, if required. Thus subject headings, notes and keywords can be assigned to each journal, or to each issue of each journal, thus increasing access through the Inquiry module. In the latter case the linking facility in normal cataloguing can then be used to associate catalogue records for individual articles with the issue. Complete control of subscriptions, holdings and claims is provided. Minimal time is required to process each incoming issue.

(e) Journal Indexing

The Journal Indexing module allows the operator to enter and index individual journal articles that can then be accessed by library users from Inquiry. Individual article information may be recorded. This includes journal, issue, article title, author, length and starting page. Multiple subjects can be added along with scanned images and extensive notes. Words in the notes can be tagged as keywords.

The library user, when conducting a search in Inquiry, can access journal information entered by the librarian. Any articles that are not held by the library may be requested from the OPAC, if this function has been authorized by the librarian. If the library uses the Periodicals module then the location and availability of an article are also displayed.

(f) Multimedia

The purpose of the Multimedia module is to allow scanned images (photographs, diagrams, maps or text), video or film, sound and slide shows (a series of images and sound), to be attached to catalogue records. The module will also allow images to be attached to borrower records. mages are created using a scanner. A Twain compatible flatbed scanner is recommended. Images, video or film, sound and slide shows can be attached to resources during the cataloguing process. These images can be accessed from cataloguing and also from the Inquiry terminals. Images may be enlarged, reduced and inverted while being viewed in Inquiry. Scanned images can be attached to article information, if used in conjunction with the Journal Indexing module. A borrower image may be attached to a borrower record. The borrower image may be viewed in borrower details and will also be displayed when the borrower's barcode is scanned in loans

(j) Multilingual Module

It is possible to run the AfW Multilingual Module with any of the minimum or recommended operating systems. However, if you require the use of Multilingual for languages such as Hebrew or Arabic you will need Windows 2000 SP4 (Professional, Server or Advanced Server) or Windows Server 2003 or Windows XP Professional SP2 or Windows Vista There is now a Unicode version of AfW. For this you require Windows 2000 SP4 or Windows XP Professional SP2 or Windows Vista.

4.1.1. Wide Area Networks and Multi-Sites

For this type of setup, Softlink recommends the use of Terminal Server with **Windows 2000 Advanced Server** or **Windows Server 2003**. Running Alice across multi-sites on a WAN has been known to cause problems, therefore it is not recommended.

4.1.2. Networking

We currently recommend the following network software:

1. Windows 2003
2. Windows 2000
3. Windows XP Professional Peer to Peer

It is possible to run Alice on other types of network, but we recommend the above as we have many clients running Alice successfully on these network types. The minimum Network Speed should be 100 Mbps for Alice to run smoothly on workstations. If you haveany further queries on network issues, please contact Softlink Support who will be able to advise you further.

4.1.3. Barcode Scanner

Libraries who wish to use Barcode Technology for fast and accurate retrieval of data should have a compatible Barcode Scanner which is able to scan Barcodes.

Flatbed/Image Scanner : If the user wishes to use the Multimedia features of Alice whereby they can attach Images to Resources and Periodical Issues, then they can use any Flatbed/ADF/Book Scanner according to their requirement. The Scanner should be compatible with the Windows Operating used by you.

Fingerprint Scanner : In place of regular Barcoded Borrower Cards, AfW has the ability to scan and save the Fingerprint of Borrowers as identity. Only U. are. U 4000B Fingerprint Reader are compatible with AfW.

4.1.4. Internet

It is possible to catalogue Web sites and then access these via Inquiry. If you wish to use this functionality, then Windows must have a default web browser set up, which can access the Internet, this is normally Internet Explorer. AfW will then spawn this browser and pass to it, the URL of the site you have catalogued.

Internet Inquiry : The Internet Inquiry module allows you to make your catalogue available over the Internet, so that anyone with a web browser and access to your web site can search our catalogue. Please note that this is separate from viewing other web sites via Inquiry, which does not require the Internet Inquiry module. The minimum System Requirements for the machine running Internet Inquiry are as follows:

- Windows 2000 SP4 or Windows XP SP2 or Windows 2003
- Internet Information Server 5.1 or later
- Public IP Address (for viewing the information on Internet)
- WAN Server
- Alice for Windows version 5.50a or later
- 50 MB available disk space
- An HTML browser with Java and JavaScript enabled (Netscape 3.0+ or Internet Explorer 5.0+)

4.2. Software For University Libraries (SOUL)

Software for University Libraries (SOUL) is state-of-the-art integrated library management software designed and developed by the INFLIBNET Centre based on requirements of college and university libraries. It is user-friendly software developed to work under client-server environment. The software is complaint to international standards for bibliographic formats, networking and circulation protocols. The software is suitable not only for the academic libraries, but also for all types and sizes of libraries, even school libraries.

4.2.1. Major Features and Functionalities of SOUL

Following are the strong features of SOUL:

a. Window based user's friendly software.

b. Well-designed schemes, logically arranged functions with extensive help messages.

c. It is based on client server architecture allowing scalability to the users.

d. Does not need extensive training.

e. Multi-user and unlimited user access.

f. Supports internationally known standards CCF, AACR-2 etc.

g. Provides export/import facility.

h. Provides comprehensive list of reports, master database and authority files.

i. Available at affordable cost.

4.2.2. Modules of SOUL

The SOUL consists of the following modules. Each module has further been divided into sub modules to cater to its functional requirements:

1. Acquisition,
2. Catalogue,
3. Circulation,
4. OPACs,
5. Serial Control, and
6. Administration.

The in-built network feature of the software will allow multiple libraries of the same university to function together as well as access to the distributed databases installed at various university libraries and union catalogue mounted at INFLIBNET using VSAT network. Barcode and Spine Labels from software database Printing by using laser printer.

Random barcode generation is also possible.

Modules Descriptions

1. Acquisition : The Acquisition module enables library staff to handle major functions related to acquisition of library material including Suggestions management, Ordering cancellation and reminders, Receiving, Payment including fund control, Master file management such as currency table, vendors, publisher, user etc. Through this module library staff can search the entire database of library holdings for the purpose of duplicate check etc. Using various combinations, number of reports could be generated.

2. Catalogues : This module is used for retrospective conversion of books; technical processing of books received from Acquisition Section, printing a range of records for verification, searching by title and accession numbers, authority files for publishers etc. One of the unique features of SOUL is accessing to authority files on screen as well as selection box in various fields of records. Once the proposed VSAT Network by INFLIBNET is commissioned this module will take care of automatic replication of data into union catalogue. This will avoid exchange of library data on physical media i.e. floppy, tape etc. This module covers Cataloguing Process, Catalogue Search, User Services, Catalogue card generation, Authority file maintenance, Retro conversion, Stock verification, Report Generation, Union database maintenance (local level), and Export/ import of records.

3. Circulation : The circulation component of SOUL is the area in which you record resource transactions. Circulation allows resources to be loaned out to borrowers and returned to the library. Circulation also maintains and follows your library policies regarding who can loan out what resource type and for how many days. When selecting Transaction, this is the window that appears. The cursor is automatically positioned in the Enter barcode field and awaits a barcode or command. To loan out a resource, scan the Document barcode and press enter than courser automatic go to the member area where scan the members' card than issue is highlighted click on this. The document is issued against the member. And software also provides the print information of the issued document if you want print than one can take and keep for record purpose. And Statistical reporting -User and usage statistics - wide variety of reports can be generated.

4. Online Public Access Catalogues (OPACs) : The Online Public Access Catalogue (OPAC) of SOUL is a window to the library collection. Using the user friendly menus, user can search for an item available in the library by author, title, corporate author, conference name, subject descriptors, class number etc. The Boolean search enables the user to conduct the search using all combinations including type of material, language, year etc. Besides, this will serve as first point of information about the library, Library profile and calendar of the institute.

5. Serial Control : The complex job of keeping track of serials can easily and effectively be handled using SOUL through its Serial Control module. This module broadly handles Suggestions, Subscription (renewal and new subscription), Payment including fund control etc., Check in of issues including prediction of issues arrival, Reminder generation, Binding management, Search status of every item, Master database management, Reports generation etc. User administration facility module is used for creating new users and giving them right for accessing different modules.

6. Administration : With the help of this module librarian can assign the each module of each staff they can use only that module. A password assign for this.

4.3. LIBSYS

LibSys is an integrated library management software package designed and developed by LibSys Corporation, New Delhi. It is the most popular library automation software in India, having served more than 2000 different libraries and information centers, both India and Internationally. Serving the library community from past 22' years with a focus to deliver user friendly and technically sound solutions. It was initially developed COBOL language but converted into C and C++ languages. The software is based on its own bibliographic database, and available for systems using ORACLE and SQL Server as back-end RDBMS (Antony,1997).

LibSys has various special features i.e., Graphic User Interface (GUI), menu driven, powerful editing facility, user-defined security, flexible operations, variable field length, help and multilingual use, etc. It is run on a wide variety of hardware and operating systems, i.e. UNIX, Linux, and Windows NT Operating System on the server side and having any version of Windows at the customer part.

Libsys follows international standards such as CCF, MARC, etc. The cataloguing data entry accepts data in standard machine readable formats such as USMARC, OCLC etc., thus facilitating import and export of bibliographic data in both MARC and non-MARC formats (Husain and Ansari, 2008).

The various modules of LibSys are as follow:

(1) Acquisition

(2) Cataloguing

(3) Circulation

(4) Serial control

(5) Article Indexing

(6) Online Public Access Catalogues (OPACs)

1. Acquisition : Acquisitions, is an essential library operation which is significant to the achievement of a library's mission. Acquisitions, studied involves a great deal of detailed and exacting paper work; materials handling in large quantities, reconciliation of orders, invoices and materials received; fiscal control and so on. Acquisitions, thus, is a highly labour intensive and therefore a prime candidate for automation support. As defined by ***James E.***

Rush "Acquisitions encompasses all aspects of the procurement of all types of library materials whether by gift or exchange, from the request stage through transfer of materials to cataloguing".

The challenges librarians face in managing multi-location libraries. With LibSys7, multi-location libraries having centralized procurement can perform hassle free operations like centralized ordering and invoice processing with flexibility for location-wise receiving. Online indenting and approval simplifies the process.

2. Cataloguing : Cataloguing module of LibSys has many unique features such as-maintenance of 'in-process title', production of catalogue by improving bibliographic data from elsewhere, facilitating the cataloguing of various user defined types of materials, updating of cataloguing details for the titles entered in 'Acquisition module', thereby avoiding the reentering of the bibliographical information, allowing modifications of bibliographic data as and when required.

The Cataloguer gets a new powerful tool 'Net cataloguing' that allows searching of catalogues of other libraries having Z39.50/ SRU-SRW/ OAI-PMH/LibSys databases. Retrieved MARC21/MARC-XML records can be edited and downloaded into Libsys7.Cataloguer works on a flexible MARC21 interface that provides quick-tips as well as in-depth online 'Help' to make the task easy. User defined iReports or AACR2 Cards provides the much desired flexibility and localization to the library.

3. Circulation : Circulation is a central and highly visible function of a typical library. Circulation, which is often compared with inventory control, involves a great deal of record keeping and correspondingly consumes staff time. Automated support for circulation control vastly improves library's ability to rapidly and accurately record the loan transactions, to monitor these transactions, to record return of lent items and to support other related circulation functions.

Libsys7 offers a new level of circulation through integration with Biometric or RFID technology. Besides the regular email reminders to patrons, options are available for instant SMS alerts and emails. Patrons can perform self-reservation and self-renewal. Support for multi-location circulation through location based checks and validations.

4. Serial Control : The term 'Serials' denotes those publications which are issued in successive parts on a recurring basis, usually, but not necessarily, at regularly scheduled intervals and usually having numerical or chronological designation. The term `Serials control' refers to those tasks which support the procurement and management of serials collection in a library.

LibSys7 builds upon the widely appreciated functional depth of serials control of earlier versions with the inclusion of MARC21 interfaces. Handling of online journals to meet changing subscription pattern of the libraries. Option to scan the cover and contents page of physical journals for publishing in OPAC. Compliance to SICI-Barcode standard.

5. Online Public Access Catalogues (OPACs) : In Libsys OPAC services include title, catalogue author cataloguing, subject catalogue, classified catalogue, publisher index, place of publication index, keyword in context/keyword out of context indexes. Boolean searches allows use of logical connections OR, AND, and NOT. It allows use of truncation, parentheses, and proximity connectors.

Libsys also allows user defined searchable fields, and stop words. OPAC provides online information on holding of current journals including recent issues received. There is also facility for online reservations, serial digital interface (SDI), conditional access system (CAS), etc. Moreover, Libsys supports defining multiple databases based on types of documents for searching in OPAC6. Other services from OPAC client includes updating subject interest profile for SDI by users themselves, request for acquisition of a document while browsing/ searching various catalogues, and facility to make request online for putting a specific title on reserve, etc. OPAC module of the software also has the multimedia interface.

A contemporary and user friendly OPAC inspired by Web/Lib 2.0 philosophy that emphasizes on meeting the needs and aspirations of the Users rather than just feeding information. Like, a suggestion list assists the user in building a search strategy. Patrons get comprehensive information through Table of Contents, Summary, Annotations, Authors Notes which can be further expanded through search links to 'Google', 'WorldCat', 'BookFinder' and 'Google Scholar'. 'Shelf Browse' provides the patrons a window to peek on titles available on shelf, nearby the searched book, which definitely enhances their online library experience. LibSys7 encourages patrons to be more participative through sharing reviews/ ratings on titles, emailing or downloading information.

4.5. SLIM++

SLIM++ is integrated, multi-user, multi-tasking library information software for the Windows environment. SLIM++ helps to users for catalogue books, films, sound recordings, drawings, clippings, articles, reports, letters, pamphlets, serials publications... all those things that contain information so vital to your organization. SLIM++ cataloguing adheres to popular international standards. This means you can exchange data with the world. Retrieval of the data is simple, fast and efficient. Even a catchy phrase in the description of the catalogued item can be used for searching.

SLIM++ is designed and developed in modules to take care of complete functionality required for automating libraries. You can configure SLIM++ software for your library by selecting one or more of these standard and add-on modules. These modules exhibit features that make SLIM++ a top class software.

SLIM++ modules work on the same data from different nodes of a network. They can be installed independent of each other on different desktops. SLIM++ works just as well on a stand-alone machine as it does in a network of Computers. Moreover, your library can be browsed through the Internet / intranet with SLIM++.

1. Acquisition : SLIM++ Acquisition system supports the entire range of activities from the time someone makes a proposal or a recommendation to acquire an item, until it is finally paid for and accessioned. It covers:

a. Proposal for acquisition
b. Inquiry to book sellers / publishers
c. Purchase orders (foreign / local)
d. Books on approval memos
e. Purchase bills
f. Payment details of purchase bills
g. Credit notes
h. Detailed information about vendors
i. Multiple currencies and conversion rates

This data is automatically picked up for generating numerous letters. These can be simply printed, signed and posted. Items on proposals may be searched using author names or titles. The items are grouped by proposers, subjects, recipients, etc. and can be retrieved in many ways:

a. Those on requests, orders, bills or approval memos
b. Those awaiting approval
c. Those received on donation or exchange basis

Associated payments information is maintained. Purchase follow-ups are made easy with:

a. Purchase order status report
b. Purchase order follow up letters
c. Payment advices

d. Entries in accession register are generated automatically.

Items under acquisition are also visible through OPAC browsers.

2. Cataloguing : SLIM++ Cataloguing is based on AACR2 (Anglo American Cataloguing Rules, 1988). Catalogue any type of material: Books, Micro-documents, Slides, Maps, Audio / video cassettes, Drawings, Films, Texts, Clippings, Serial publications and more. Descriptions of AACR2 areas / subareas / other categories are available on-line. MARC fixed fields are provided. Data entry for a card is entirely menu driven. Rules of punctuation are programmed to give consistent and accurate cards. The cards are available in the standard 5" x 3" size. Analytical entries, 'See', 'See also' references and multiple catalogues are available. Unlimited numbers of added entries (access points) per card are allowed such as title, uniform titlc, multiple keywords, place of conference, etc. Any subject classification system such as UDC, DDC, or CC is permissible.

Other Features

(a) Authority control on author / publisher name / keyword

(b) Accession details of items

(c) Cardex for bound volumes of journals

(d) Micro-document cataloguing (article indexing)

(e) Bibliographic details of serials

(f) Accession register

(g) Catalogues and labels printing

3. Circulation : SLIM++ Circulation system is based on lending rules that you can define and change. It covers: Member information / registration card,Subjects of interest for members (SDI),and Loans and reservations data retrieval by borrower identification

Front desk operations

a. Issues, returns, reissues
b. Reservations / cancellations
c. Bulk transactions for a borrower
d. Backdated transaction

Other Features

a. Inventory / circulation status
b. Physical stock verification
c. Binding (issues / receipts)
d. Shelf list
e. Calendar master for maintaining institute / library holidays
f. Deferred reservations to ensure availability of an item on shelf at a specified future date
g. Transaction logging
h. Rules based computation of fines for overdue items
i. Tracking fines and fees due
j. Prioritized reservation queues
k. Inter library loan monitoring system

Letters Generation

i. Collect reserved item
ii. Overdue loans notice
iii. No dues certificate
iv. Membership renewal reminder
v. Recall a book in circulation
vi. SDI (selective dissemination of information)

The Issue / Return Application

It provides an easier interface to the **barcode** system, offering basic transactions like Issue and Return. You may also print transaction report for a borrower.

4. Serials Control : SLIM++ serials control system helps achieve an effective utilization of periodicals budget. It allows for tracking receipts of issues, filing claims for issues not received, preparing binding orders, etc. It includes:

Journal title and related information

Publisher / agent	Periodicity
Delivery mode	Subject
Gratis / exchange	Addresses for communication
Subscription order.	Subscription payment details

Issue details

a. Cardex for loose issues
b. Issues arrived
c. Issues not received
d. Missing / damaged issues
e. Duplicate issues
f. Issues in bindery
g. Issues borrowed

5. OPAC (On-line Public Access Catalogue) : LIM++ OPAC offers powerful on-line search facilities to search through library catalogues:

Author	Keyword	Subject class
Title	Publisher	Place of publication
Main entry	Material type	Place of conference
Subject name	ISBN / ISSN	Year of conference
Series Titles	Serials Title	Year of publication

Fig. 2.1. OPACs Search Elements

The repository of words, names, titles, keywords, etc. is available for on-line browsing while the search phrase is being entered. This enables display of alternate spellings; words derived from same root and help the searcher by providing a view of the data. In addition to these conventional searching methods, OPAC indexes every word in the description of the item. Thus, to conduct a search one need not be aware of the cataloguing style of the library.

6. Web Aware OPAC : SLIM++ has the capability of putting your library information on the WWW / INTRANET. This module allows the user to login as a library member and view his/her loans and reservations. He/She can even reserve an item in the library through the internet. Along with all these features, catalogue browsing, circulation details, word/phrase search, view card etc. are also available.

All this information appears as different web pages on the NET. The appearance of these pages can be customized by you.

Retrieval of the data is simple, fast and efficient. Even a catchy phrase in the description of the catalogued item can be used for searching.

Bulletin Printing (CAS Current Awareness Service) : SLIM++ helps in the publication of an information bulletin containing particulars of the latest additions of books or articles. The list in the bulletin is arranged in the order of subjects. The particulars of the items can include abstracts besides the standard bibliographic data and library call numbers. A Keyword or an author name index to the list is also prepared.

This report can be prepared either in the Rich Text Format or the HTML Format. The report when created in the HTML format gets automatically linked to the Web Aware OPAC module of SLIM++.

SDI (Selective Dissemination of Information Service) : This application lets you prepare a bibliography report per library member:

This report contains the bibliography of those recently acquired library items in which the member is interested. The generated report can be printed, stored into a file or can be mailed to the borrower.

WEB Proposals : Web Proposals covers:

a. View Proposals List.

b. Propose an Item online.

c. View the list of Proposals proposed only by the member.

d. View List of items for approval if the member is an approver.

e. View the details of item.

7. Statistical Analysis : This Module produces different statistical information required for library management such as:

a. Distribution of transactions over working-hours, week-days, or months

b. Distribution of loans and overdue loans for a borrower category

c. Distribution of loans and overdue loans for a subject group Reservation queue sizes and average waiting period

4.6. VIRTUA

Virtua is designed for libraries that expect more than meets the eye. Providing full multilingual support and leveraging a solid Oracle™ foundation. Virginia-Tech Library System (VTLS), Blacksburg, Virginia, USA, has developed an Integrated Library System (ILS) known as 'Virtua' set a new standard of excellence for the library world. With advanced features such as FRBR (Functional Requirements for Bibliographic Records), Update Notifications through SDI, User Reviews & Ratings, and support for mobile computing. Virtua Library Software package is a Windows based Client/ Server application. The Virtua software is based on six key technologies: relational database management systems, rapid development tools, three tier client/server architecture, database warehousing, Unicode support and ATM network optimized applications. These technologies facilitate handling data management, software development and network delivery.

Support of Unicode, multilingual dialogue, access to external tools such as OCLC, RLIN, unique data entry templates, adherence to a variety of international MARC formats are special features of the cataloguing module of Virtua.

Easy to learn and easy to use, Virtua offers integrated functionality that includes OPAC, cataloging, acquisitions, serials, circulation and reporting. Other components include FRBR, Consortium Databases, Union Catalogs, SDI, Open URL and a lot more. With our fully integrated, single-client approach, switching from one module to another is as seamless as a keystroke or a click of the mouse.

4.6.1. History

Virginia Tech Library System (VTLS) Inc. located in Blacksburg, Virginia, is the offspring of a project launched in 1974 at Virginia Polytechnic Institute and State University's Newman Library, a member of the Association of Research libraries with more than 1.5 million catalogued volumes. Having studied available library automation alternatives and having realized no system perfectly suitable for the needs of its libraries, Virginia Tech initiated a project to develop an automated library system. This forerunner of VTLS, comprising an OPAC and an automated circulation system, was installed at Virginia-Tech's Newman Library in 1975. By 1985, the software had grown into the integrated library system known as VTLS. In the same year, VTLS Inc. was formed as a subsidiary corporation of Virginia Tech Intellectual Properties (VTIP), which granted VTLS Inc. exclusive worldwide rights to market VTLS products. In 1998, VTLS Inc. introduced Virtua library automation software5. VTLS Inc is an ISO 9001 certified company. Significantly, more than 1000 libraries in around 40 countries have chosen Virtua software for automation purpose.

Virtua has many modules, viz., acquisition and fund accounting, cataloguing, circulation, serials control, OPAC, chameleon gateway, statistic and reporting, and system profiling. VTLS also manage collection through radio frequency identification (RFID) technology. Furthermore, company specialises in microfilm scanning and digital library techniques.

The various modules of Virtua are as follows:

(1) Acquisition

(2) Cataloguing

(3) Circulation

(4) Serial control

(5) OPAC

(6) Statistics and reporting

(7) Chameleon Gateway.

1. Cataloguing : Cataloguing module of Virtua is equipped with seamless access to tools and resources from a unified set of screens. Cataloguers can directly access external copy cataloguing data from within the Virtua software. Interfaces are available for a variety of sources such as online bibliographic utilities and CD ROMs including Bibliofile, OCLC, RLIN etc. This software provide services like electronic version of cataloguing services such as Library of Congress (LC) cataloguer's Desktop can be searched directly without coming out from the software.

Virtua supports all formats, character sets, and classification schemes. The system can accommodate all MARC21 bibliographic formats for Serials, Music, maps, mixed materials, books, etc. It is accommodates different versions of the MARC standard such as USMARC, UKMARC, CANMARC, SWEMARC etc. the software is compatitable to the MARC 21 formats for authority data, community information and holding data.

Virtua cataloguing system is compatible with the character repertoire of the Unicode standard. The Unicode supports hundreds of characters while the key board can be used for a single language. To facilitate the editing of records having words and characters from many languages, Virtua allows for switching of keyboards. It is also facilitates entry of the Arabic, Persian, Hebrew, and Urdu records preserving their original scripts. Significantly these records can be viewed by the users in OPAC in the natural scripts.

2. Serial Control : Virtua is packed with time-saving features. Virtua's EDI-compliant serial module, for example, features the serial pattern editor, an easy-to-use GUI interface for generating and editing prediction patterns. It also offers an easy way to save them to a serials pattern database so that they can be retrieved for re-use, eliminating the need for complex coding.

REFERENCES

1. Antony, J. (1997). *Libsys-a selection for library automation and networking*. Paper presented at National Seminar on Library Automation-Problems and Prospects, Roorkee, India.
2. Harinarayana, N. S. (1991). Concept of library automation. *Herald of Library Science*, 30 (3/4), 176-177.
3. Husain, S. and A., Mehtab Alam. (2008). Library automation software packages in India: A study of the cataloguing modules of Alice for Windows, Libsys and Vitua. *Annals of Library and Information Studies, 54*, 146-151.
4. Kumar, P. S. G. (1987). *Computerization of Indian libraries*. New Delhi: B.R. Publishing Corporation.
5. Wikipedia. (2012). *Automation* Retrieved 15 March, 2012, from http://en.wikipedia.org/wiki/Automation

3

Database Management Systems (DBMS)

0. INTRODUCTION

The word data is the plural of datum, but some people prefer to use it in singular form. It may be defined as "data are qualitative or quantitative attribute of a variable or set of variables". Also, data are representations of a fact, figure, and idea. Such usage is the origin of data as a concept in computer science: data are numbers, words, images, etc., accepted as they stand. Data is organized into 'data fields'. A 'data field'is a component of a record corresponding to an attribute. One record may have several data fields. For example, a record of a book has several fields such as 'Field for Author', 'Field for Title', Field for Edition Statement', Field for Publisher', 'Field for Place of Publication', 'Field for Year of Publication', and so on. These fields taken together make a record. Collection of related records, all conforming to the same type and format, form a data file. For example, a file on 'Bibliography of OPACs', contains records of reading material on this subject. All the records in this file have a common subject, and are interrelated. Each record contains such information as author, title, place of publication, publishers, year of publication, edition, pages, etc. This file is given a name for its storage and retrieval. A collection of such interrelated records, with a given structure for acceptance, storage, and retrieval and dissemination of data, on demand, for multiple users for one or more applications produces a database.

1. DATABASE MANAGEMENT SYSTEM (DBMS)

International Encyclopedia of Information and Library Science focuses that "a database management system (DBMS) is a program that can input, edit and retrieve information from a database. A database is a collection of information organized into records and fields, and stored as files on a computer". Another word we can say that Database Management System (DBMS) is a set of computer programs that controls the creation, maintenance, and the use of a database. It allows organizations to place control of database development in the hands of database administrators (DBAs) and other specialists. A DBMS is a system software package that helps the use of integrated collection of data records and files known as databases. It allows different user application programs to easily access the same database. In large systems, a DBMS allows users and other software to store and retrieve data in a structured way. Instead of having to write computer programs to extract information, user can ask simple questions in a query language. Thus, many DBMS packages provide Fourth-generation programming language (4GLs) and other application development features. A DBMS also provides the ability to logically present database information to users. (Wikipedia, 2010)Presently there are hundreds of DBMSs. dBase, Foxbase, Sybase, Informix, Delphi, etc. are well known DBMSs, while LibSys, Alice for Windows and SOUL are the examples of library-oriented DBMSs.

1.1. Concepts, Design and Development of Database

The DBMSs are categorized according to their data structures or types. The DBMS is a collection of programs that enables information to be stored in, modified, and extracted from a database. There are many different types of DBMSs, ranging from small systems that run on personal computers to huge systems that run on mainframes. From a technical standpoint, the systems can differ widely. The terms relational, network, flat, and hierarchical all refer to the way a DBMS organizes information internally. This internal organization affects how quickly and flexibly the information can be extracted when the DBMS processes requests for information from a database. The requests are made in the form of a query, which is a stylized question.

A DBMS includes four main parts: modeling language, data structure, database query language, and transaction mechanisms. Components of DBMS are:

1. **DBMS engine** accepts logical requests from various other DBMS subsystems, converts them into physical equivalents, and actually accesses the database and data dictionary as they exist on a storage device.

2. **Data definition subsystem** helps the user create and maintain the data dictionary and define the structure of the files in a database.

3. **Data manipulation subsystem** helps the user to add, change, and delete information in a database and query it for valuable information. Software tools within the data manipulation subsystem are most often the primary interface between user and the information contained in a database. It allows the user to specify its logical information requirements.

4. **Application generation subsystem** contains facilities to help users develop transaction-intensive applications. It usually requires that the user perform a detailed series of tasks to process a transaction. It facilitates easy-to-use data entry screens, programming languages, and interfaces.

5. **Data administration subsystem** helps users manage the overall database environment by providing facilities for

backup and recovery, security management, query optimization, concurrency control, and change management.

A data modeling language to define the schema of each database hosted in the DBMS, according to the DBMS database model. The four most common types of models are:

1. **Hierarchical database model :** A hierarchical database model is a data model in which the data is organized into a tree-like structure. The structure allows representing information using parent/child relationships: each parent can have many children, but each child has only one parent (also known as a 1-to-many relationship). All attributes of a specific record are listed under an entity type. In a database an entity type is the equivalent of a table. Each individual record is represented as a row, and each attribute as a column. Entity types are related to each other using 1:N mappings, also known as one-to-many relationships. This model is recognized as the first database model created by IBM in the 1960s. Currently the most widely used hierarchical databases are IMS developed by IBM and Windows Registry by Microsoft.

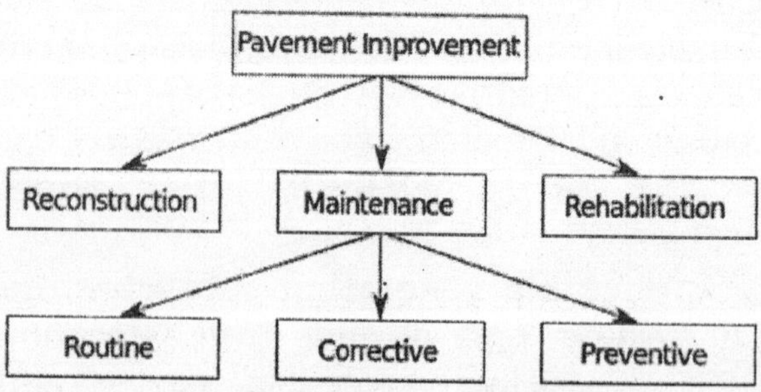

Fig. 3.1. Hierarchical Model

2. **Network model :** The network model is a database model conceived as a flexible way of representing objects and their relationships. Its distinguishing feature is that the

schema, viewed as a graph in which object types are nodes and relationship types are arcs, is not restricted to being a hierarchy or lattice. The network model's original inventor was Charles A. Bachman (USA), and it was developed into a standard specification published in 1969 by the CODASYL (Conference on Data Systems Languages) Consortium.

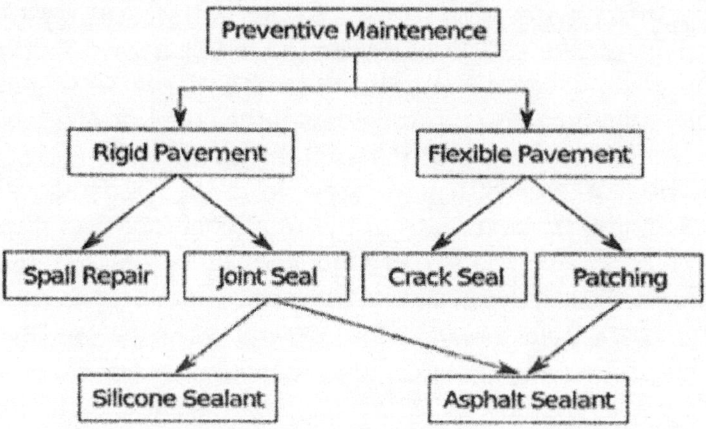

Fig. 3.2. Network Model

3. Relational model : The relational model's central idea is to describe a database as a collection of predicates over a finite set of predicate variables, describing constraints on the possible values and combinations of values. The content of the database at any given time is a finite (logical) model of the database, i.e. a set of relations, one per predicate variable, such that all predicates are satisfied. A request for information from the database (a database query) is also a predicate.

The relational model for database management is a database model based on first-order predicate logic, first formulated and proposed in 1969 by Edgar F. Codd. The purpose of the relational model is to provide a declarative method for specifying data and queries: users directly state what information the database contains and what information they want from it, and let the database management system software take care of describing data structures for storing the data and retrieval procedures for answering queries.

IBM's original implementation of Codd's ideas was System R. There have been several commercial and open source products based on Codd's ideas, including IBM's DB2, Oracle Database, Microsoft SQL Server, PostgreSQL, MySQL, and many others. Most of these use the SQL data definition and query language. A table in an SQL database scheme corresponds to a predicate variable; the contents of a table to a relation; key constraints, other constraints, and SQL queries correspond to predicates. However, SQL databases, including DB2, deviate from the relational model in many details; Codd fiercely argued against deviations that compromise the original principles.

Data items organized as a set of formally described tables from which data can be accessed or reassembled in many ways without having to reorganize the database tables. Each table (sometimes called a relation) contains one or more data categories in columns. Each row contains a unique instance of data for the categories defined by the columns.

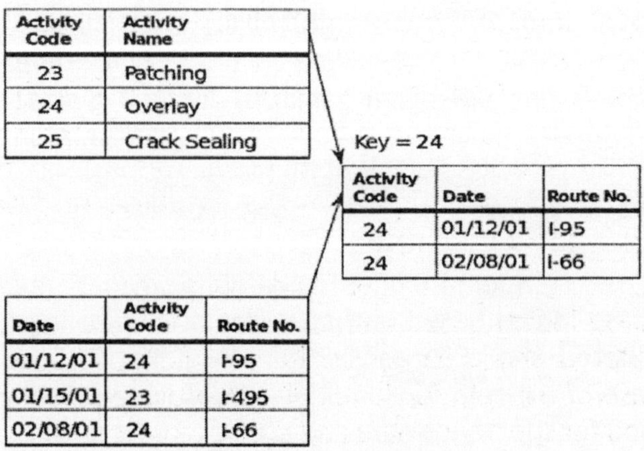

Fig. 3.3. Relational Model

4. Multidimensional databases : Multidimensional databases are a type of database that is optimized for data warehousing and online analytical processing (OLAP) applications. Multidimensional databases are frequently created using input from existing relational databases. MDB denotes the ability to process the data in the database quickly so that answers can be generated immediately.

Multidimensional structure is defined as "a variation of the relational model that uses multidimensional structures to organize data and express the relationships between data". The structure is broken into cubes and the cubes are able to store and access data within the confines of each cube. "Each cell within a multidimensional structure contains aggregated data related to elements along each of its dimensions". Even when data is manipulated it remains easy to access and continues to constitute a compact database format. The data still remains interrelated. Multidimensional structure is quite popular for analytical databases that use online analytical processing (OLAP) applications (O'Brien & Marakas, 2009). Analytical databases use these databases because of their ability to deliver answers to complex business queries swiftly. Data can be viewed from different angles, which gives a broader perspective of a problem unlike other models.

A simple example would be a cube that contains a store's sales as a measure, and Date/Time as a dimension. Each Sale has a Date/Time label that describes more about that sale. Any number of dimensions can be added to the structure such as Store, Cashier, or Customer by adding a foreign key column to the fact table. This allows an analyst to view the measures along any combination of the dimensions.

For example:

```
 Sales Fact Table
+-------------+----------+
| sale_amount | time_id  |
+-------------+----------+                Time Dimension
|      2008.10|     1234 |---+     +---------+-------------------+
+-------------+----------+   |     | time_id | timestamp         |
                             |     +---------+-------------------+
                             +---->|   1234  | 20080902 12:35:43 |
                                   +---------+-------------------+
```

5. Object database : An object database (also known as Object-Oriented Database Management System) is a database management system in which information is represented in the form of objects as used in object-oriented programming. Object databases have been considered since the early 1980s and 1990s, and main usage is in object oriented areas.

When database capabilities are combined with object-oriented programming language capabilities, the result is an object-oriented database management system (OODBMS). OODBMS allow object-oriented programmers to develop the product, store them as objects, and replicate or modify existing objects to make new objects within the OODBMS. Because the database is integrated with the programming language, the programmer can maintain consistency within one environment, in that both the OODBMS and the programming language will use the same model of representation. Relational DBMS projects, by way of contrast, maintain a clearer division between the database model and the application.

As the usage of web-based technology increases with the implementation of Intranets and extranets, companies have a vested interest in OODBMS to display their complex data. Using a DBMS that has been specifically designed to store data as objects gives an advantage to those companies that are geared towards multimedia presentation or organizations that utilize computer-aided design (CAD).

Some object-oriented databases are designed to work well with object-oriented programming languages such as

Delphi, Ruby, Python, Perl, Java, C#, Visual Basic .NET, C++, Objective-C and Smalltalk; others have their own programming languages. OODBMSs use exactly the same model as object-oriented programming languages.

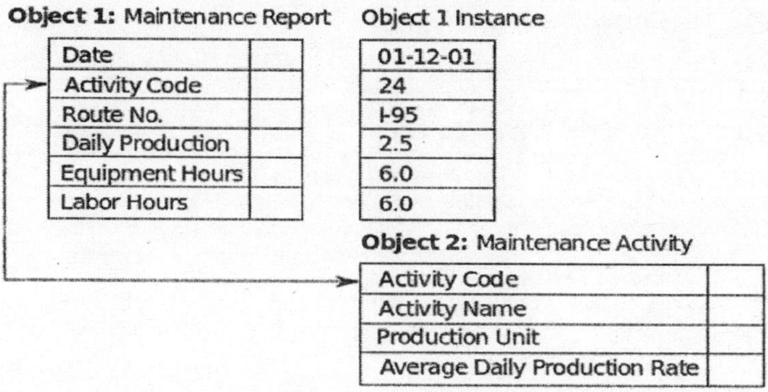

Fig. 3.4. Object-Oriented Model

There are many DBMS software with variety of features. Such as: Oracle, MS SQL Server, MY SQL Server, WINISIS, etc.

2. MS SQL/MYSQL SERVER

2.1. MS SQL Server

Microsoft SQL Server is a relational database server, developed by Microsoft. It is a software product whose primary function is to store and retrieve data as requested by other software applications, be it those on the same computer or those running on another computer across a network (including the Internet). The MSSQL Server aimed at different audiences and for different workloads ranging from small applications that store and retrieve data on the same computer, to millions of users and computers that access huge amounts of data from the Internet at the same time. Microsoft SQL Server's primary query languages are T-SQL and ANSI SQL.

Table 3.1. SQL Server Release History

Year	Version	Release Name	Code Name
1989	1.0 (OS/2)	SQL Server 1.0 (16bit)	–
1991	1.1 (OS/2)	SQL Server 1.1 (16bit)	–
1993	4.21 (WinNT)	SQL Server 4.21	SQLNT
1995	6	SQL Server 6.0	SQL95
1996	6.5	SQL Server 6.5	Hydra
1998	7	SQL Server 7.0	Sphinx
1999		SQL Server 7.0 OLAP Tools	Plato
2000	8	SQL Server 2000	Shiloh
2003	8	SQL Server 2000 64bit Edition	Liberty
2005	9	SQL Server 2005	Yukon
2008	10	SQL Server 2008	Katmai
2010	10.25	SQL Azure	Matrix (aka CloudDB)
2010	10.5	SQL Server 2008 R2	Kilimanjaro (aka KJ)
2012	11	SQL Server 2012	Denali

A number of different versions of MS SQL Server have been released by Microsoft Company and of course it runs in the windows environment. Its first edition was released in 1989 based on version 1.0 (OS/2) 16bit. In the year 1991 the next version 1.1 16bit was released. After that in almost every year it has been updated and a new version with some advanced and new features are being released. The latest version 11.5 is currently in the market which was released in 2012.

2.1.1. Data Storage in MS SQL

The main unit of data storage is a database, which is a collection of tables with typed columns. SQL Server supports different data types, including primary types such as *Integer*, *Float*, *Decimal*, *Char* (including character strings), *Varchar* (variable length character strings), binary (for unstructured blobs of data), *Text* (for textual data) among others. The rounding of floats to integers uses either Symmetric Arithmetic Rounding or Symmetric Round Down

(*Fix*) depending on arguments: SELECT Round (2.5, 0) gives 3. It is

Microsoft SQL Server also allows user-defined composite types (UDTs) to be defined and used. It also makes server statistics available as virtual tables and views (called Dynamic Management Views or DMVs). In addition to tables, a database can also contain other objects including views, stored procedures, indexes and constraints, along with a transaction log.

2.1.2. Full Text Search Service

SQL Server Full Text Search service (fig.3.5) is a specialized indexing and querying service for unstructured text stored in SQL Server databases. The full text search index can be created on any column with character based text data. It allows for words to be searched for in the text columns. While it can be performed with the SQL LIKE operator, using SQL Server Full Text Search service can be more efficient.

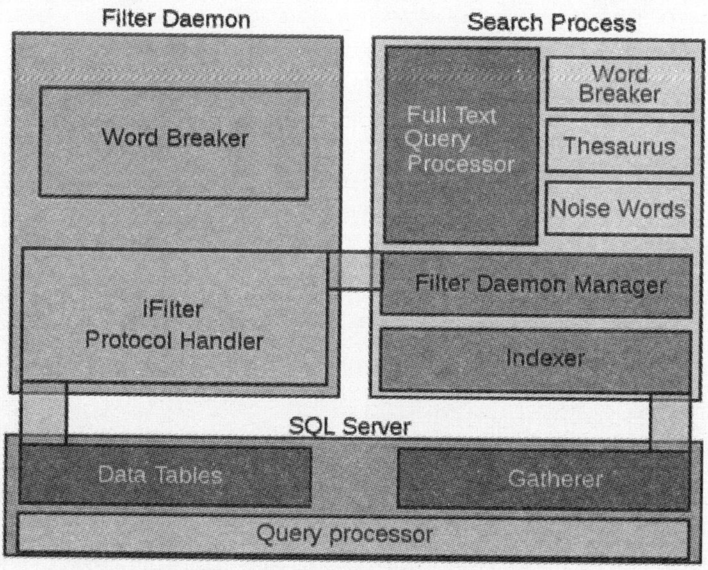

Fig. 3.5. The SQL Server Full Text Search service architecture

The Full Text Search engine is divided into two processes - the Filter Daemon process (msftefd.exe) and the Search process (msftesql.exe). These processes interact with the SQL Server. The Search process includes the indexer (that creates the full text indexes) and the full text query processor. The indexer scans through text columns in the database. It can also index through binary columns, and use iFilters to extract meaningful text from the binary blob (for example, when a Microsoft Word document is stored as an unstructured binary file in a database). The iFilters are hosted by the Filter Daemon process. Once the text is extracted, the Filter Daemon process breaks it up into a sequence of words and hands it over to the indexer. The indexer filters out noise words, i.e., words like A, And etc., which occur frequently and are not useful for search. With the remaining words, an inverted index is created, associating each word with the columns they were found in. SQL Server itself includes a Gatherer component that monitors changes to tables and invokes the indexer in case of updates.

2.2. MySQL Server

My SQL Server is a Relational Database Management System (RDBMS) that runs as a server providing multi-user access to a number of databases. MySQL development project has made its source code available under the terms of the GNU General Public License, as well as under a variety of proprietary agreements. MySQL was owned and sponsored by a single for-profit firm, the Swedish company MySQL AB, now owned by Sun Microsystems, a subsidiary of Oracle Corporation.

Free-software projects that require a full-featured database management system often use MySQL. Such projects include (for example) WordPress, phpBB, Drupal and other software built on the LAMP (LAMP is an acronym Linux, Apache, MySQL, Perl/PHP/Python) software stack.

MySQL is also used in many high-profiles, large-scale World Wide Web products including Wikipedia, Google and Face book and Twitter. This software has been written in C, C++ languages and initial released in May 23, 1995. This is cross-platform based software and the latest version is 5.1.20 has been released in January 20, 2010. MySQL Workbench lets users manage the following:

- Database design & modeling
- SQL development - replacing MySQL Query Browser
- Database administration - replacing MySQL Administrator

MySQL Workbench is available in two editions, the regular free and open source Community Edition which may be downloaded from the MySQL website, and the proprietary Standard Edition which extends and improves the feature set of the Community Edition.

MySQL can be built and installed manually from source code, but this can be tedious so it is more commonly installed from a binary package unless special customizations are required. On most Linux distributions the package management system can download and install MySQL with minimal effort, though further configuration is often required to adjust security and optimization settings.

2.2.1. Features of MySQL

As of April 2009, MySQL offered MySQL 5.1 in two different variants: the open source MySQL Community Server and the commercial Enterprise Server. It 5.5 is offered under the same licenses. They have a common code base and include the following features:

- A broad subset of ANSI SQL 99, as well as extensions
- Cross-platform support
- Stored procedures
- Triggers
- Cursors

- Updatable Views
- Information schema
- Strict mode[further explanation needed]
- X/Open XA distributed transaction processing (DTP) support; two phase commit as part of this, using Oracle's InnoDB engine
- Independent storage engines (MyISAM for read speed, InnoDB for transactions and referential integrity, MySQL Archive for storing historical data in little space)
- Transactions with the InnoDB, and Cluster storage engines; savepoints with InnoDB
- SSL support
- Query caching
- Sub-SELECTs (i.e. nested SELECTs)
- Replication support (i.e. Master-Master Replication & Master-Slave Replication) with one master per slave, many slaves per master, no automatic support for multiple masters per slave.
- Full-text indexing and searching using MyISAM engine
- Embedded database library
- Partial Unicode support (UTF-8 and UCS-2 encoded strings are limited to the BMP)
- ACID compliance when using transaction capable storage engines (InnoDB and Cluster)[27]
- Partititoned tables with pruning of partitions in optimiser
- Shared-nothing clustering through MySQL Cluster
- Hot backup (via mysqlhotcopy) under certain conditions[28]

The developers release monthly versions of the MySQL Server. The sources can be obtained from MySQL's website or from MySQL's Bazaar repository, both under the GPL license.

3. CDS/ISIS & WINISIS

CDS/ISIS stands for Computerized Documentation Service / Integrated Set of Information Systems. CDS/ISIS for Microcomputers was released by UNESCO in 1985. It was called officially CDS/ISIS Mini-Micro Version but is usually called CDS/ISIS or simply ISIS. In Latin America, where the minicomputer package MINISIS (developed in Ottawa, Canada, by the International Development Research Centre) is prevalent, the original DOS version was always called Micro-ISIS; the Windows version is called Micro-ISIS or WINISIS. Versions have been produced in Arabic, Chinese, English, French, German, Portuguese, Russian and Spanish amongst other languages. UNESCO makes the software available free for non-commercial purposes, though distributors are allowed to charge for their expenses.

3.1. Features of the CDS/ISIS Software

The major features of the CDS/ISIS software are:

1. The handling of variable length records, fields and sub fields, thus saving disk space and making it possible to store greater amounts of information;
2. The handling of repeatable fields;
3. A data base definition component allowing the user to define the data to be processed for a particular application;
4. A data entry component for entering and modifying data through user-created data base specific worksheets;
5. An information retrieval component using a powerful search language providing for field-level and proximity search operators, in addition to the traditional and/or/not operators, as well as free-text searching;
6. A powerful sort and report generation facility allowing the user to easily create any desired printed products, such as catalogues, indexes, directories, etc.;

7. A data interchange function based on the ISO 2709 international standard used by leading data base producers;
8. An integrated application programming language (CDS/ISIS Pascal and the ISIS_DLL), allowing the user to tailor the software to specific needs;
9. Functions allowing the user to build relational data bases, though CDS/ISIS is not based over a relational model;
10. Powerful hypertext functions allow designing complex user interfaces.

3.2. What is Database?

The bellow example shows that the term "database" denotes a collection of structured information. It contains data elements called "records". Each record in the database has the same structure. Some units of information in a record may be absent, some others may occur more than once (a book may have more than one author or may not have an ISBN). The data unit in a record is called "fields", and fields may contain independent data elements called "subfields".

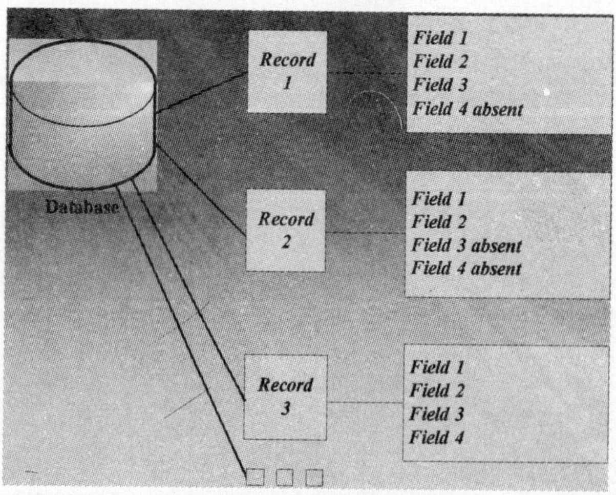

Fig. 3.6. Database Structure

3.4. Installations CDS/ISIS for Window

CDS/ISIS for Windows is, as its name implies, a Windows-based system. Windows programs have many distinctive features as a result of the Windows operating system. Microsoft Windows is described as a graphical user environment which gives you more control over the way you work as well as enabling you to use more of the power of the computer. It allows you, for example, to run more than one program at the same time. Thus it allows you to have more than one CDS/ISIS database open. Your work appears in a window which may be enlarged, diminished, activated or put on hold whilst other windows are opened and programs there run. Because more than one program may be available on the screen it is possible to transfer data or images from one to another. As well as using the computer's keyboard, the user can employ a mouse to move windows around the screen and to activate or de-activate windows. Within a Window there are drop down menus also activated by the mouse. A number of drop-down menus are accessible from the bar at the top of each window. They are accessed by a single click of the mouse with the pointer controlled by the mouse on the relevant word at the top of the window. Alternatively pressing the {Alt} key and keying the underlined letter in that word will 'open' the menu.

To install CDS/ISIS for window insert the disk1 in your drive from window 95 start menu run **a:\setup.exe.** The following screen will be appear, to chose "Continue" to start installation procedure and follow the instructions on the screen: usually you may just click "OK" to each installation question

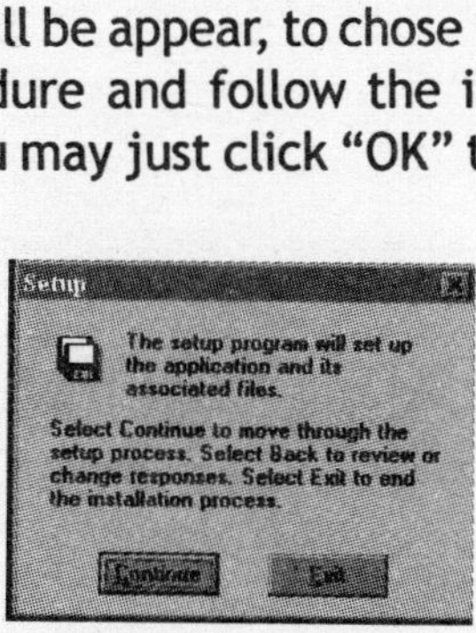

3.5. CDS/ISIS-Running

To launch the CDS/ISIS for Windows (Winisis):Locate the program shortcut. In Windows 95 it is in the Start menu, folder programs.

Click the item to run Winisis

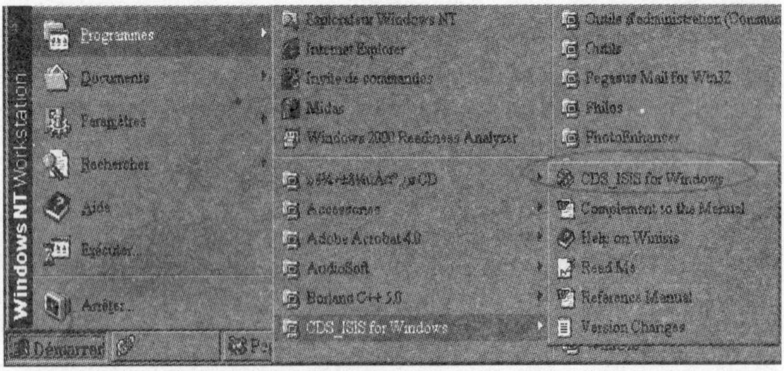

The following screen will appear:

In case of problems, please read the "readme.wri" file.

Use **menus and buttons** to access the CDS/ISIS services:

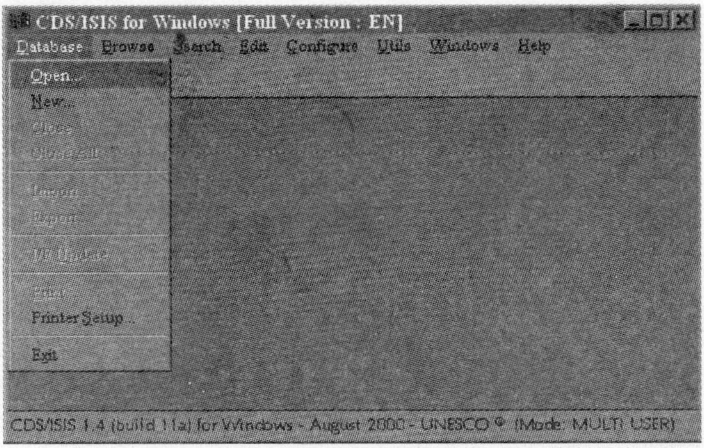

In order to get familiar with the system, two databases are provided as examples. The most important is CDS.

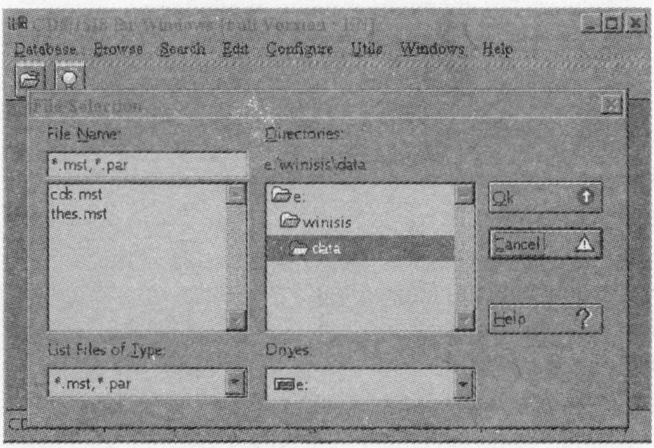

To open an existing database select the menu option File Open. Double-click on "CDS" from the database list.

The database "CDS" is now open and you may start using the CDS/ISIS services:

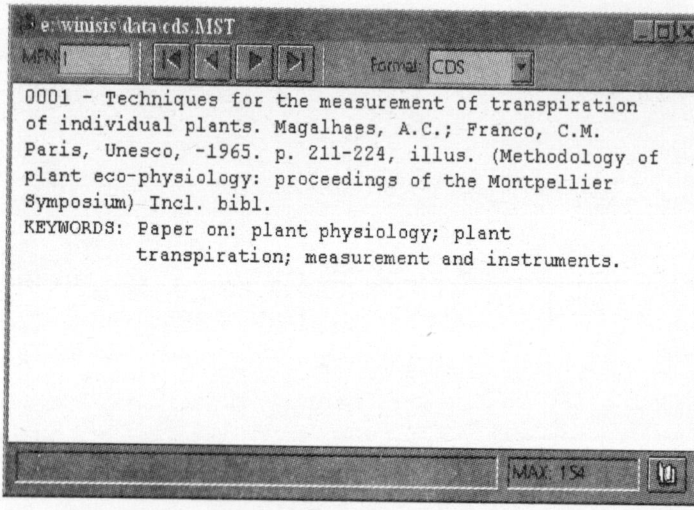

The CDS/ISIS interface is multi-lingual. UNESCO's version comes with menus and messages in:

English, Spanish (2 Versions), French and Italian. Users may create their own language versions by translating system messages to another language. This procedure is quite simple and is explained in the Reference Manual. Among other available languages are: Portuguese, Dutch, Polish, Vietnamese, German and Slovak. Other language versions of CDS/ISIS are under development or its feasibility study has been completed: Russian, Kazak, Armenian, and Azeri. A successful effort has been made to develop a complete Arabic version of CDS/ISIS in co-operation with the Arab League Documentation Centre.

At any time you may configure CDS/ISIS for Windows using the "Configure - System Settings" menu:

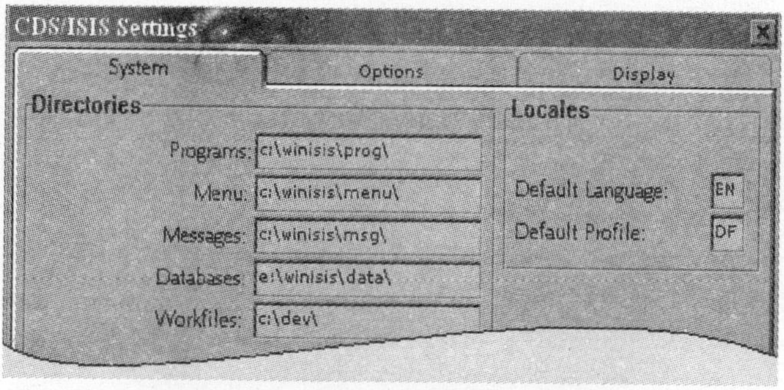

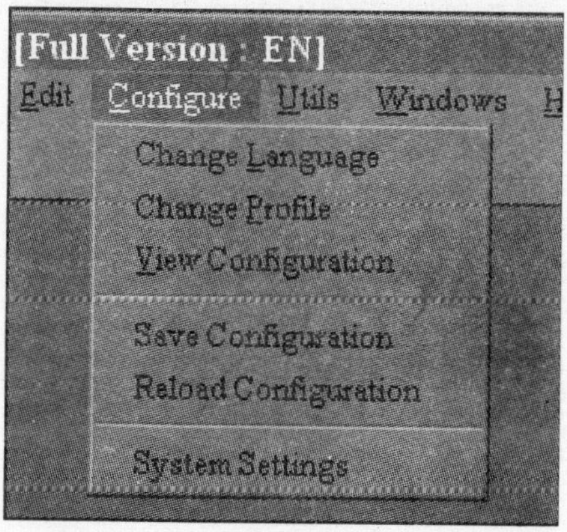

Use the menu "Configure" to change the current interface language and profile at any time

3.6. CDS/ISIS - Basic Information retrieval

3.6.1. To browse the content of an existing database:

Open the database file (ex. CDS.MST)

Use the arrows to move within the records sequentially, just as the pages of a book

You may select different views by choosing a different display format

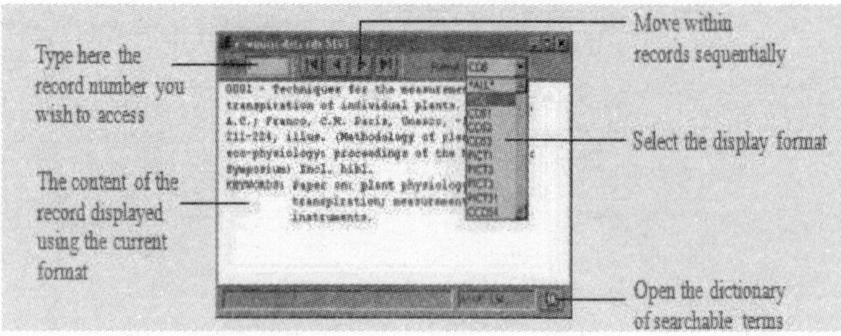

3.6.2. To search an existing database:

Open the corresponding file (ex. CDS.MST. Select option "**Search - Expert Search**".

Select option "Search - Expert Search". Select option "Search - Expert Search".

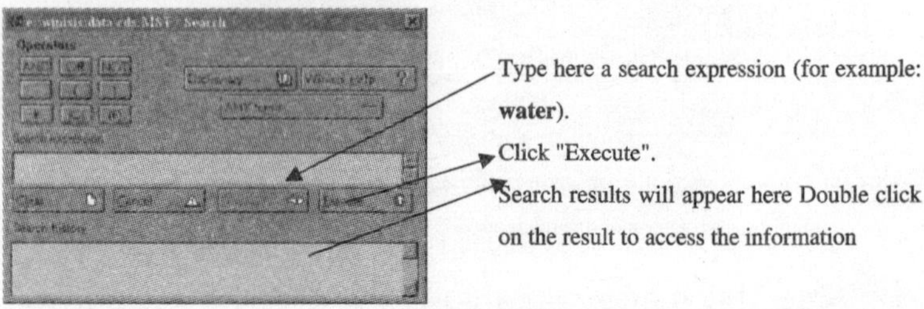

Congratulations, you made your first search with CDS/ ISIS!

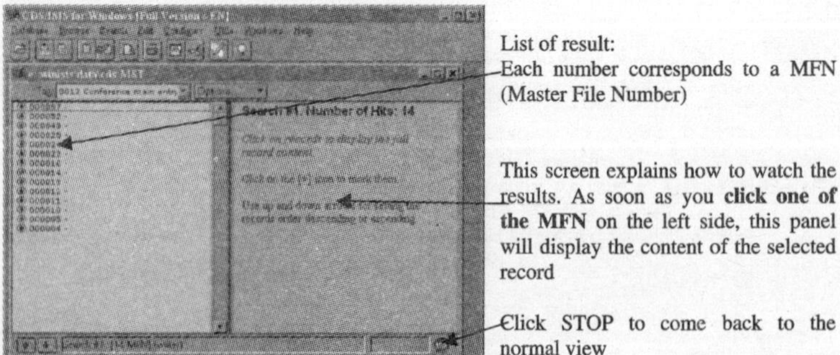

To make a new search select option "Search" again

In order to get an idea of what the content of database CDS is, you may display its dictionary of searchable terms. This will help you to find out what can we ask to CDS/ISIS and how:

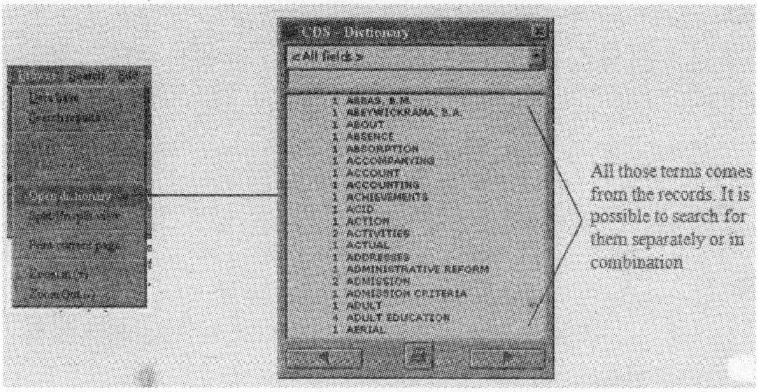

The dictionary of searchable terms, also called Inverted File, is built following the directives given by the **database creator** .Those directives instruct CDS/ISIS on how to extract the search terms from a record. The directives are collected in the Field Selection Table (FST)

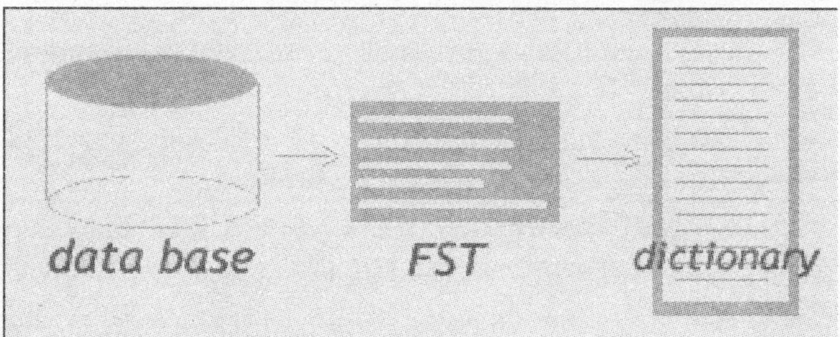

3.6.3. CDS/ISIS - Basic Data Editing

You may update the information contained in a given record by using the CDS/ISIS Data Entry option

Selecting this option will open the **Data Entry window**

which allows to modify the content of every single field.

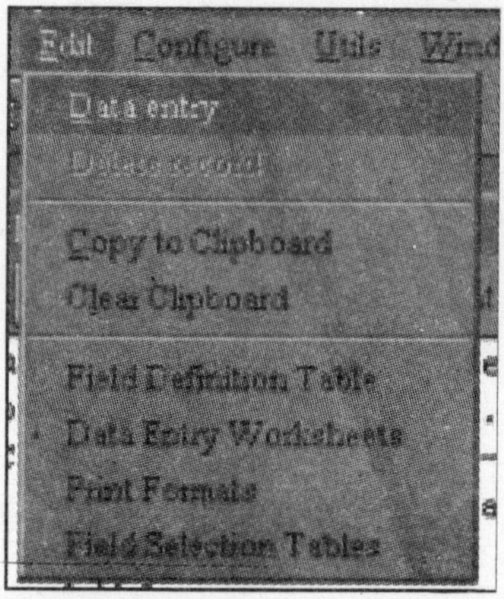

This window also enables access to further options:

Creation of new records

Deletion of existing records

Add./Deletion of fields, new repetitions, etc

When editing a record, the system will automatically check for some kind of errors, for example:

- Attempt to insert invalid subfield elements
- Attempt to repeat non-repeatable fields
- Other validation restrictions foreseen by the database manager

Each time the record is stored (saved) to the disk, the new content becomes available for browsing

You must ensure that the **Inverted File** has been updated in order to be able to search for terms in the new record

- Several **Data Entry worksheets** may be available for a given database, in order to insert different data elements.
- Each time the record is **stored** (saved) to the disk, the new content becomes available for browsing
- You must ensure that the **Inverted File** has been

updated in order to be able to search for terms in the new record

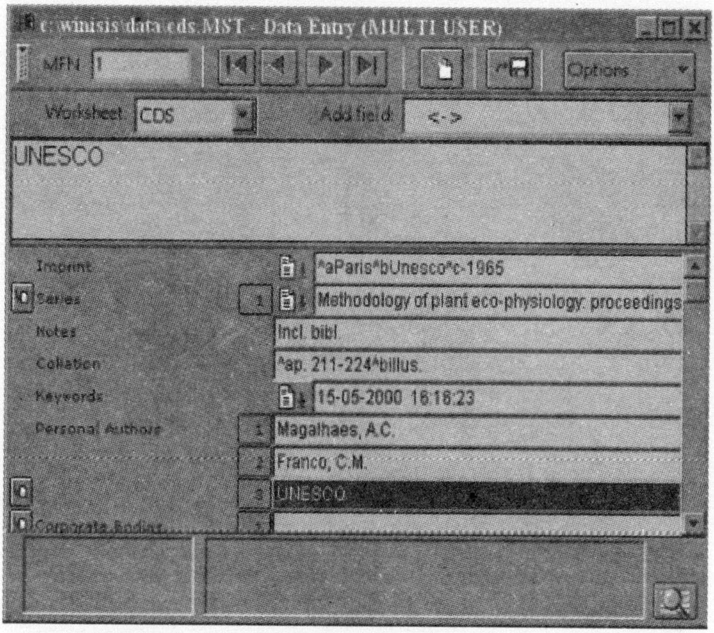

3.6.4. *CDS/ISIS* - Functioning scheme

- To resume, the following figure shows the role of the different components of a CDS/ISIS database

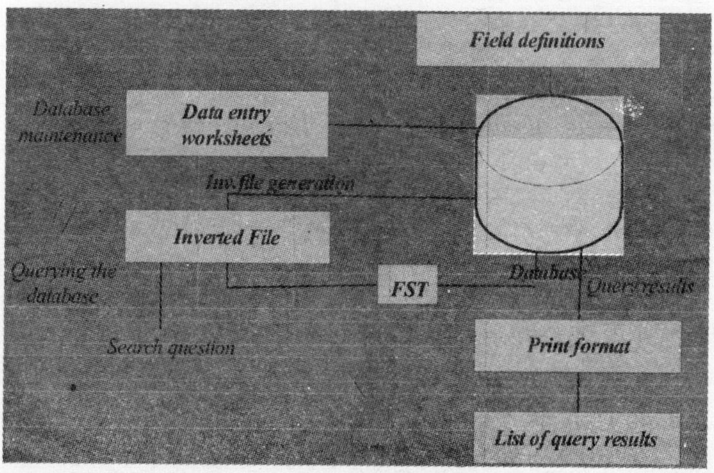

3.6.5. CDS/ISIS - Beyond my own computer

There are several ways to **share** information with others:

- Publish diskettes or **CD-Roms** containing the database(s)
- Share them in a **Local Area Network** (LAN)
- Share them in Remote Private Networks (through **TCP/IP**)
- Publish them to the **World Wide Web**
- Mix all the solutions above!!

4. CONCLUSION

A database management system (DBMS) is a program that can input, edit and retrieve information from a database. A database is a collection of information organized into records and fields, and stored as files on a computer. Sometimes the term database is used to include the DBMS as well.

Relational model, multi-dimensional, object-oriented, network, flat and hierarchical is all types of DBMS. They differ in how they organize information for storage. Retrieval from a DBMS requires a query language, a structured way for expressing search requests. Relational DBMS alone have a standard query language called SQL (structured query language). My SQL Server is a Relational Database Management System (RDBMS) that runs as a server providing multi-user access to a number of databases.

In this chapter discusses as regards CDS/ISIS & WINISIS software packages. Unlike Dbase or MS-Access, CDS/ISIS is not a relational database system, although it provides some relational facilities. It deals with questions like: "which research projects deal with basic education in India?" It also allows the user to design the record structure of each database.

REFERENCES

1. O'Brien, J. A., & Marakas, G. M. (2009). *Management information systems* (9 ed.). Bostan, MA: McGraw-Hill/Irwin.
2. Poulter, A. (2003). Database Management Systems (DBMS). In J. F. a. P. Sturges (Ed.), *International Encyclopedia of Information and Library Science*. London: Routedge, pp.126.
3. UNESCO. (2001). CDS/ISIS Retrieved 17, 2012, from www.unesco.org/isis/files/winisis/windows/doc/.../ Isis_Tutorial2. ppt
4. UNESCO. (2012). CDS/ISIS database software, from www.unesco.org/webworld/isis/
5. Wikipedia. Database Management System (DBMS) Retrieved 5 March, 2012, from http://en.wikipedia.org/wiki/ Database_management_ system
6. Williams, C. hi*et al*. (1994). Multidimensional models boost viewing options. *InfoWorld, 16*(4).

4

Open Source Software (OSS) Tools for Digital Library Management

0. INTRODUCTION

Now-a-days Information Technology (IT) becomes an indispensable concern of developing countries like India. One of the vital components of IT is software (Das, 2007). A feature of the software world over the past years has been the rise of Open Source Software (OSS) including using and developing OSS-names like Google, eBay and Facebook. Now, such software is increasing being used in the library environment. Today's libraries are faced with the challenges of integrating traditional and emerging formats, balancing resource allocation between traditional and upcoming technologies and building new information management processes and procedures. The explosion of the web, the internet and information technology in general has provided huge opportunities for those working in library and information professions in higher education (Wei, 2011).

The open source software phenomenon has over the last decade had a significant impact, not only on the software industry, but also on software-intensive organizations in both the public and private sector. In a library environment, budget, time, and staffing either predicate or prevent technological initiatives. While users' needs are growing, library budgets are shrinking. Libraries are increasingly looking for methods to meet user demands while simultaneously providing less costly quality systems and resources. In this context of an ever increasing need for technology and ever decreasing resources to acquire these new products, OSS offers libraries an attractive solution. Library end users with technical and nontechnical skills can participate in OSS installation and maintenance, librarians can engage in OSS development and modifications, and library user groups can often customize OSS environments. Moreover, OSS is an important library solution, for there exists a large user base for OSS applications, a wide variety of available OSS tools, and a multitude of OSS support channels. Additionally, OSS systems assist in the collection, maintenance, storage, and access of library materials, which fulfills the primary objectives of many library institutions. The benefits of OSS are compelling more active engagement between librarians and OSS communities, and the result is the adaptation of OSS applications at a rapidly increasing rate (Payne & Vandana Singh, 2010).

1. THE OPEN SOURCE MOVEMENT

The open source movement is a broad-reaching movement of individuals who feel that software should be produced altruistically. The open source movement started in the 1980s. In this era, computer manufacturers tended to create their own proprietary operating systems for their computers. They also produced their own software applications or sometimes allowed software companies to do as well. Rarely, they bought in a proprietary operating system from a software company. This is how Microsoft achieved its position, by making its proprietary Windows operating system ubiquitous and using that as a platform to sell its proprietary applications, like Office.

In 1985 *Richard Stallman* was a highly regarded programmer, who worked at MIT's artificial intelligence lab, established the Free Software Foundation (FSF) as non-profit body dedicated to the development of free Software. Mr. Stallman resigned from MIT and founded the GNU project, hold the copyright in software created for it and enforce the licences. Under the GNU general licence, users were free to use and modify source code,

In a way analogous to the web making content publishing open to all, the open source movement blossomed into an enormous range of software, for all types of computer. Stallman had himself created a text editor called EMACS and a compiler called GNU C. A Finn called Linus Torvalds used these two software tools to build an entire open source operating, called Linux, based on Unix, thus realising Stallman's ambition for GNU. Now Lunix is available in a number of different versions/distributions, called "distros", Torvalds is only loosely in charge. Another important open source application is Apache, which is a web server and currently the most popular one in use on the World Wide Web. It is managed by the Apache Software Foundation, which pools funding donated to the project and runs the development of the software according to a business plan. Apache is one of a "stack" (i.e. collection of applications) which together create a platform for the creation and implementation of just about any large-scale application: this is the Linux, Apache HTTP Server, MySQL and PHP/Perl/Python (LAMP) stack, consisting of Linux, Apache, MySQL and PHP/Perl/Phython. The latter three are programming languages, while MySQL is a database. The website **http://sourceforge.net/** is the hub of the global open source community and contains a massive collection of open source applications. Because of its ubiquity, there cannot be any computer user today who, albeit unknowingly, has not used some OSS. Without OSS, today's networked environment would not be possible.

2. WHAT IS OPEN SOURCE SOFTWARE?

Open source is a development method for software

that harnesses the power of distributed peer review and transparency of process. The promise of open source is better quality, higher reliability, more flexibility, lower cost, and an end to predatory vendor lock-in. Open Source Software" (OSS) is computer software that is underlying 'source-code' made available under license. OSS is a marketing name for Free Software, coined in Feb 1998 as an attempt to overcome the confusion over the word "free" in the English language. Open Source refers to the fact that the source code of the software is open to and for the world to take, to modify and to reuse. Open Source Software, as used in this chapter, refers to software distributed in source form which can be freely modified and redistributed, i.e. OSS is freely modifiable and redistributable software. More precisely, it refers to four kinds of freedom, for the users of the software:

- The freedom to run the program, for any purpose.
- The freedom to study how the program works, and adapt it to specific needs.
- The freedom to redistribute copies of the original or modified programs, so one can help another.
- The freedom to improve the program and release your improvements to the public, so that the whole community can get the benefits. Access to the source code is a precondition for this (www.gnu.org/philosophy/free-sw.html).

A program is Open Source Software if users have all of these freedoms. Thus, users should be free to redistribute copies, either with or without modifications, either gratis or charging a fee for distribution, to anyone anywhere. Being free to do these things means that the developer does not have to ask or pay for permission. The license must allow modifications and derived works, and must allow them to be distributed under the same terms as the license of the original software.

Therefore, another group has been using the term Free Software instead of Open Source Software. They consider the Open Source Software is something close to Free Software, but not identical. They prefer the term 'Free Software' because, once we have heard that it refers to freedom rather than price, it calls to mind freedom. The word 'open' never refers to freedom. OSS is copyrighted and distributed with General Public License (GPL) terms to design to ensure that the source code will always be available.

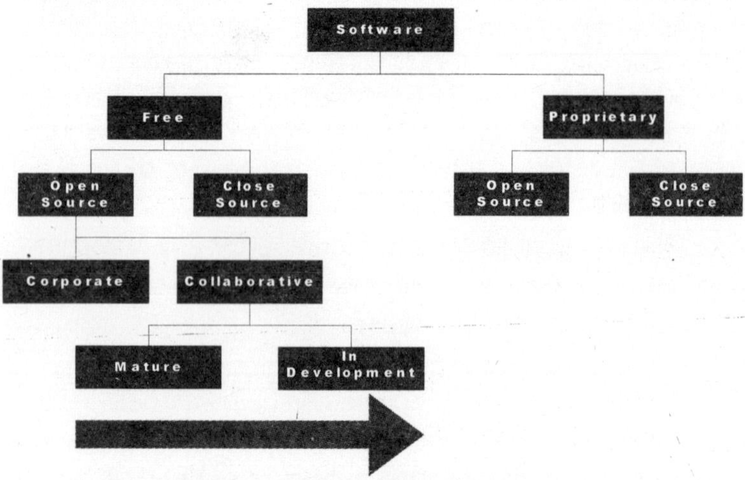

Fig. 4.1. Software Classification

Wikipedia (2007) offers a simple definition that is taken from Time Magazines, Dec. 25, 2006.It states: Open source software is computer software whose source code is available under a license (or arrangement such as the public domain) that permits users to use, change, and improve the software, and to redistribute it in modified or unmodified form. It is often developed in a public, collaborative manner. It is the most prominent example of open source development and often compared to user generated content (Wikipedia, 2006).

As described in the Open Source Definition (OSD), the idea of OSS promotes software reliability and quality by supporting peer review and rapid evolution of source code. To be certified as open source software, the license of a program must guarantee the right to access, redistribute, modify, and use it freely (OSI, 2006).

The *Open Source Initiative (OSI)* is the steward of the Open Source Definition (OSD) and part of its function is to review and approve licences conforming to the OSD. Many different licences satisfy the OSD, but the types of obligations they impose can vary quite widely. The OSD has developed ten criteria to determine whether a licence for software is open source (see Fig1.) (Wei, 2011).

1. **Free redistribution**: the software to be available for distribution without payment.
2. **Source code**: the soft to be distributed with the source or well-publicized access to it.
3. **Derived works**: the license must allow modifications and derived works, and must allow them to be distributed under the same terms as the license of the original software.
4. **Integrity of the author's source code**: distribution of "patch files" used to recreate derived works to be permitted.
5. **No discrimination against persons or groups**: the license must not discriminate against any person or group of persons.
6. **No discrimination against fields of endeavour**: for example, it may not restrict the program from being used in a business, or from being used for genetic research.
7. **Distribution of license**: the rights attached to the program must apply to all to whom the program is redistributed without the need for execution of an additional license by those parties.
8. **License must not be specific to a product**: license rights must not depend on the software being distributed with the other specific software.
9. **License must not restrict other software**: the license must not place restrictions on other software that is distributed along with the licensed software.
10. **License must be technology**-neutral: No provision of the license may be predicated on any individual technology or style of interface.

Fig. 4.2. The Open Source Definition

Harrod's Librarians' Glossary and Reference Book defines "Open source software (OSS) (*www.opensource.org*) that provides access to the source code, does not restrict any party from selling or giving away the software and whose license does not require a royalty or other fee and permits the creation of modifications and derived works to be distributed under the same terms as the license of the original software".

In conclusion, The OSS offer attractions to the libraries as majority libraries around the world, especially in developing countries, do not afford to purchase costly commercial software. Nevertheless OSS offer cheap alternatives to expensive commercial software with freedom from vendor lock-in and facilitate flexibility to modify for local needs. In this context it was felt that a study is deemed necessary to measure the perceptions of LIS community towards OSS.

2.1. The LAMP Model of Open Source Software

The LAMP model has shown influence on the information industry than anything else in the open source community, particularly in this age of World Wide Web and digital era. In this chapter, the acronym LAMP refers to a set of OSS programs used together to support dynamic websites or servers. The L in the acronym stands for the Linux operating system, which serves as the core of the LAMP model, the A represents the Apache Web server, which makes dynamic websites available from the Linux server so that users can access and interact with the Web pages with their Web browsers, the M refers to the database server MySQL, which is necessary for developing dynamic database-driven Websites; the P stands for one or more of the following scripting and programming languages: PHP, Python, or Perl, which can be used to create interactions between the end-users and the databases. With the rapid development of OSS, these components have been fairly mature and stable today, and the applications based on the LAMP model have been largely adopted by enterprises, institutes and governments. A low-cost LAMP Brower/Server (B/S) model for libraries can be simply described in the following diagram. The implementation of OSS packages discussed in the following sections is based on this structure (White & balsam, 2005).

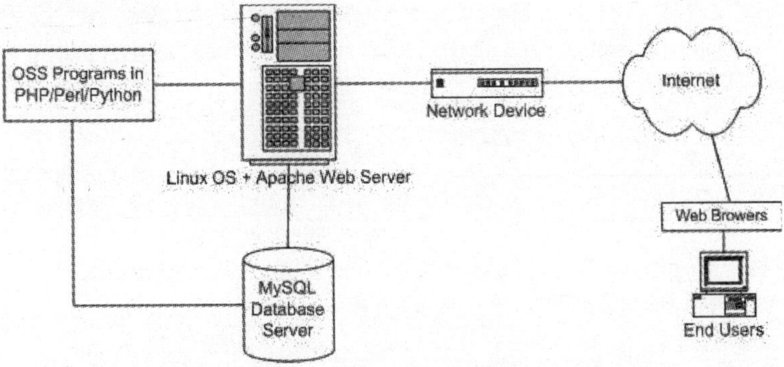

Fig.4.3 The B/S structure based on the LAMP model

In order to install and configure OSS packages for libraries described in this chapter, some basic knowledge about Linux, Apache, MySQL and PHP/Perl/Python should be comprehended. For the Linux operating system, the prerequisite knowledge includes how to choose a distribution and install it, some basic commands (e.g. *ls, man, mkdir, rmdir, cd, cp, mount, tar, ifconfig*, etc.), and X-window desktops (e.g. GNOME and KDE). Most Linux reference books cover these topics.

For the Apache Web server, it is necessary to know how to find the configuration files and how to modify them. The most predominant configuration file is named "*httpd.conf*" and normally can be found under the */etc/httpd/conf* directory in the Linux system. More detailed information on this topic can be found from the Apache's documentation site, http://httpd.apache.org/docs/2.2/.

In addition, it is also important to understand major administrative commands and SQL statements (e.g. *select, create, insert, delete, update*, etc) for the MySQL database system, which are covered by the online MySQL Reference Manual (AB, 2006).

Most scripts and programs mentioned in the following sections are written in Perl and PHP. Therefore, good knowledge of these languages is very helpful for customizing these programs for a specific library. The manuals of these languages can be easily found from their websites, http://www.php.net/docs.php and http://www.perl.org/docs.html.

Table 4.1: Open Source Software tools

Operating Systems	Linux (or GNU/Linux), FreeBSD/OpenBSD, NetBSD, GNU/Hurd, etc.
Windowing Systems	The X Window System, XFree86, etc.
Desktop Environments	GNOME, KDE, GNUStep, XFce, etc.
Languages	GNU C/C++ , Perl , Python , Tcl, etc.
Web Browsers	Mozilla (Netscape 6), etc.
Server-type software	Samba, Apache, PhP, Zope, MySQL, PostgreSQL, etc.
Office Suites	Open Office, KOffice, etc.
Productivity Applications	ABIWord, GNU Image Manipulation Program, Dspace, GSDL, KOHA, etc.
General Utilities	GNU Utilities, etc.

2.2. Use of Open Source Software in Digital Libraries

In the present day context due to the wide use of information and communication technology and digital/electronic storage media, it becomes a challenge to the library professionals how to acquire, organize, store and retrieve various information available in digital form. This has initiated the concept of creation of 'digital library'. *Harrod's librarians' glossary and reference book* define "Digital library is an umbrella term a) for conceptual models of libraries of the future that focus on the provision of services associated almost totally with digital content, and b) used to describe those aspects of existing library services that have a significant digital component". According to *Bhattacharya* (2004), digital libraries are managed collections of digital objects, created or acquired according to the principles of collection development, in which information is stored and distributed in digital form with the associated value-added services necessary to allow users to retrieve and exploit the resources just as in a traditional library. *Digital Library Foundation (DLF)* has defined, "Digital libraries are organizations that provide the resources, including the specialized staff, to select, structure, offer intellectual access to, interpret, distribute, preserve the integrity of, and ensure the persistence over time of collections of digital works so that they are readily and economically available for use by a defined community or set of communities". Digital library has a number of machine readable study materials as well as other publications such as text, images, sound, videos, and any combination of text, images, sound, videos etc. in digital form and facilitates remote access to several databases. The basic concept behind a digital library is to exploit the facilities of information technology with a mission of sharing resources available globally for providing nascent information to the users' community at right time.

Hence, a typical digital library has a media server connected to high speed networks, and we also call it 'Virtual Library'. Unlike a conventional library where users are provided with physical materials from many sources, a digital library is a group of attributed repositories that users see as single repository in a digital form. The functioning of a digital library is controlled by machines with minimum human interventions.

Nowadays, digital libraries provide an integrated set of services for capturing, cataloguing, storing, searching, protecting, and retrieving information, which provide a coherent organization and convenient access to typically large amounts of digital information. The OSS Library portal includes a number of library-related projects and some of these are detailed in Table 2. These range from simple scripts to produce statistics to integrated library systems to institutional repository software. Such as CDSware, developed by CERN and Fedora developed jointly by the University of Virginia and Cornell University, with funding from the Andrew W. Mellon Foundation. Fedora - Flexible Extensible Digital Object and Repository Architecture - is an open-source digital object repository management system that "demonstrates how distributed digital library architecture can be deployed using web-based technologies, including XML and Web services.[13]This chapter describes DSpace, E-Prints and Greenstone etc. Digital Library Software which is all widely used OSS for digital libraries. The digital library and repository software available can be broadly classified into:

(a) **Open Source Software (OSS),** such as DSpace, ePrints, Fedora, ARNO, i-TOR, CDSware, and Greenstone Digital Library (GSDL).

(b) **Commercial software**, such as DigiTool from ExLibris, and digital library software developed by VTLS Inc, etc.

(c) **Custom-made software**, Major digital library initiatives in India, such as the Kalasampada (www.ignca.nic.in/dlrich.html) and Digital Library of India (http://www.dli.ernet.in/) are using custom-made software or OSS that has been highly customized.

The Indian Institute of Information Technology and Management (IIITM), Trivandrum, has digital library software known as ABCD developed by BIREME, Brazil in association with UNESCO. Commercially available off-the-shelf digital library solutions are not known to be popular among libraries for the creation of digital libraries and repositories in India. This differs from the situation with library management systems (LMS) where a number of commercial LMS packages are used such as LibSys, SLIM++, Alice for Windows, SOUL, etc. This chapter describes Koha, DSpace, E-Prints and Greenstone Digital Library Software which is all widely used OSS for digital libraries.

Table 4.2: The Open Source Software Library Portal

Name	*URL*	*Types of Projects*
Uportal	www.jasig.org	The open source enterprise portal framework
GridSphere	www.gridsphere.org	The open-source portlet based Web portal
My Library	–	A Digital Library Framework and Toolkit
iVai	–	Based Web Digital Library portal
DSpace	www.dspace.org	Digital library software
E Prints	www.eprints.org	Digital library software
CDS invenio	http://invenio-software.org/	integrated library systems
Greenstone	www.greenstone.org	Digital library software
Apache	www.apache.org	Web server
PHP	www.php.net	OS programming tool
Linux	www.linux.org	Unix operating system
My SQL	www.mysql.org	Database
Mozilla	www.mozilla.org	Web browser
GIMP	www.gimp.org	OS image manipulation software
GNOME	www.gnome.org	Unix desktop environment

2.2.1. KOHA: First Open Source ILS

Koha (the Maori word for "gift" or "donation") is the first open source Integrated Library System (ILS), used world-wide by library and information centers. It is a one of the digital library open source programs for acquiring, organizing, storing and distributing the documents in digital format. It is built using library standards and protocols to ensure interoperability with other systems and technologies and provide a platform-independent solution. In 1999 when the Horowhenua Library Trust (HLT) in New Zealand, was looking for a year 2000 compliant replacement for their library system, using open-source tools to be released under the general public licence (GPL). In 2001, Paul Poulain (of Marseille, France) began adding many new features to Koha, most significantly support for multiple languages. By 2010, Koha has been translated from its original English into French, Chinese, Arabic and several other languages. Support for the cataloguing and search standards MARC and Z39.50 was added in 2002 and later sponsored by the Athens County Public Libraries. In 2005, an Ohio-based company, trading as LibLime, was established to support Koha and added many new features, including support for Zebra sponsored by the Crawford County Federated Library System. Zebra support increased the speed of searches as well as improving scalability to support tens of millions of bibliographic records. LibLime had registered a US trademark and replaced the Koha.org website at short notice· LibLime's "Enterprise Koha" hosted service (known as LEK) used code that significantly diverged from released Koha source code. With its advanced feature set, LibLime koha is the most functionally advanced open source ILS on the market today.

The current version is Koha-3.0.4 (Linux platform only) and Koha 2.2.9 (for Windows and other platforms) (http://koha.org). It runs on different platforms, including Linux, MacOSx, FreeBSD, Solaris, and Windows. Originally developed on the Linux OS, Koha is written in Perl, uses the Apache web server, and has better support for multi-RDBMS like MySQL, PostgreSQL. The OPAC interface is in CSS with XHTML. It supports all major library standards such as MARC record import/export, Z39.50 and SRU/Wfeature. Koha-3.x supports the Zebra full-text search engine as a backend, in addition to MySQL/PostgreSQL. Records are stored internally in an SGML-like format and can be retrieved in MARCXML, Dublin Core, MODS, RSS, Atom, RDF-DC, SRW-DC, OAI-DC, and Endnote; and the OPAC can be used by citation tools such as Zotero. Koha's default installation supports running Zebra which is configured to support SRU queries on bibliographic and authority data. Zebra itself is capable of detecting Z39.50 or HTTP and responding with SRU if the incoming request is HTTP.

2.2.2. Features of Koha

Koha has most of the features that would be expected in an ILS, including:

- Simple, clear interface for librarians and members (patrons)
- MARC based cataloging
- Various Web 2.0 facilities like tagging and RSS feeds
- Union Catalog Facility
- Customizable search
- Circulation and borrower management
- Cataloging module with integrated Z39.50 client
- Full acquisitions system including budgets and pricing information (including supplier and currency conversion)
- Simple acquisitions system for the smaller library
- Ability to cope with any number of branches, patrons, patron categories, item categories, items, currencies and other data
- Serials system for magazines or newspapers
- Reading lists for members

2.2.3. Greenstone Digital Library (GSDL)

The Greenstone Digital Library Software (GSDL) is a suite of software for building and distributing digital library collections. It provides a new way of organizing information and publishing it on the Internet or on CD-ROM. Greenstone is produced by the New Zealand Digital Library Project at the University of Waikato headed by Prof. Ian H. Witten in the early 2000s, and provides a suite of open source software for building and distributing digital library collections.

Greenstone is now developed and distributed in co-operation with UNESCO and the Human Info nongovernmental organization. It is open-source, multilingual software, issued under the terms of the GNU

(General Public License).Greenstone is powerful and flexible software which is of great potential interest to libraries and information centers and public private institutions in the world. It provides a new way of organizing information and making it available over the Internet. Collections of information comprise large numbers of documents (typically several thousand to several million), and a uniform interface is provided to them. The structure of a collection is determined by a configuration file. The collections range from educational journals to oral history, from newspaper articles to technical documents, from visual art to videos, from pop music collections to ethnic folksongs, etc.

Information available on Greenstone, it is used to create large, searchable collections of digital documents. In addition to command line tools for digital collection building, Greenstone has a graphical Greenstone Librarians Interface (GLI) used to build collections and assign metadata. Through user selected plugins, Greenstone can import digital documents in formats including text, html, jpg, tiff, MP3, PDF, video, and Word, among others. The text, PDF, HTML and similar documents are converted into Greenstone Archive Format (GAF) which is an XML equivalent format (Zhang, *et al.*, 2008).

There are six stages in developing a digital library using GSDL:(1) Collect information.(2) Describe the data.(3) Configure the collection.(4) Build the collection.(5) View the collection, and (6) Working with exiting collection.

Greenstone constructs full-text indexes from the document text, and from metadata elements such as title and author. Indexes can be searched for particular words, Boolean combinations, or phrases and results are ranked by relevance or sorted by a metadata element. There are several ways for user to find information, although they differ between collections depending on the metadata available and the collection design. The system is widely used internationally- the first few responses to a call on the Greenstone mailing list for testers for a new version of the software came from India, Pakistan, USA, Australia, Indonesia, The Netherlands and Canada. Nowadays, Greenstone 3 is a complete redesign and re-implementation of the original Greenstone digital library software and incorporates all the features of the existing system, and is backward compatible, that is, it can build and run existing collections without modification. Written in Java, it is structured as a network of independent modules that communicate using XML. A number of examples of libraries around the world that have implemented GSDL are provided on the website (www.greenstone.org); these include Human Rights in Argentina, Kyrgyz Republic National Library, Philippine Research, Education and Government Information Network and the Sudan Open Archive (Witten, *et al.*2003).

2.2.4. DSpace

DSpace is an open source software package that provides the tools for management of digital assets, and is the software of choice for academic, non-profit, and commercial organizations building open digital repositories. It is free and easy to install "out of the box" and completely customizable to fit the needs of any organization. DSpace system was developed in cooperation between Massachusetts Institute of Technology Library (MIT Libraries) and the U. S. Hewlett-Packard Labs about more than two years and put into using in October 2002.On November 4, 2002, MIT Library provided the first real-time service with the system and published its system source code under the BSD license agreement on open source. The system can collect, store, index, preserve, and redistribute any digital format and the data of hierarchical structure and permanent identity character (Wikipedia, 2012). It supports a wide variety of data, including books, theses, 3D digital scans of objects, photographs, film, video, research data sets and other forms of content. The data is arranged as community collections of items, which bundle bitstreams together. Its main features are: the storage-based asset management; the workflow mechanism constructed based on event triggering; the hierarchical access control management system (Ye & Huang, 2006).

The DSpace architecture consists of three layers: application layer; business layer; storage layer. The *application layer* is the user interface to use, and still provides a series of interface services, such as WEB user interface, OAI metadata harvest service, input/output data items. WEB user interface provides the user with an easy-to-use Windows. The *business layer* is the area of DSpace function integration, including the workflow, content operation, management systems and retrieval, browsing and authorize modules, each module has an API which allows the DSpace users to modify or expand function according to his own need. The *storage layer* is a document management system, which is managed by the PostgreSQL—Relational Database Management System. The main code was implemented by JAVA language in the overall system, which had selected JDBC the (JAVAAPI) actuation to connect database; On the one hand the storage layer is responsible for the backstage data bank operation to complete the organization and preservation of content, content metadata, electronic user, authorization, workflow and retrieval index; On the other hand, it is responsible for the binary stream (Bitstream) preservation, which is achieved by the file system and the storage Resource agency services (Storage Source Broker)(Wei-bo *et al.*, 2011).

However, DSpace system is an open source software platform, which can help users divide a variety of workflow modules, content models and digital resources, and publish figures through online search and browsing system. It is the best software system to achieve long-term preservation and open access in the digital space of academic achievements. DSpace provides the basic functions needed run agency's digital resources and will be the base for development to solve the long term preservation and public access in the future. The latest version of DSpace is 1.6.2, which was released on June 13, 2010.

2.2.5. E-Prints

EPrints is a free and open source software package for building open access institutional repositories that are amenable with the Open Archives Initiative (OAI) Protocol for Metadata Harvesting. EPrints has been developed at the University of Southampton School of Electronics and Computer Science, (UK) and released under a General Public Licence (GPL). E-Prints was designed initially to create a pre-print institutional repository for scholarly research, but is now used for other material including reprints, technical reports, conference publications or other means of electronic communication. On its website (www.eprints.org) this OSS is described as "a flexible platform for building high quality, high value repositories. It is recognized as the easiest and fastest way to set up repositories of research literature, scientific data, student theses, and project reports, multimedia, teaching materials, scholarly collections, digitized records, exhibitions and performances". E-Prints is written in Perl, require installation of the Apache web server and a number of Perl modules, and uses the MySQL database as a back-end.

EPrints is a Web and command-line application based on the LAMP architecture (but is written in Perl rather than PHP). It has been successfully run under Linux, Solaris and Mac OS X. A version for Microsoft Windows was released 17th May 2010. Version 3 of the software introduced a (Perl-based) plugin architecture for importing and exporting data, converting objects (for search engine indexing) and user interface widgets (Wikipedia, 2012).

Configuring an EPrints repository involves modifying configuration files written in Perl or XML. The appearance of a repository is controlled by HTML templates, CSS stylesheets and inline images. While EPrints is shipped with an English translation it has been translated to other languages through (redistributable) language-specific XML phrase files. Existing translations include Bulgarian, French, German, Hungarian, Italian, Japanese, Russian, Spanish and Ukrainian.

E-Prints have been installed and is running in over two hundred repository systems worldwide. Most repositories hold only electronic publications, but a number have been developed specifically to support research output. These include the Southampton Crystal Structure Report Archive, the National Aerospace Laboratories Institutional Repository, and the IUBio Software Archive. Simpson describes the use of the E-Prints software for the institutional repository at the University of Southampton.

In September 2002 ePrints@IISc (http://eprints.iisc.ernet.in) is India's first interoperable, open-access institutional repository to have been established. From the researchers' perspective, the Institute is trying to impress on them the advantages that they stand to gain by depositing their research papers in the open-access, interoperable institutional repository by stressing the following points:

- helps in establishing priority for research findings;
- being interoperable, metadata from the repository are available through cross
- archive service providers like OAIster;
- indexed by Google Scholar, Microsoft's Windows Live Academic Search, Scirus;
- better visibility and wider access;
- better impact and citations;
- rapid communication of research;
- long-term preservation;
- integrated view of IISc research publications;
- value-added services like individual and department-wise publication listings; and

- graphical view of usage statistics.

2.2.6. Fedora

Fedora (Flexible Extensible Digital Object Repository Architecture) was originally developed by researchers at Cornell University as an architecture for storing, managing, and accessing digital content in the form of digital objects. Fedora defines a set of abstractions for expressing digital objects, asserting relationships among digital objects, and linking "behaviors" (i.e., services) to digital objects.

The Fedora Repository Project (i.e., Fedora) implements the Fedora abstractions in a robust open source software system. Fedora provides a core repository service (exposed as web-based services with well-defined APIs). In addition, Fedora provides an array of supporting services and applications including search, OAI-PMH, messaging, administrative clients, and more. Fedora provides RDF support and the repository software is integrated with semantic triple store technology, including the Mulgara RDF database. Fedora helps ensure that digital content is durable by providing features that support digital preservation.

The Fedora Commons refers to the community surrounding the Fedora Repository Project. This community joins together with common needs, use cases, and projects. The Fedora Commons community is very active in producing additional tools, applications, and utilities that augment the Fedora repository. Many of these creations are available to the entire community as open source.

The Fedora Repository software has been installed by institutions, worldwide, to support a variety of digital content needs. The Fedora Repository is extremely flexible and can be used to support any type of digital content. There are numerous examples of Fedora being used for digital collections, e-research, digital libraries, archives, digital preservation, institutional repositories, open access publishing, document management, digital asset management, and more. The following is a short categorical list of the types of organizations in the Fedora Commons user community (alphabetically ordered): broadcasting and media, consortia, corporations, government agencies, IT-related institutions, medical centers and libraries, museums and cultural organizations, national and public libraries and archives, professional societies, publishing research groups and projects, semantic and virtual library projects, university libraries and archives (http://fedora-commons.org).

2.2.7. WEBLIS

WEBLIS is a Web-based library Integrated System based on CDS/ISIS. The system has been developed by the Institute for Computer and Information Engineering (ICIE) of Poland, based on their experience in building library systems for international organizations such as FAO, IFAD and GTS. It is run through WWW-ISIS engine, also develop by ICIE. The current version of WEBLIS, available in English, consists of four modules: Cataloguing system, OPAC (search), LOAN and Statistical module. In brief we can say WEBLIS is a freeware, implemented on WWW-ISIS as a platform. Its functionality and user interface is just "coded" by HTML, print formatting language, definition files and HTP files (http://portal.unesco.org/ci/en).

2.3. Software Security

To increase the reliability and security of code, OSS depends directly on the programmer's competence, experience and professional methodology such as peer review, testing, quality audits alpha and beta versioning etc. However, for the library' security enforcement, high-quality expertise is scarce and may often have to be developed to adequately cope with the increased responsibilities that OSS-based systems will require. Access to source code can also be an advantage to an attacker who can try to develop more elaborate attacks on the open source code. For example by malicious developers who could install backdoors or other undesirable functionalities may result in massive data losses in library.

2.4. Software Licences

Most countries' copyright laws have for a generation or more protected computer programs by subsuming them under the class of literary works for copyright purposes. As such, the holder of copyright in original software has the exclusive rights include to reproduce the copyrighted work and prepare derivative works based on it. Nowadays, Open Source Software (OSS) scope is set to increase. There are many different types of OSS licences. However, it coupled with a lack of settled case law and rapidly developing market practice, so libraries should also consider their procurement operations to make sure they have effective ways of verifying that code they buy or license in does not contain unexpected OSS and other necessary contractual cover

3. IMPACT OF OSS IN LIBRARY AND INFORMATION CENTERS

Two things distinguish the market for library systems in general. One is that "library automation", as it was called back in the 1960s, is something that, to their credit, libraries have engaged for a long time. The early days were characterized by library co-operatives pooling resources to share systems development, support and records. The venerable MAchine-Readable Cataloging (MARC) record, for example, dates from 1968. The second is that software customised for libraries has a very small market, relatively speaking.

This means that companies supplying library management systems (also known as integrated library systems) tend to be small, specialised and dependent on this one source of income, despite trying to generalise their products as "information management" tools. Some of the early library automation co-operatives (e.g. BLCMP,VTU) transformed into businesses. Continuing the venerable traditions of library automation, there is an impressive and growing range of open source applications available for libraries, from complete library management systems to utilities to support specific tasks (e.g. editing MARC records), or to add functionality (e.g. Z39.50 clients and servers). Koha was the first open source library management system. Developed in 1999 by Katipo Communications for the Horowhenua Library Trust in New Zealand, it first went live in January 2000. It has customers all over the world. The other main open source learning management system (LMS) is public information network for electronic services which was developed by Georgia Public Libraries. It is now supported by a consortium of 251libraries, covering a wide variety of types and sizes of library. Just as with open source in general applications, the range of utilities is vital in providing facilities which support core networked functions. And as with mainstream open source, there is a community supporting open source applications in libraries. For example, the website and associated mailing list at oss4lib.org has acted as an entire port for OSS applications: it mission is to build better and free systems for use in libraries. Toward this end, it maintain a listing of free software and systems designed for libraries [the physical, books-on shelves kind], and it track news about project updates or related issues of interest. oss4lib started at the Yale Medical Library in early February 1999 thinking there were probably other folks like us out there who might be working on free library software or looking for same.

Libraries tend to be reliant on other bodies to provide their information technology infrastructure, having usually no specialist systems staff. Thus, libraries tend to expect far more from library management system vendors than just software: they need quality support and guaranteed continued development of systems relative to new requirements and standards. This perception of better vendor support, rightly or wrongly, keeps them firmly wedded to the existing range of proprietary systems. Since this market is a niche one, there is unlikely to be any commercial drive to move in and upset the market for the established companies. What is a small market, will stay a small market.

This is unfortunate as there are strategic reasons for libraries to adopt OSS. The development of the internet has created a public information landscape which has isolated libraries by bypassing their aging commercial systems and undercut the value of their services. Rather than pay for the maintenance of existing systems and functions, by adopting OSS resources money could be directed into research and development of better library systems and services, to try to win a secure place and a bright future for libraries in the new networked world. Any new solutions discovered should be shareable by all. A thriving OSS community would be vital for this development. The development of digital library initiatives exemplify the potential opportunities for adopting OSS: for example, software for the open archives initiative is largely OSS. As XML moves into the mainstream, it is an ideal environment for OSS.

As Google seeks permission for its proposed massive digitization program of books, it presents an obvious threat of redundancy to libraries. It would be ironic indeed if the corporate champion of OSS was also the agent of destruction for libraries, wedded to commercial systems to the last.

4. CONCLUSION

Remember a time when doing research required us to have to go to the library? Your school/college had one, and that's probably where you spent most of your library time. If it wasn't your school/college, then it was probably your local town or city library. Some of these libraries may have been tiny little holes in the wall with just a few thousand books while others were huge university libraries with 10,000 of books, magazines, newspapers, cd, microfiche, and more.

The depth a library can have can range greatly; it all depends on how much money that library gets in funding. The big college libraries obviously get the most due to the fact that they are part of an actual business model that produces a significant amount of money. Public libraries on the other hand only get what the government gives them, which in smaller municipalities can be very little.

For many libraries, organizing books and other media can be a daunting task, especially as the library grows with more material. Years ago we had crude card catalog systems (remember the Dewy Decimal System) that kept things organized, but were difficult to maintain. With today's computing technology, organizing our libraries has never been easier or more efficient. Gone is the card catalog and in some libraries, it's much easier to locate a book through an internet connection and picking it up upon your arrival, rather than wasting the time scouring the aisles looking for your next read.

Now just because the world has been blessed with wonderful software solutions that make everything easier to do, doesn't mean that every library in the universe is using these solutions. As noted above, many libraries do not have huge amounts of money to burn, and any that they do get usually goes to purchasing additional resources for you to have at your disposal (think about how many books get printed in a year).

Because of this need for software (and the installation and training costs associated with any), and the lack of money available to spend on it, many libraries are left to fend for themselves when it comes to staying up-to-date with the latest technology. Unless, of course, they embrace the open source movement and use some of the countless software solutions available to help out. "Open Source" you say? If you are unaware what open source is, then let me briefly enlighten you.

Most software that we all use every day is known as

"proprietary", which in a nutshell means that it costs money and that the actual code of the software is restricted, in that the code of the software cannot be modified, copied, or changed from its original construction. The code is "unreadable" and pretty much is what it is.

Open source software, on the other hand, is quite the opposite. The open source mentality revolves around sharing and collaboration, and these two important elements describe open source software perfectly. First and foremost, open source software is free for anyone to have; more importantly, not only is the software free, but it is also free for anyone to copy, hack, modify, etc. This increases the possibilities of a software program's potential because of this free-thinking model. Many large groups of programmers have customized basic open source programs into whatever they deemed necessary, and have in turn given these modifications back to the open source community for free where others can continue to build on their work.

There are many different kinds of open source software solutions out there today that could be embraced by the library. There are basic operating systems and document processing programs. Then there's many web-based content management solutions and database driven organization software. So why aren't libraries using these free, open programs to make their lives easier and their libraries better? The answers you'll find lie in an area that one would think to be ironic given the situation - the lack of information. It will be our goal here to outline some of the prominent players in the open source software game and offer solutions to not only portray their role in the modern library, but offer the means to get these programs installed and up and running.

REFERENCE

1. AB, M. (2006). MySQL Documentation Retrieved 5 May, 2012, from http://dev.mysql.com/doc/
2. Bhattacharya, P. (2004).Advances in digital library initiatives: a

developing country perspective. *International Information & Library Review, 36* (3), 165-75.

3. Das, N. (2007). *Open Source Software and building digital library using GSDL software*. Paper presented at the 5th Convention PLANNER -2007, Guwahati University, Guwahati.
4. Digital Library of India. Retrieved 9 May, 2012, from http://www.dli.ernet.in/
5. DLF. (1998). A working definition of digital library Retrieved 11 May, 2012, from http://old.diglib.org/about/dldefinition.htm
6. DSpace (2006). DSpace repository Retrieved 5 May, 2012, from http://www.dspace.org/whos-using-dspace/Repository-List.html
7. ePrints@IISc. Retrieved 9 May, 2012, from http://eprints.iisc.ernet.in
8. Fedora Commons. Retrieved 9 May, 2012, from http://fedora-commons.org
9. IGNCA. Retrieved 7 May, 2012, from http://www.ignca.nic.in/
10. IIIMT-K. Retrieved 8 May, 2012, from http://www.iiitmk.ac.in/iiitmk-services/library-services
11. Janamanchi B, K. E, Raghupathi, W.& Gao, W.(2009). The state and profile of Open Source Software projects in health and medical informatics. *Int J Med Inform*, *78*,457-472.
12. Koha. LibLime Koha Retrieved 9 May, 2012, from http://www.koha.org/
13. OSI. (2006). Open Source Software Definition Retrieved 5 May, 2012, from http://www.opensource.org/docs/definition.php
14. Payne, Alexandria & Vandana Singh (2010). Open Source Software use in libraries. *Library Review, 59*(9), 708-717. doi: 10.1108/00242531011087033.
15. Prytherch, R. J. (Ed.) (2005) Harrod's librarins' glossary and reference book. Hampshire, England: Ashagate Pub. Comp.
16. Sandra, P. (1998).Flexible and extensible object and repository architecture (Fedora). *Lect Notes Comput Sc.*, 15(13), 41-59.
17. Tansley, R. & Harnad, S. (2000). Eprints.org Software for Creating Institutional and Individual Open Archives. *D-Lib Magazine*,*6*(10).
18. WEBLIS. Retrieved 10 May, 2012, from http://portal.unesco.org/ci/en
19. Wei, Z. (2011). Research on the application of Open Source Software in Digital Library. *Procedia Engineering, 15*, 1662-1667. doi: 10.1016/j.proeng.2011.08.310
20. Wei-bo, Lin; Cheng, Yi; & Chun, Li (2011). Establishing a university

library institutional repository based on DSpace and DIPS. *Energy Procedia, 13, 9322-9329.*

21. White, A., & Balsamo, J. (2005). Using LAMP to make our library shine. *Computers in Libraries, 25*(5), 6.
22. Wikipedia. (2012). DSpace Retrieved 5 May, 2012, from http://en.wikipedia.org/wiki/DSpace
23. Wikipedia. (2012). EPrints Retrieved 5 May, 2012, from http://en.wikipedia.org/wiki/EPrints
24. Wikipedia. (2012). Open Source Software Retrieved 5 May, 2012, from http://en.wikipedia.org/wiki/Open_source
25. Witten, I.H. and David, B.2003. *How to build a digital library.* San Francisco: Morgan Kaufmann Publishers.
26. Ye Ying, H.C. (2006). DSpace-based Lib2·0. *Journal of Academic Libraries, Beijing*, 2-5.
27. Zhang, A. B. and Don, G. (2008). *Creating digital collections: a practical guide*. Oxford, England: Chandos Publishing.

5

RFID in Libraries and Information Centers

0. INTRODUCTION

Radio Frequency Identification (RFID) systems is the use of a wireless non-contact system that uses radio-frequency electromagnetic fields to transfer data from a tag attached to an object, for the purposes of automatic identification and tracking (Wikipedia, 2012). RFID systems were developed about 30 years ago and were originally niche products. They were used for "radio tracking" of wild and agricultural animals and evolved later into a technology, which is used in many industrial applications today. For instance, all car keys of major car manufactures contain a little transponder (Sender) which sends a radio signal to the car steering wheel lock and to the car's electronics, resulting in a very efficient theft control. Also RFID systems are used for building access control, e.g. with "smart cards" for identification at doors. Another popular application is "Easy-Pass" used on tall motorways and bridges.

RFID systems have been in use in libraries for five years for book identification, for self checkout, and for sorting and conveying of library books and AV materials. These applications can lead to significant savings in labour costs, enhance customer service, and lower book theft and can provide a constant record update of media collections.

RFID is a combination of radio-frequency based technology and microchip technology. The information contained on microchips in the tags affixed to library materials is read using radio frequency technology regardless of item orientation or alignment (i.e., the technology does not require line-of-sight or a fixed plane to read tags as do traditional theft detection systems). The corridors at the library exist(s) can be as wide as four feet because the tags can be read at a distance of up to two feet by each of two parallel exit sensors.

1. BARCODE AND RFID TECHNOLOGY

Computer technology has helped libraries to perform their jobs efficiently and to the ultimate satisfaction of their users. Computers have revolutionised the work culture of modern day libraries. The growth in number and variety of computer-based technologies are playing important role in the efficient working of a library. Barcode technology is one such technology being implemented in the libraries at an accelerated pace. Barcodes are self-contained machine-readable identification labels with information encoded in a series of black bars and white spaces of varying widths that represent digits and other punctuation symbols. These are readable only through a reader or a scanner. A basic barcode scanner consists of a decoder and a scanner. The basic operation of a scanner is to scan a barcode symbol and provide an electrical output that corresponds to the bars and spaces of a barcode. Barcode scanner acts in much the same way as a keyboard. (Seema & Maninder, 2010)

Barcodes especially the UPC - have slowly become an essential part of modern civilization. Their use is widespread, and the technology behind barcodes is constantly improving. The application of barcodes in information management is incredible especially in easy issue/return, stock verification, user card, library clearance report, etc. There are two types of barcode, i.e. Linear barcode (UPC, Codabar, code 25, 39, 128) and Matrix 2d barcode (3-DI, ArrayTag, Aztec Code)

2. RFID TECHNOLOGY

As a general definition, radio transmissions containing some type of identifying information are considered as radio frequency identification. RFID is about devices and technology that use radio signals to exchange identifying data. In the usual context, this implies a small tag or label that identifies a specific object.

Radio frequency identification is a relatively new automatic identification system (auto-Id). Auto-Id refers to the methods of recognizing objects, getting information about them, and entering that data or feeding it directly into computer systems without any human involvement. Automatic identification and data capture technologies include barcodes, optic character recognition (OCR), magnetic stripes, smart cards, and biometrics. Typically, RFID systems consist of a microchip with a coiled antenna and a reader (Fig. 1). Data and energy are transmitted without any contact between the microchip and the reader. The reader sends out electromagnetic waves that form a magnetic field so that the microchip's circuits are powered. The chip modulates the waves and sends back to the reader. The reader converts the new waves into digital data.

Some of the current uses of RFID technology include point of sale (POS), automated vehicle identification (AVI) systems, access control within buildings, animal identification, asset tracking, warehouse management and logistics, product tracking in a supply chain, and raw material tracking/parts movement within factories.

Fig. 5.1. Components of an RFID system

2.1. What is RFID?

RFID (Radio Frequency Identification) is a wireless data collection technology that uses electronic tags for storing data. Like bar codes (those boxes of vertical bars and spaces that represent numbers and other symbols), they are used to identify items. Unlike bar codes, which must be brought close to the scanner for reading, RFID tags are read when they are within the proximity of a transmitted radio signal. RFID is sometimes called dedicated short range communication (DSRC). According to the *Harrod's Librarian's Glossary and Reference Book* "RFID an alternative to the bar code that uses tiny microchips in tags to hold and transmit detailed data about the item tagged". *Dictionary for Library & Information Science* defines RFID as " the use of microchips to tag library materials and library card, enabling patrons to check out items by walking through a self-service station equiped with an antenna that emits low frequency radio waves".

In other word we can say that RFID is a technology that incorporates the use of elecromagnetic or electrostatic coupling in the radio frequency portion to uniquely identify objects.

2.2. RFID History

As a basic concept; radio is the wireless transmission of signals, by modulation of electromagnetic waves with frequencies below those of visible light. The radio frequency (RF) area is broken down into a number of grouped frequencies that are called "bands". Very high frequency

(VHF) band covers from 30 megahertz (MHz) to 300 MHz. For RFID, most systems utilize one of three general bands: low frequency (LF) at 125-134 kHz, high frequency (HF) at 13.56 MHz, and ultra HF at 860-930 MHz. There may be some variation of frequency use, depending on the local regulations. RFID equipments are generally manufactured utilizing a specified band according to their potential usage environment. In the late 1940s, the scientist Harry Stockman published a paper about RFID, which he said is related to the "friend or foe transponder identification system" (IFF) used in World War II (John, 1993). In the IFF system, a coded interrogation signal is sent out on a particular RF, which the transponder receives and decodes. The transponder then replies with encrypted identifica- tion information. Each transponder has a unique identifier; however, some secondary information could be manually set by the pilot. In the late 1960s to the early 1970s, RFID developed its first commercial application, the electronic article surveillance (EAS) system, which uses a simple form of RFID with 1-bit tags to prevent shoplifting (i.e., everyone walks through EAS system panels when entering and leaving stores). Other RFID commercial uses followed, including livestock tagging, toll road payment.

3. THE RFID SYSTEMS

RFID systems consist of three components in two combinations; a transceiver (transmitter/receiver) and antenna are usually combined as an RFID reader. A transponder (transmitter/responder) and antenna are combined to make an RFID tag. An RFID tag is read when the reader emits a radio signal that activates the transponder, which sends data back to transceiver.

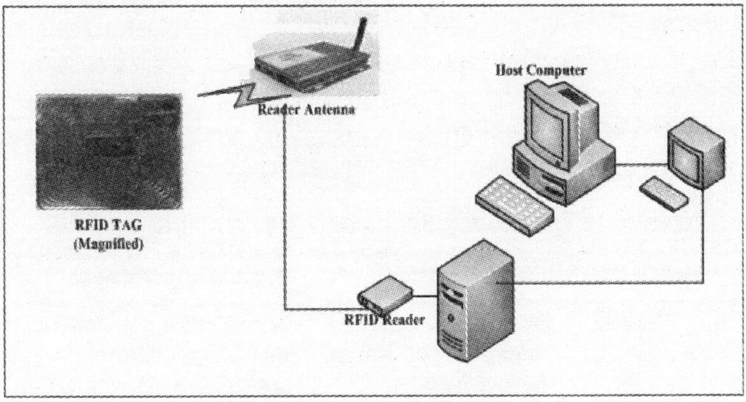

Fig. 5.2. RFID Systems

3.1. RFID Tags

The heart of the system is the RFID tag which can be fixed inside a book's back cover directly onto CDs and Videos. This tag is equipped with a programmable chip and an antenna. Each paper-thin tag contains an engraved antenna and microchip with a capacity of at least 64 bits. There are three types of tags: "read only", "WORM," and "read/write." Tags are "read only" if the identification is encoded at the time of manufacture and not rewritable. It can be used for EAS (Electronic Article Surveillance) or anti-theft devices. "WORM" (Write-Once-Read-Many)" tags are programmed by the using organization. They can be used a retrospective conversion of a collection. "Read/write tags," which are chosen by most libraries, users have access to read and write into the tag's memory. Tags have more memory and can used as data loggers. For example, in manufacturing line, data can be updated at every step of production.

All of the tags used in RFID technology for libraries are "passive" tag. The power to read the tags comes from the reader or exit sensor, rather than from a battery within the tag. "Active" tags, which have their own power supply, are substantially larger and more expensive than the tags used in library RFID applications. Low-frequency RFID systems (30 KHz to 500 KHz) have short transmission ranges of generally less than six feet. High-frequency RFID systems (850 MHz to 950 MHz and 2.4 GHz to 2.5 GHz) offer longer transmission ranges. In general, RFID systems are more expensive if they operate on higher frequencies.

Table 5.1: Frequency Bands and Applications of RFID

Frequency Band	*Characteristics*	*Typical Applications*
Low30-500 kHz	Short to medium read range Inex pensive low reading speed	Access control Animal identification Inventory control Car immobiliser
Intermediate 10-15 MHz	Short to medium read range potentially inexpensive medium reading speed	Access control Smart cards
High 850-950 MHz2.4-5.8 GHz	Long read range High reading speed Line of sight required Expensive	Railroad car monitoring Toll collection systems

3.2. RFID Readers

RFID readers or receivers are composed of a radio frequency module, a control unit and an antenna to interrogate electronic tags via radio frequency (RF) communication. The reader powers an antenna to generate an RF field. When a tag passes through the field, the information stored on the chip in the tag is decoded by the reader and sent to the server, which in turn, communicates with the automated library system when the RFID system is interfaced with it.

RFID exist gate readers at exists are two types. One type reads the information on the tags going by and communicates that information to a server. The server, after checking the circulation database, turns on an alarm if the material is not properly checked out. Another type relies on a "theft" byte in the tag that is turned on or off to show that the item has been charged or not, making it unnecessary to communicate with the circulation database.

Readers in RFID library are used in the various ways i.e., conversion station, staff workstation at circulation, self-checkout station, exist sensors, book-drop reader, sorter and conveyor and hand-held reader.

3.3. Antenna

The antenna uses radio frequency waves to transmit signal that activate the transponder. Antenna is the channel between the tag and the reader, which controls the system's data acquisitions and communication. The electromagnetic field produced by an antenna can be constantly present when multiple tags are expected continually. Antennas can be built into a doorframe to receive tag data from person's things passing through the door.

3.4. Server

The Server is the heart of some comprehensive RFID systems. It is the communications gateway among the various components. It receives the information from one or more of the readers and exchanges information with the circulation database. Its software includes the APIs (Applications programming Interface) necessary to interface it with the automated library system.

4. RFID ISSUES

4.1. New Technology for Efficiency in Operations

New technologies have always been of libraries, both for the potential of increasing the quality of service and for improving efficiency of operations. At the present time when, libraries of all kind (public, research, special) are facing economical for cost savings in the operations and the management of material flows.

4.2. Looking Back at Bar Codes

RFID is an identification technology; it does the same job as bar codes but offers potentially a lot more. It can therefore fruitful to look back at bar code technology and learn its application in library operations. Bar codes is fundamental technology for library operations and flow managements, it provides the coupling between the information system (the ILS, or Integrated Library System) and the physical flow of library material. In applications at circulation desk bar code technology has been proven to be robust, reliable and efficient. In the effort to extend bar code technology to self-service stations, which is one major direction for achieving better efficiency in operations, the experiences have been less than satisfactory.

4.3. Electromagnetic Security Systems

Bar codes cannot be the signal feed for anti-theft system so the usual combination is to have a combination of bar codes for identification, and some electromagnetic (EM) system must interact with the anti-theft system, so that items have the correct EM state after the circulation transactions, i.e. checked-out item must be deactivated, and returned items activated. The signal source for the anti-theft system, i.e. the magnetic stripe, label, or rod, there is a danger of a technology trap: once the magnetic device is attached to the library item it should, ideally, not be possible to take it away.

4.4. Interoperability through the supply chain

It can be tricky to set up antenna fields. Tags use reflected power and modulate the reflections to respond to reader inquiries. However, just about any object can cause of degree of reflection and noise.

4.5. IT infrastructure to handle large amounts of data

Since RFID tags contain much more information than bar codes, many IT infrastructures may have to be upgraded.

4.6. Change of work practices

In some supply chain or manufacturing instances, the

RFID tag might be updated with new information as the object it's attached to works its way along the chain or assembly line. Changes in work flow and work habits could result.

5. ADVANTAGES OF RFID SYSTEMS

There are the following advantages of RFID systems:

5.1. Self-charging/Discharging

The use of RFID reduces the amount of time required to perform circulation operations. This technology helps librarians eliminate valuable staff time spent scanning barcodes while checking out and checking in borrowed items. For the users, RFID speeds up the borrowing and return procedures. Library employees are released for more productive and interesting duties. Staffs are relieved further when readers are installed in book drops.

5.2. Reliability

The readers are highly reliable. Several vendors of RFID library systems claim an almost 100 percent detection rate using RFID tags. Some RFID systems have an interface between the exit sensors and the circulation software to identify the items moving out of the library. Were a library user to leave the library and not be caught, the library would at least know what had been stolen. If the user card also has an RFID tag, the library will also be able to determine who removed the items without properly charging them.

Other RFID systems encode the circulation status on the RFID tag. This is done by designating a bit as the "theft" bit and turning it off at time of charge and on at time of discharge. If the material that has not been properly charged is taken past the exit gate sensors, an immediate alarm is triggered. Another option is to use both the "theft" bit and the online interface to an automated library system, the first to signal an immediate alarm and the second to identify what has been taken out.

5.3. High-Speed Inventorying

A unique advantage of RFID systems is their ability to scan books on the shelves without tipping them out or removing them. A hand-held inventory reader can be moved rapidly across a shelf of books to read all of the unique identification information. Using wireless technology, it is possible not only to update the inventory, but also to identify items, which are out of proper order.

6.4. Automated Materials Handling

Another advantage of RFID technology is automated materials handling. This includes conveyor and sorting systems that can move library materials and sort them by category into separate bins or onto separate carts. This significantly reduces the amount of staff time required to ready materials for re-shelving.

6.5. Long Life Tag

RFID tags last longer than barcodes because the technology does not require line-of-sight. Most RFID vendors claim a minimum of 100,000 transactions before a tag may need to be replaced.

6. DISADVANTAGES OF RFID SYSTEMS

The following are the disadvantages of RFID systems:

6.1. High Cost

The major disadvantage of RFID technology is its cost. While the readers and gate sensors used to read the information are comparable in cost to the components of a typical EM or RF theft detection system, cost around $2,000 to $3,500 each; and the tags cost $.40 to $.75 each.

6.2. Accessibility to compromise

It is possible to compromise an RFID system by wrapping the protected material in two to three layers of ordinary household foil to block the radio signal. It is also possible to compromise an RFID system by placing two items against one another so that one tag overlays another. That may cancel out the signals. This requires knowledge of the technology and careful alignment.

6.3. Chances of Removal of Exposed Tags

RFID tags are typically affixed to the inside back cover and are exposed for removal. This means that there would be problems when users become more familiar with the role of the tags. In Indian libraries, it is a major challenge to keep the tags intact.

6.4. Exit Gate Sensor (Reader) Problems

While the short-range readers used for circulation charge and discharge and inventorying appear to read the tags 100 percent of the time, the performance of the exit gate sensors is more problematic. They must read tags at up to twice the distance of the other readers. There is no library that has done a before and after inventory to determine the loss rate when RFID is used for security.

6.5. User Privacy Concerns

Privacy concerns associated with item-level tagging is another significant barrier to library use of RFID tags. The problem with today's library RFID system is that the tags contain static information that can be relatively easily read by unauthorized tag readers. This allows for privacy issues described as "tracking" and "hot listing".

Tracking refers to the ability to track the movements of a book (or person carrying the book) by "correlating multiple observations of the book's bar code" or RFID tag. Hot listing refers to the process of building a database of books and their associated tag numbers (the hot list) and then using an unauthorized reader to determine who is checking out items in the hot list.

6.6. Reader Collision

The signal from one reader can interfere with the signal from another where coverage overlaps. This is called reader collision. One way to avoid the problem is to use a technique called time division multiple access, or TDMA. In simple terms, the readers are instructed to read at different times, rather than both trying to read at the same time. This ensures that they don't interfere with each other. But it means any RFID tag in an area where two readers overlap will be read twice.

6.7. Tag Collision

Another problem readers have is reading a lot of chips in the same field. Tag clash occurs when more than one chip reflects back a signal at the same time, confusing the reader. Different vendors have developed different systems for having the tags respond to the reader one at a time. Since they can be read in milliseconds, it appears that all the tags are being read simultaneously.

6.8. Lack of Standard

The tags used by library RFID vendors are not compatible even when they conform to the same standards because the current standards only seek electronic compatibility between tags and readers. The pattern of encoding information and the software that processes the information differs from vendor to vendor; therefore, a change from one vendor's system to the other would require retagging all items or modifying the software.

7. RFID OF INDIAN LIBRARIES/ INFORMATION CENTERS

Today's libraries in adopting RFID system are the need to increase efficiency and reduce cost. Automation and self-service can help libraries of all size to achieve, their operations, and the flexibility of tagging all kinds of media easily, are important criteria in choosing an RFID system.

The products of six manufacturers of library RFID systems are available in India through their business associates: Bibliotheca, checkpoint, ID systems, 3M, Edutech, X-ident technology GmbH represented by Infotek software and systems in India and TAGSYS - the last represented by Tech Logic, Vernon, Libsys in India and VTLS. There are several other companies that provide products that work with RFID, including user self - charging stations and materials handling equipments.

RFID technology has been introduced in a few Indian libraries. Edutech in India have done: Indian Institute of Technology, Madras (Chennai); Indian Institute of Management, Indore. Some other sites claimed by Libsys in India like University of Jammu (Jammu & Kashmir); Bank of Baroda, Mumbai; Indian Institute of Science, Banglore (only pilot project with 5000 books); Indian Institute of Technology, Kharagpur (West Bengal); IGCAR, Kalpakkam near Chennai (Tamil Nadu) yet to go live.

8. CONCLUSION

RFID (Radio Frequency Identification) is a technology that incorporates the use of electromagnetic or electrostatic coupling in the radio frequency portion of the electromagnetic spectrum to uniquely identify an object, animal, or person. RFID systems consists of three components (1) RFID tags that are electronically programmed with unique information (2) readers or sensors to interrogate the tags and (3) a servers or docking station on which the software that interfaces with the automated library system is loaded. This RFID technology may eventually replace the bar code and optical technology in library circulation systems. Tags are available in various shapes and sizes for use in a wide range of applications, with read/write capability for interactive application. The fact that high frequency radio waves can be used to track moving objects at a distance has raised concerns about privacy.

There are still many issues that must be addressed before RFID hits the big time like bar codes have some of those issues include: new technology for efficiency in operations, looking back at bar codes, electromagnetic security systems, IT infrastructure to handle large amounts of data etc.

RFID has advantages over bar code such as the ability to held more data, the ability to change the stored data as processing occurs, it does not require line-of-sight to transfer data and is very effective in harsh environments where bar code labels may not work. However, a lack of standardization, particularly in the commercial sector is currently delaying take up.

REFERENCES

1. Boss, R. W. RFID Technology for Libraries Retrieved 7 May, 2012, from http://www.ala.org/pla/tools/technotes/rfidtechnology
2. Cobb, M.). RFID projects: Implementation considerations, RFID security concerns Retrieved 15 May, 2012, from http://searchsecurity.techtarget.co.uk/tip/RFID-projects-Implementation-considerations-RFID-security-concerns
3. Hussain, A. (2007). RFID Technology for Libraries. *IASLIC Bulletin*, 52(1), 49-56.
4. Kabachinski, J. (2005). An introduction to RFID. *Biomedical Instrumentation & Technology*, 1-4.
5. Kern, C. (2004). Radio-frequency-identification for security and media circulation in libraries. *Electronic Library*,22(4),317-24.
6. Lindquist, M. G. (2003). *RFID in libraries-introduction to the issues.* Paper presented at the Biomedical Instrumentation & Technology, Berlin, Germany. http://www.ifla.org
7. PC Magazine. RFID Retrieved 11 may, 2012, from http://www.pcmag.com/encyclopedia_term/0%2C1237%2Ct%3DRFID&i%3D50512%2C00.asp
8. Prytherch, R. J. (Ed.) (2005) Harrod's librarins' glossary and reference book. Hampshire, England: Ashagate Pub. Comp.
9. Reitz, J. M. (Ed.) (2004) Dictionary for library and information science. Channai: Rain Tree.
10. Shahid, S. M. (2005). Use of RFID Technology in Libraries: a New Approach to Circulation, Tracking, Inventorying, and Security of

Library Materials. *Library Philosophy and Practice 8*(1).

11. Vasishta, S. and Dhanda, M.K. (2010). Transferring a traditional library to modern library using barcode technology: an experience of central library, PEC University of Technology, Chandigarh *DESIDOC Journal of Library & Information Technology, 30*(1), 44-48.

12. Wikipedia. Radio-frequency identification Retrieved 13 May, 2012, from http://en.wikipedia.org/wiki/Radio-frequency_identification

6

Social Networking Tools for Libraries and Information Services

0. INTRODUCTION

In the knowledge society in addition to technical skills and access to information technologies, it is becoming increasingly important for people to have diversified and supportive social connections. Social Networking-It is the way the 21st century communicates now. The term social networking service is an online service, platform, or site that focuses on building and reflecting of social networks or social relations among people. A social network service consists of a representation of each user his/her social links, profile, and a variety of additional services. Most social network services are web-based and provide means for users to interact over the Internet, such as e-mail and instant messaging. Online community services are sometimes considered as a social network service, though in a broader sense, social network service usually means an individual-centered service whereas online community services are group-centered. The various important types of social networking services are those that connect with friends (usually with self-description pages), and a recommendation system linked to trust. Popular methods now combine many of these, with Facebook, Google+, Hi5, Orkut, MySpace, and Twitter widely used worldwide. *The Oxford English Dictionary Online* (2010) defines "social networking as... the use or establishment of social networks or connections; (now esp.) the use of Web sites which enable users to interact with one another, find and contact people with common interests, etc." Another word we can say that social networking sites allow users to share ideas, activities, events, and interests within their individual networks (Dickson & Holley, 2010).

In general social networking services allow users to create a profile for themselves and can be broken down into two bread categories. Internal Social Networking (ISN) and External Social Networking (ESN) (MySpace, Facebook, Twitter and Bebo etc). An ISN is a closed /private community that consists of a group of people within a company, association, society, education provider and organization or even an "invite only" group created by a user in a ESN. ESN's can be smaller specialized communities or they can be large generic social networking sites.

Though, whether specialized or generic there is commonality across the general approach of social networking sites. Users can upload a picture of themselves create their 'profile' and can often be "friends" with other users. In most social networking services, both users must confirm that they are friends before they are linked. For example, if Duncan lists Molder as a friend, then Molder would have to approve Duncan's friend request before they are listed as friends. Some social networking sites have a "favorites" feature that does not need approval from the other user. Social networks usually have privacy controls that allow the user to choose who can view their profile or contact them, etc.

The varied social networking tools are increasingly used by individuals of all ages but are especially popular among young people and college students. Due to high use among these two groups, many academic librarians advocate using these new social Web platforms to reach out to student populations.

1. IMPACT OF SOCIAL NETWORKING

Web-based social networking services make it possible to connect people who share interests and activities across political, economic, and geographic borders.[7] Facebook and other social networking tools is increasingly the object of scholarly research. Scholars in many fields have begun to investigate the impact of social-networking sites, investigating how such sites may play into issues of identity, privacy social capital, youth culture, and education.

Social networks are providing a different way for individuals to communicate digitally. These communities of hypertexts allow for the sharing of information and ideas, an old concept placed in a digital environment (Zyl, 2009).

2. FEATURES OF SOCIAL NETWORKING

Much of the buzz in the online world today is about social networking sites (SNS). The likes of the video sharing site YouTube, community sites like MySpace, Facebook, Friendster, photo sharing sites Flickr, photobucket, user tagging/sharing sites del.ilcio.us, digg, LinkedIn have made a strong impact among internet users around the world. According to the Alexa.com - premier web site ranking i.e. Wikipedia, MySpace, YouTube, Orkut, Facebook and Friendster and similar social networking sites which have been ranked highly receive the highest hits compared with any other sites. The uniqueness of these social networking sites is to share information among users ranging from highly personal to academic interests of the participants.

Many sites allow users to post blog entries, search for others with similar interests and compile and share lists of contacts. User profiles often have a section dedicated to comments from friends and other users. To protect user privacy, social networks typically have controls that allow users to choose who can view their profile, contact them, add them to their list of contacts, and so on.

Some social networks have additional features, such as the ability to create groups that share common interests or affiliations, upload or stream live videos, and hold discussions in forums. Another social network allows professionals to exchange information, opportunities and ideas. Professionals are able to stay informed with new knowledge about their field.

Moreover, Geosocial networking co-opts Internet mapping services to organize user participation around geographic features and their attributes. There is a trend towards more interoperability between social networks led by technologies such as OpenID and OpenSocial. Lately, mobile social networking has become popular. In most mobile communities, mobile phone users can now create their own profiles, make friends, participate in chat rooms, create chat rooms, hold private conversations, share photos and videos, and share blogs by using their mobile phone. Some companies provide wireless services that allow their customers to build their own mobile community and brand it; one of the most popular wireless services for social networking in North America is Facebook Mobile.

3. EMERGENCE OF SOCIAL NETWORKING

The increase in popularity of social networking is on a constant rise, new uses for the technology are constantly being observed. The forefront of emerging trends in social networking sites is the concept of "real-time web" and "location-based." Real-time allows users to contribute content, which is then broadcast as it is being uploaded, the concept is analogous to live radio and television broadcasts. *Twitter* set the trend for "real-time" services, wherein users can broadcast to the world what they are doing, or what is on their minds within a 140-character limit. *Facebook* followed suit with their "Live Feed" where users' activities are streamed as soon as it happens. While Twitter focuses on words, *Clixtr*, another real-time service, focuses on group photo sharing wherein users can update their photo streams with photos while at an event.

Companies have begun to merge business technologies and solutions, such as *cloud computing*, with social networking concepts. Instead of connecting individuals based on social interest, companies are developing interactive communities that connect individuals based on shared business needs or experiences. Many provide specialized networking tools and applications that can be accessed via their websites, such as *LinkedIn*. Others companies, such as *Monster.com*, have been steadily developing a more "socialized" feel to their career center sites to harness some of the power of social networking sites. These more business related sites have their own nomenclature for the most part but the most common naming conventions are "Vocational Networking Sites" or "Vocational Media Networks", with the former more closely tied to individual networking relationships based on social networking principles.

Foursquare gained popularity as it allowed for users to "check-in" to places that they are frequenting at that moment. *Gowalla* is another such service that functions in much the same way that Foursquare does, leveraging the *GPS* in phones to create a location-based user experience. *Clixtr*, though in the real-time space, is also a location-based social networking site, since events created by users are automatically geo tagged, and users can view events occurring nearby through the Clixtr iPhone app. Recently, Yelp announced its entrance into the location-based social networking space through check-ins with their mobile app; whether or not this becomes detrimental to Foursquare or Gowalla is yet to be seen, as it is still considered a new space in the Internet technology industry.

One popular use for this new technology is social networking between businesses. Companies have found that social networking sites such as Facebook and Twitter are great ways to build their brand image. According to Jody Nimetz, author of Marketing Jive, there are five major uses for businesses and social media: to create brand awareness, as an online reputation management tool, for recruiting, to learn about new technologies and competitors, and as a lead generation tool to intercept potential prospects. These companies are able to drive traffic to their own online sites while encouraging their consumers and clients to have discussions on how to improve or change products or services.

3.1. Science & Technology

Julia Porter Liebeskind *et al.* (1996) have published a study on how new biotechnology firms are using social networking sites to share exchanges in scientific knowledge. They state in their study that by sharing information and knowledge with one another, they are able to "increase both their learning and their flexibility in ways that would not be possible within a self-contained hierarchical organization." Social networking is allowing scientific groups to expand their knowledge base and share ideas, and without these new means of communicating their theories might become "isolated and irrelevant".

3.2. Education

Social networks are also being used by teachers and students as a communication tool. Because many students are already using a wide-range of social networking sites, teachers have begun to familiarize themselves with this trend and are now using it to their advantage. Teachers and professors are doing everything from creating chat-room forums and groups to extend classroom discussion to posting assignments, tests and quizzes, to assisting with homework outside of the classroom setting. Social networks are also being used to foster teacher-parent communication. These sites make it possible and more convenient for parents to ask questions and voice concerns without having to meet face-to-face. The advent of social networking platforms may also be impacting the ways in which learners engage with technology in general.

The use of online social networks by libraries is also an increasingly prevalent and growing tool that is being used to communicate with more potential library users, as well as extending the services provided by individual libraries.

3.3. Grassroots Organizing

Social networks are being used by activists as a means of low-cost grassroots organizing. Extensive use of an array of social networking sites enabled organizers of the 2009 National Equality March to mobilize an estimated 200,000 participants to march on Washington with a cost savings of up to 85% per participant over previous methods. The August 2011 England riots were similarly considered to have escalated and been fuelled by this type of grassroots organization.

3.4. Employment

A social network use is being driven by college students using the services to network with professionals for internship and job opportunities. Many schools have implemented online alumni directories which serve as makeshift social networks that current and former students can turn to for career advice. However, these alumni directories tend to suffer from an oversupply of advice-seekers and an undersupply of advice providers. One new social networking service, Ask-a-peer, aims to solve this problem by enabling advice seekers to offer modest compensation to advisers for their time.

3.5. Hosting Service

A social network hosting service is a web hosting service that specifically hosts the user creation of web-based social networking services, alongside related applications. Such services are also known as vertical social networks due to the creation of SNSes that cater to specific user interests and niches; like larger, interest-agnostic SNSes, such niche networking services may also possess the ability to create increasingly niche groups of users. An example for this is Ning.

3.6. Business Model

Few social networks currently charge money for membership. In part, this may be because social networking is a relatively new service, and the value of using them has not been firmly established in customers' minds. Companies such as MySpace and Facebook sell online advertising on their site. Their business model is based upon large membership count, and charging for membership would be counterproductive.

Social networks operate under an autonomous business model, in which a social network's members serve dual roles as both the suppliers and the consumers of content. This is in contrast to a traditional business model, where the suppliers and consumers are distinct agents. Revenue is typically gained in the autonomous business model via advertisements, but subscription-based revenue is possible when membership and content levels are sufficiently high.

3.7. Social Interface

Social networking is a way for one person to meet up with other people on the Net. That's not all though. Some people use social networking sites for meeting new friends on the Net. Other's use it to find old friends. Then there are those who use it to find people who have the same problems or interests they have, this is called niche networking. Following this trend is the emerging trend of people meeting online to meet offline. More and more relationships and friendships are being formed online and then carried to an offline/in person setting.

Social networking sites play a vital role in this area as well, being able to meet someone as a "friend" and see what common interests you share and how they have built up their friend base and "likes" you can truly see a more whole picture of the person you are talking with and most sites are free instead of being pay based which allows younger people with stricter budgets to enjoy some of the same features. While not the intended or original use for these social sites a large area of their current function has stemmed from people wanting to meet other people in person and with so many of us so busy it is a fast reliable and easy way in which to do so that costs you little time and money.

4. APPLICATION DOMAINS

There are various application domain of social networking as follow:

4.1. Government Applications

Social networking is more recently being used by various government agencies. Social networking tools serve as a quick and easy way for the government to get the opinion of the public and to keep the public updated on their activity. The Centers for Disease Control demonstrated the importance of vaccinations on the popular children's site Whyville and the National Oceanic and Atmospheric Administration has a virtual island on Second Life where people can explore underground caves or explore the effects of global warming. Likewise, NASA has taken advantage of a few social networking tools, including Twitter and Flickr. They are using these tools to aid the Review of U.S. Human Space Flight Plans Committee, whose goal it is to *ensure that the nation is* on a vigorous and sustainable path to achieving its boldest aspirations in space.

4.2. Business Applications

The use of social networking services in an enterprise context presents the potential of having a major impact on the world of business and work. Social networks connect people at low cost; this can be beneficial for entrepreneurs and small businesses looking to expand their contact bases. These networks often act as a customer relationship management tool for companies selling products and services. Companies can also use social networks for advertising in the form of banners and text ads. Since businesses operate globally, social networks can make it easier to keep in touch with contacts around the world.

Two examples of social networking being used for business purposes are LinkedIn.com and Youngblack professionals.org. LinkedIn aims to interconnect professionals.

Another is the use of physical spaces available to members of a social network such as Hub Culture, an invitation-only social network for entrepreneurs, and other business influential's, with Pavilions in major cities such as London, UK. Having a physical presence allows members to network in the real world, as well as the virtual, adding extra business value.

Applications for social networking sites have extended toward businesses and brands are creating their own, high functioning sites, a sector known as brand networking. It is the idea a brand can build its consumer relationship by connecting their consumers to the brand image on a platform that provides them relative content, elements of participation, and a ranking or score system. Brand networking is a new way to capitalize on social trends as a marketing tool.

4.3. Dating

Social networks provide an online environment for people to communicate and exchange personal information for dating purposes.

These social networks, such as online dating services, require users to give out certain pieces of information. This usually includes a user's age, gender, location, interests, and perhaps a picture. Releasing very personal information is usually discouraged for safety reasons. Online dating sites are similar to social networks in the sense that users create profiles to meet and communicate with others, but their activities on such sites are for the sole purpose of finding a person of interest to date. Social networks do not necessarily have to be for dating; many users simply use it for keeping in touch with friends, and colleagues.

Therefore, the difference between social networks and online dating services is the fact that online dating sites usually require a fee, where social networks are free. This difference is one of the reasons the online dating industry is seeing a massive decrease in revenue due to many users opting to use social networking services instead. Many popular online dating services such as Match.com, Yahoo Personals, and eHarmony.com are seeing a decrease in users, where social networks like MySpace and Facebook are experiencing an increase in users.

4.4. Education

Social networks focused on supporting relationships between teachers and their students are now used for learning, educator professional development, and content sharing. Ning for teachers, TermWiki, Learn Central, TeachStreet and other sites are being built to foster relationships that include educational blogs, eportfolios, formal and ad hoc communities, as well as communication such as chats, discussion threads, and synchronous forums. These sites also have content sharing and rating features.

Social networks are also emerging as online yearbooks, both public and private. One such service is MyYearbook, which allows anyone from the general public to register and connect. A new trend emerging is private label yearbooks accessible only by students, parents, and teachers of a particular school, similar to Facebook's beginning within Harvard.

4.5. Finance

The uses of virtual currency systems inside social networks create new opportunities for global finance. Hub Culture operates a virtual currency Ven used for global transactions among members, product sales and financial trades in commodities and carbon credits. In May 2010, Carbon pricing contracts were introduced to the weighted basket of currencies and commodities that determine the floating exchange value of Ven. The introduction of carbon to the calculation price of the currency made Ven the first and only currency that is linked to the environment.

4.6. Medical and Health

Social networks are beginning to be adopted by healthcare professionals as a means to manage institutional knowledge, disseminate peer to peer knowledge and to highlight individual physicians and institutions. The advantage of using a dedicated medical social networking site is that all the members are screened against the state licensing board list of practitioners.

A new trend is emerging with social networks created to help its members with various physical and mental ailments. For people suffering from life altering diseases, PatientsLikeMe offers its members the chance to connect with others dealing with similar issues and research patient data related to their condition. For alcoholics and addicts, SoberCircle gives people in recovery the ability to communicate with one another and strengthen their recovery through the encouragement of others who can relate to their situation. DailyStrength is also a website that offers support groups for a wide array of topics and conditions, including the support topics offered by PatientsLikeMe and SoberCircle.

Some social networks aim to encourage healthy lifestyles in their users. SparkPeople offers community and social networking tools for peer support during weight loss.

Fitocracy is focused on exercise, enabling users to share their own workouts and comment on those of other users.

4.7. Social and Political

Social networking sites have recently showed a value in social and political movements. In the Egyptian revolution, Facebook and Twitter both played a pivotal role in keeping people connected to the revolt. Egyptian activist have credited social networking sites with providing a platform for planning protest and sharing news from Tahrir Square in real time. By presenting a platform for thousands of people to instantaneously share videos of mainly events featuring brutality, social networking proves to be a vital tool in revolutions.

5. SOCIAL NETWORKING: IT'S IMPACT ON OUTREACH

The rise of online social networking tools is rooted in the emergence of Web 2.0. Web 2.0 can be "loosely defined as the evolution to a social and interactive Web that gives everyone a chance to participate" (Kroski, 2007). The web is no longer the domain of those who possess computer programming skills. Average "internet users are creating knowledge repositories on Wikis, developing bibliographies through social bookmarking sites, building historical and cultural collections through media sharing applications, and forming relationships with like-minded individuals in social networking communities (Kroski, 2007).

With the enormous popularity of Web 2.0's social networking platforms, libraries of all types have embraced them as a method of promoting themselves within their communities. This new method of providing library services is referred to as Library 2.0. Academic library outreach is not a new phenomenon. Several outreach methods exist with the goal of encouraging library usage by faculty and students. Some outreach methods focus on programs aimed at faculty with the hope that faculty will encourage library use among their students. Other approaches focus more on the student population, including embedded librarians and collaboration with student organizations. Thus, the use of social networking is only the latest example of academic library outreach to students.

Student-based outreach is encouraged because college students today are less dependent upon the traditional library. With the rise of electronic and Internet resources, students may never feel the need to step inside the physical library or use a librarian in their research. Thus, many academic librarians advocate reaching students in their preferred environments in order to extend library services beyond the traditional library walls. Academic librarian Meredith Farkas (2007) is a strong advocate of reaching patrons where they are *"If libraries are not the first place our prospective users go to do research, they will likely miss any marketing we do on our own Web sites. This is why we must start looking beyond these sites and toward putting our content where our users actually are"*.

Online social networking provides such an avenue to reach college students in their own environments. The goal among academic libraries is to reduce the need for users to come to the library and "to repackage our materials into an environment that is more familiar to specific users" (Mathews, 2007). Based on a review of the relevant literature, the major social networking tools used today for social networking by academic libraries is the mainstream social networking web sites, blogs, wikis, social media web sites, and social bookmarking web sites.

6. WEB 2.0 TECHNOLOGY

The term "Web 2.0" was coined in January 1999 by Darcy DiNucci. It is popular when O' Reilly Media and MediaLive organized the first Web 2.0 conference. The term is closely associated with Tim O'Reilly because of the O'Reilly Media Web 2.0 conference in 2004. O'Reilly, define as a Web 2.0 is "the business revolution in the computer industry caused by the move to the internet as platform, and an attempt to understand the rules for success on that new platform. Chief among those rules is this: Build applications that harness network effects to get better the more people use them". A much simpler definition of Web 2.0 is "a space that allows anyone to create and share information online - a space for collaboration, conversation, and interaction; a space that is highly dynamic, flexible, and adaptable (Coombs, 2007). A key feature of Web 2.0 technologies is "philosophy of mutually maximizing collective intelligence and added value for each participant by formalized and dynamic information sharing and creation" (Meckel et al., 2006).

Web 2.0 is the popular term for advanced Internet technology. Owing to the extensive research in computer networking and internet use, more and more advancements are being developed in the communication technologies that enable people to become closer and participate in many local and global communities interactively. Fast and easier access to the internet through computers and the handheld mobile devices, and the interactive characteristics of recently developed Web 2.0 technologies have enabled people to collaborate in virtual societies more easily than ever. Web 2.0 is a collaborative web development platform that refers to the cumulative changes in the ways software developers and end-users achieve benefits from the web (O'Reilly, 2005). In the recent years, Web 2.0 technologies have become popular among the younger generation to make communication and effective and interactive.

Social networking applications such as blogs, forums, podcasts, and wikis are the successful implementations of the new generation Web 2.0 technologies. These provide web 2.0-based applications, programs, and services including web hosting, text-audio-video sharing, communication, social interaction, and many more.Web 2.0-based applications such as Facebook, Hi5, LinkedIn, MySpace, Nexopia, Twitter, and YouTube enable users to share ideas, opinions, interestswithin their individual networks over the internet in convenient ways. The free, open, collaborative, and interoperable features of Web 2.0 technologies allow users to create many virtual communities at home and abroad free of charge. The use of syndication technology such as RSS to notify users of content changes.

The two major components of Web 2.0 are the technological advances enabled by Ajax and other new applications such as RSS and Eclipse and the user empowerment that they support. The term Web 2.0 is commonly associated with web applications that facilitate interactive information sharing, interoperability, user-centered design, and collaboration on the World Wide Web.

Macaskill and Owen (2006) have defined Web 2.0 tools as a "web-based platform which allows users to gain access, contribute, describe, harvest, tag, annotate and bookmark web mediated content in various formats, such as text, video, audio, pictures and graphs." Stuart (2010) has defined Web 2.0 tools as sites which share stuff. Some of the Web 2.0 based popular websites are Flicker which can be used to share Photos, YouTube for sharing videos, Last.fm for sharing audio, and MySpace for sharing text based information.

But today it is the time of web 3.0 technology and the definitions of Web 3.0 vary greatly. Amit Agrawal states that Web 3.0 is, among other things, about the Semantic Web and personalization. Conrad Wolfram has argued that Web 3.0 is where "the computer is generating new information", rather than humans. And after that another term is raised that is Cloud computing, it is Internet-based computing, whereby shared resources, software, and information are provided to computers and other devices on demand, like the electricity grid.

6.1. Tools of Web 2.0 Technology

There are a number of Web-based services and applications that demonstrate the foundations of the Web

2.0 concept, and they are already being used to a certain extent in education and research. These are not really technologies as such, but services (or user processes) built using the building blocks of the technologies and open standards that underpin the Internet and the Web. These include blogs, wikis, multimedia sharing services, content syndication, podcasting and content tagging services. (Anderson, 2007)

6.2. Application of Web 2.0 Technology in Libraries/ Information Centers

Web 2.0 is a new trend in communication technology that has become a basis of the new generation internet to make it a more mature and distinctive medium of communication by facilitating user to develop web application interactively and interoperable (O'Reilly, 2005). Technologies listed in web 2.0 bellow, such as RSS, wikis, blogging; tagging and social networking software could be used for building up an active, institutional environment driven by libraries.

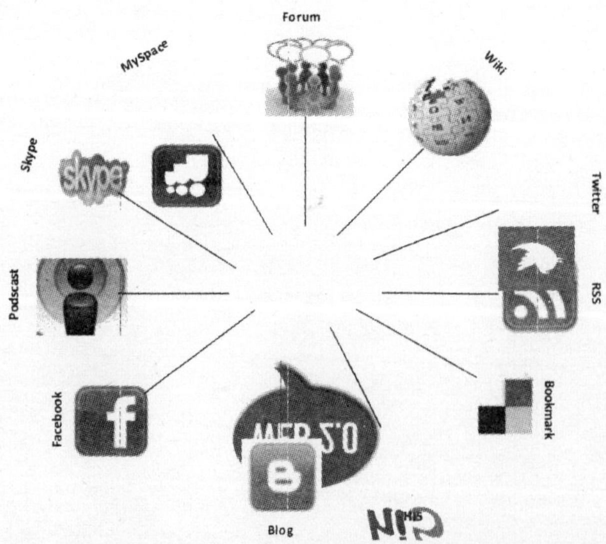

Fig. 6.1. Web 2.0 Services in Libraries and Information Centers

There are following essential facets of the Web 2.0 Technology in libraries/information centers.

1. Forum : Social Media Glossory (2008) define a " forum is an online community discussion group, usually centered around one topic or theme, where people can post messages or comment on other messages". Forum provides a meeting point for collaboration. Instead of linking to another piece of information, they are the starting point of a discussion or communal task. Forum is the easiest way to start working actively in Web 2.0 because there is a need to click a reply button and express the thought. Forum can be used in the three ways. (1) Act as an electronic medium for quick exchange of informal information and experiences related to new initiatives, plans, projects, information sources and services, forthcoming events and international developments (2) Purpose of forum is not only delivery of data in response to query but also supports communication among a large number of people belonging to different parts of the world within a short duration, and (3) Find new peer workers and enable posting problems (does anybody know?) and seek solutions. For instance LIS Forum, Digilib etc.

2. Blogs : A blog, an acronym for web log, or *blog*, was coined by Jorn Barger in 1997 and refers to a simple webpage consisting of brief paragraphs of opinion, information, personal diary entries, or links, called *posts*, arranged chronologically with the most recent first, in the style of an online journal. A blog takes in a user-friendly commentary format with separate postings rather than a threaded discussion board (Richardson, 2006). Users' ability to leave comments is the distinct feature of a blog. A typical blog combines text, images and links to other web pages, blogs, and contents related to the topic. A blog usually provides news or comments on a particular subject or a person's opinion in text, picture, audio, and video formats. Creating or editing a blog requires only basic computing knowledge. Blogs can be visited by local and global communities.

Libraries utilize blogs in a novel way that allows them to disseminate information to their patrons. Libraries are using blogs as a way to share information, to encourage feedback from their users, to highlight services or new materials, and more. Blogs have an impact on the activities of information professionals and they are a novel information channel for transferring information both to fellow professionals and to other users of the Web. In addition they also serve as an efficient tool for "marketing" library events and resources. Librarians use blogs to disseminate professional and general information, while libraries often use blogs for announcements. Librarians have taken to blogs like ducks to water. Peter Scott's list of Library Weblogs.

3. **Wikis :** A wikis have installed it on the Internet domain c2.com on March 25, 1995 and since then growing by leap and bound. A wiki is a collaborative web page that allows users to create and easily edit any number of interlinked web pages using a traditional web browser (Achterman, 2006). A wiki can be developed through the WYSIWYG (what you see is what you get) format that allows users to view its contents very similar to the end result while it is created. Wikis allow users to have different levels of access to edit or delete content. Creating or editing a wiki requires only basic computing knowledge - no programming knowledge at all. Wikipedia, the online encyclopedia, is a great example of a wiki that is created and constantly developed by its users.

This wiki was created to be a one-stop shop for great ideas and information for all types of librarians. All over the world, librarians are developing successful programs and doing innovative things with technology that no one outside of their library knows about. There are lots of great blogs out there sharing information about the profession, but there is no one place where all of this information is collected and organized. That's what we're trying to do.

If you have done something at your library that you

consider a success, please write about it in the wiki or provide a link to outside coverage. If you have materials that would be helpful to other librarians, add them to the wiki. And if you know of a librarian or a library that is doing something great, feel free to include information or links to it. Basically, if you know of anything that might be useful to other librarians (including useful websites), this is the place to put it. I hope this wiki will be a venue where people can share ideas with one another, and where librarians can learn to replicate the successes of other libraries.

As more educators and librarians collaborate in an online environment, wikis provide users with a tool that can be easily accessed, edited, and updated; and it provide an opportunity for students, teachers, parents, administrators, and community members to actively create new information for others.

4. Podcast : The term "podcasting" was first mentioned by Aled Williams in *The Guardian* newspaper in a February 2004 article, along with other proposed names for the new medium. A podcast is a series of digital media files in audio or video format. It allows users to publish their audio and video recordings over the Internet, episodically and to download them through multiple devices including cell phones, iPods, net books, laptops, desktops, and similar handheld devices (Richardson, 2006). Publishing audio and video recordings of lecture materials and class discussion on a podcast is a popular way of information sharing among the new generation of students, teachers and social workers. The *New Oxford American Dictionary* provides a broad, inclusive definition, stating that a podcast is "a digital recording of a radio broadcast or similar program, made available on the internet for downloading to a personal audio player" (Oxford University Press, 2010, p. 1348).*Online Dictionary of Library and Information Science* define, "A podcast is a series of digital media files (either audio or video) syndicated over the Internet and often downloaded through RSS feed."

Potential areas of application of podcasts in libraries as suggested by Abram (2006) are: story hours/story time (record your kiddy librarians); information literacy and research help; collecting and indexing good free podcasts (found through the podcast search engines); local history (collected from veterans, pioneers, local characters, etc.); teen book/DVD/game reviews (collected by the circulation desk);.music collections; audio book collections (on iPods and MP3 players);library events (like Science Fair help, Literacy nights, author readings); library debates; archiving class lectures; library marketing podcasts (how to use RSS, databases, VR, etc.); training; library gadget petting zoos (for staff and patrons); and public speaking training (partnering with groups).

The Library of Congress (The National Library of USA, Washington, D.C.) is offering podcast services such as voices from the days of slavery (stories, songs and memories), music and brain, digital preservation, national book festival etc. The British Library (The national Library of U.K., London) is offering podcast services for instance Talks, discussion and performance, tour and general information, events and exhibitions, planning your visit etc.

An example of weekly library instruction podcasts can be found on the Curtin University of Australia's web site at http://library.curtin.edu.au/podcast/index.html. Two examples of New Zealand academic libraries with instructional podcasts are Wintec in Hamilton with a library orientation podcast, hosted externally by Odeo here http://odeo.com/channel/128395/view and Unitec Library in Auckland with a library orientation tour and guide to the NewzText database available here http://www.unitec.ac.nz/library2/Podcasts/podcastindex.htm.

5. RSS Feeds : RSS stands for 'Really Simple Syndication', 'Rich Site Summary' or, 'RDF Site Summary'. RSS is a family of formats which allow users to find out about updates to the content of RSS-enabled websites, blogs or podcasts without actually having to go and visit the site. Instead, information from the website (typically, a new story's title and synopsis, along with the originating website's name) is collected within a feed (which uses the RSS format) and 'piped' to the user in a process known as syndication.

The RSS feed, in the form of an XML file, is made available on the web site, a site with one or more feeds is said to be syndicated.Users subscribe to the feed using an aggregator or newsreader that polls the site on a regular basis, maybe once a week, maybe once every quarter of an hour. The aggregator displays feeds and enables users to organize them and to access related Web pages when these are available. For example, the *New York Times* circuits feed summarizes the newspaper's most recent computer technology-related articles and provides links back to NYTimes.com for the full article.

The benefits of having an RSS are: libraries can inform others of purchases, exhibitions, or other events of the library, RSS save the time of librarian and user community as librarian has choice which links can be distributed. It is a very tool to bring the latest stories, updates from news groups, magazines, journals and blogs. In a recent study of Australian University Libraries, RSS was found the most widely applied technology (Linh, 2008). It creates a feed from a site that readers can then add into an aggregator to create one point of access for many sources (Davison-Turley, 2005).

6. Mashups : Mashup is a Web page or application that uses and combines data, presentation or functionality from two or more sources to create new services (Wikipedia, 2011). They are apparently hybrid applications, where two or more technologies or services are conflated into a completely new, novel service. *Retrivr*, for example, conflates Flickr's image database and an experimental information architecture algorithm to enable users to search images not by metadata, but by the data itself. Users search for images by sketching images. Another example is *WikiBios*, a site where users create online biographies of one another, essentially blending blogs with social networks.

It is a hybrid of blogs, wikis, streaming media, content aggregators, instant messaging, and social networks. Library 2.0 remembers a user when they log in. It allows the user to edit OPAC data and metadata, saves the user's tags, IM conversations with librarians, wiki entries with other users (and catalogs all of these for others to use), and the user is able to make all or part of their profile public; users can see what other users have similar items checked-out, borrow and lend tags, and a giant user-driven catalog is created and mashed with the traditional catalog.

Library 2.0 is completely user-centered and user-driven. It is a mashup of traditional library services and innovative Web 2.0 services. It is a library for the 21st century, rich in content, interactivity, and social activity.

7. Instant Messaging (IM) : Instant messaging (IM) is a form of real-time direct text-based chatting communication in push mode between two or more people using personal computers or other devices, along with shared clients. The user's text is conveyed over a network, such as the Internet. More advanced instant messaging software clients also allow enhanced modes of communication, such as live voice or video calling and inclusion of links to media.

IM falls under the umbrella term online chat, since it is communication also text-based as well as bi-directionally exchanged in real-time. IM is distinct in that it is based on clients that facilitate connections between specified known users (often using contact list, buddy list, or friend list), whereas online 'chat' also includes web-based applications that allow communication between (often directly addressed, but anonymous) users in a multi-user environment.

IM offered on the web by provider such as AIM, MSN, Yahoo, Skype, Facebook, and Google etc., which can provide the real-time face to face virtual reference services to the users. More and more libraries are using instant messaging (IM) as a way to chat with their users. It trend have been adopted by developed and European countries. But present period it trends have been developed developing countries.

Instant messaging is faster in terms of interaction between the librarian and the user than vendor-based chat, and it is free. In terms of training, it takes less time to train staff, as they are either already aware of IM or can learn to use it quickly because it is simple and straightforward. IM is also familiar to users; it encourages repeat use through the buddy list, and it is perceived as friendly.

8. Others Tools : The web 2.0 technology can be heavily used in the field of library today. More recently the term Library 2.0 is also available and a number of studies are taking place here and there every day. Library 2.0 is a loosely defined model for a modernized form of library service that reflects a transition within the library world in the way that services are delivered to users. The focus is on user-centered change and participation in the creation of content and community. The concept of Library 2.0 borrows from that of Business 2.0 and Web 2.0 and follows some of the same underlying philosophies. This includes online services like the use of OPAC systems and an increased flow of information from the user back to the library. With Library 2.0, library services are constantly updated and reevaluated to best serve library users. Library 2.0 also attempts to harness the library user in the design and implementation of library services by encouraging feedback and participation. Proponents of this concept, sometimes referred to as Radical Trust expect that the Library 2.0 model for service will ultimately replace traditional, one-directional service offerings that have characterized libraries for centuries.

7. CONCLUSION

Social networking sites are the Web 2.0-based applications that allow users to share personal information with each other in convenient ways. Social networking sites focus on building and reflecting upon social relations and interactions among people who possess the same interests. Social network sites essentially represent individuals' profiles, social links, and a variety of additional services. They enable users to share ideas, opinions, activities events, and interests within their individual networks over the internet through e-mailing and instant messaging. Facebook, Google+, Hi5, LinkedIn, MySpace, Nexopia, Twitter, YouTube, Picasa, Flicker, etc. are popular applications of social networking services. They emphasize online collaboration, social collaboration, and resource sharing among users free of charge.

On the other hand, Maness, 2006 focuses the social networking could facilitate librarians and users not only to interact, but to share and change resources dynamically in an electronic medium. Users can create accounts with the library network, see what other users have in common to their information needs, recommend resources to one another, and the network recommends resources to users, based on similar profiles, demographics, previously-accessed sources, and a host of data that users provide. And, of course, these networks would enable users to choose what is public and what is not, a view that could help avoid the privacy issues Library 2.0 raises and which well enumerates.

REFERENCE

1. Aalexa. (2021). Retrieved 12 May, 2012, from www.alexa.com
2. Abram. (2006). Podcasts and libraries Retrieved 11 May, 2012, from http://stephenslighthouse.sirsidynix.com/
3. Abram. (2006). Podcasts and libraries Retrieved 14 May, 2012, from http://stephenslighthouse.sirsidynix.com/archives/2006/11/podcasts_and_li.html
4. Achterman, D. (2006). Beyond Wikipedia. *Teacher Librarian, 34*(2),

19-22.

5. British Library. (2012). Podcasts Retrieved 8 May, 2012, from http://www.bl.uk/podcast
6. Carlson, B. (2010). March 2.0: Success of the National Equality March relied on social media tools Retrieved 11 May, 2012, from http://www.mediabullseye.com/mb/2010/04/march-2-0-success-of-the-national-equality-march-relied-on-social-media-tools.html#idc-container
7. Comscore. Introducing Mobile Metrix 2.0 Retrieved 10 May, 2012, from http://www.comscore.com/
8. Coombs, K. A. (2007). Building a library web site on the pillars of Web 2.0. Computers in Libraries, 27.
9. Davison-Turley, W. (2005). Blogs and RSS: powerful information management tools. *Library Hi Tech News*, 22(10), 28-29.
10. Dickson, A. & Holley, R. P. (2010). Social networking in academic libraries: the possibilities and the concerns. *New Library World*, 111(11/12), 468-479.
11. Farkas, M. (2007). Your stuff, their space. *American Libraries*, 38(11), 36.
12. German Xing Plans Invasion of LinkedIn Turf. (2007). *Marketingvox*. Retrieved from http://www.marketingvox.com/german-xing-plans-invasion-of-linkedin-turf-030727/
13. Hi5 popular in Europe. (2008). *Mediashift*. Retrieved from http://www.pbs.org/mediashift/2007/06/orkut-friendster-get-second-chance-overseas166.html
14. Kroski, E. (2007). The social tools of Web 2.0: opportunities for academic libraries. *Choice*, 44(12), 2011-21.
15. Libdex. Retrieved from http://www.libdex.com/weblogs.html
16. Library of congress. Podcasts Retrieved 8 May, 2012, from http:// www.loc.gov/podcasts/
17. Library Success: A Best Practices Wiki. Retrieved 13, 2012, from http://www.libsuccess.org/index.php?title=Library_Success:_A_Best_Practices_Wiki
18. Liebeskind, J.P., *et al.* (1996). Social Networks, Learning, and Flexibility: Sourcing Scientific Knowledge in New Biotechnology Firms. *Organization Science*, 7(4), 428-443.
19. Linh, N. C. (2008). A survey of the application of Web 2.0 in Australasian university libraries. *Library Hi Tech*. 26(4), 630-653.
20. Macaskill, W., and Owen, D. (2006). *Web 2.0 to go*. Paper presented at the Proceedings of LIANZA Conference 2006, Wellington.

21. Maness, J. (2006). Library 2.0 Theory: Web 2.0 and Its Implications for Libraries. *Webology, 3*(2).Retrieved from http://www.webology.org/2006/v3n2/a25.html

22. Mathews, B. (2007). Moving beyond the reference desk: being where users need us. *The Reference Librarian,48*(2), 9-13.

23. Meckel, M., Stanoevska-Slabeva, K. and Martignoni, R. (2006). *Overview of business models for Web 1.0 communities.* Paper presented at the Proceedings of GeNeMe.

24. Online, O. E. D. (2010). Social networking, from www.dictionary.oed.com

25. O'Reilly, T. (2005). What Is Web 2.0:Design Patterns and Business Models for the Next Generation of Software Retrieved 12, 2012, from http://oreilly.com/web2/archive/what-is-web-20.html

26. Reitz, J. M. (Ed.) Online Dictionary for Library and Information Science. Retrieved 12,2012,from http://www.abc-clio.com/ODLIS/odlis_p.aspx

27. Retrievr. (2011). Retrieved 11 May, 2012, from http://labs.systemone.at/retrievr/

28. Social Media Glossary. (2008). Forum Retrieved 7 may, 2012, from http://www2.capilanou.ca/help/login-page/active-cms/glossary.html

29. Stuart, D. (2010). What are libraries doing on Twitter? *Information Today, 34*, 41-45.

30. Sweney, M. (2007, 24 December). Elevator Pitch: Why Badoo wants to be the next word in social networking, *The Guardian*.

31. Times, N. Y. (2012). RSS feeds, *New York Times*. Retrieved from http://www.nytimes.com/services/xml/rss/index.html

32. Veneziani, V. (2007). Windows Live Messaging Coming To Bebo Retrieved 5 May, 2012, from http://techcrunch.com/2007/08/20/windows-live-messaging-coming-to-bebo/

33. Wikipedia. (2012). Mashup, from http://en.wikipedia.org/wiki/Mashup_%28web_application_hybrid%29

34. Wikipedia. (2012). Social networking service Retrieved 11 May, 2012, from http://en.wikipedia.org/wiki/Social_networking_service

35. Zyl, A.S.V. (2009).The impact of Social Networking 2.0 on organizations. *Electronic Library*, 27(6), 906 - 918.

7

Innovative Technology based Online Library Services

0. INTRODUCTION

In the olden times the books were kept under lock and key why because these were considered to be the pride of Emperors. The simple reason behind it was that the knowledge should not flow to masses and to avoid awakening among them so that the autocratic set-up should continue to function smoothly. Only few reputed persons in the court of ruler had privilege to access these books. As the time changed, the concept of library also changed accordingly. With the advent of democracy the more stress was given to the use of books. In India the whole credit goes to Dr. S. R. Ranganathan, the Father of Indian Librarianship. The library professionals are trying to make all efforts to save the time of users. Even though with manual facilities, a lot of time was wasted to find out required reading materials, Journals subscribed were received not in time or very late due to sea mail delivery or through agency which they take their own time for delivery. The desired document which was not available in the library, could be had from other library, took a long time to reach the destination. Thus, the library's users were suffered a lot and had to wait for long time to get the required information resources. Their research/ teaching works were also suffered a lot due to slow pace of flow of information.

Information is a vital resource for any kind of activity and it is more so in the field of advance scientific research, where new innovations, new methods, new techniques, new instruments, new products are discovered everyday in the globalised society. Scientists need to keep pace with the information explosion, they need to interact with the peers in their respective fields, they need to know their competitors and their achievements. The Internet is one of the sources which may help them in such situations and which is comparatively cheaper and faster. A connection to internet gives a user a real time access to online databases, library catalogues, software archives, full text reports/ journals and many other kinds of information. The Librarian has to play a major role of making sure that the people use not only traditional means but also digital systems to the best effect.

Infusion of technological elements in creative pursuit leads to the emergence of a new technology which becomes a part of varied spheres at varying speed over different routes. Today it appears that each new advance in technology centers on new ways to store, retrieve and transmit information. The Personal Computer (PC) can now deliver all types of information i.e. text, still images, graphics audio, etc. More particularly, the PCs have the ability to present all types of information in two different ways; for example in an integrated way and in an interactive way. It is quite clear that qualitative changes in the nature of information storage and retrieval have taken place. Internet has come in a big way for retrieval of enormous output of information combining the concepts of time, space and precision.

1. WHAT IS ONLINE SERVICES?

Online services employ online systems technology to

provide remote users with access to information organized in databases with greater flexibility, precision and speed than comparable print resources can (East, 2003). Online is a general term for devices and peripherals which are interacting directly and simultaneously with a computer in real time. Other word we can say that online is a reference to or the act of undertaking, online information retrieval (Prytherch, 2005). During period of 1960-70, the state of art on computer technology for accessing the databases was Batch Processing. It was expansive and unsatisfactory method in which programs or data accumulated and inputted to the computer in a single block. This processing always involves delay between the occurrences of the event and processing of the resultant transactions. In this type of search, the data was loaded into a computer and compared with the query of the user which selected the items. In this process the output was a subset of the data which covered the subject of the query.

The development of magnetic disc memory and the availability of computer file on disc media enabled the emergence of online search services. The term online now embodies many concepts. Literally it means that the user is in direct contact with databases user wishes to interrogate and to the computer on which it is loaded. The interaction between searcher and system is effected through terminals connected to the computer through communication lines (telex, telephone or satellite).

The alliance of computers and tele-communication has dramatically improved the potentialities of computer in the information transmission process cutting across geographical boundaries. As a result, several national and international networks have become available for data transmission. These computer networks made available online access to the users. This online access is called online services, through them we can access databases existing elsewhere in the world.

The online service is a business that provides its subscribers with a wide variety of data transmitted over telecommunications lines. Online services provide an infrastructure in which subscribers can communicate with one another, either by exchanging e-mail message or by participating in forums. In addition, the services can connect users with an almost unlimited number of third-party information providers. Subscribers can get up-to-date stock quotes, news stories hot off the wire, articles from many magazines and journals, in fact, almost any information that has been put in electronic form. Of course, accessing all this data carries a price. In short we can say it is nothing but networked and paperless work. (Webopedia, 2010)

Thus online means the state of being in direct immediate communication with the computer on which the database is loaded. It is interactive system, i.e. an online system allows the user to input instructions, receive response and then modify or manipulate the retrieval results. By using online system search can be perform more quickly and accurately, and the search of information can be wider and exhaustive.

2. FEATURES OF ONLINE SERVICES

Moreover the move toward an online environment has resulted in a shift form the systematic one-to-one information flow of the post to a new model in which the users and providers of information are able to relate in a many to many dynamic relationship. For e.g. in the traditional model, a librarian provides a bridge learners and information providers by selecting and cataloguing resources and assist in these resources. In the new model the library serves as a facilitator by offering ongoing support enabling learners to interact and exchange knowledge with others, to communicate directly with the publishers and vendors of information sources and to participate in the collaborative endeavor to make available rich collection on online scholarly information resources.

Librarians have traditionally selected and organized resource. In providing online service librarians have the opportunity to provide the e-learners with direction and to reduce those from information overload. Some of the online library services can link their users to library catalogue, licensed journal databases, electronic book collections, selected Internet resources and tutorials and forums for communication and interaction with librarians.

This online library permits users to access library and networked resources and services anytime and anywhere that an Internet connection and computing equipment are available. All users are not the same. While providing these services it is important to bear in mind the elements covering end user services. End user search training; End user access to online tools and electronic full text; and the facility for direct user requesting of materials.

These are policy implications for what people can and cannot have access to circulation policies, loan periods, borrowing limits and other related matters. Libraries that participate in such schemes need to show commitment to consortia users not just local users. User support and training must also be increased in the electronic environment so that clients can effectively use the online services that have been put in place.

3. FUNCTIONS OF ONLINE SERVICES

Most database producers, particularly those compiling bibliographic databases, license their databases to other organizations called 'online services' or 'host computer services' or simply a host, which provide the computer, software and telecommunications support that enables remote users to access the databases. The larger hosts provide access to several hundreds of databases in a wide range of subject areas (they are sometimes called 'supermarket' hosts). The operation of such services requires large investments in hardware and software.

The functions of hosts are structuring, loading and

subsequently updating the databases into large timesharing computers; maintaining 24-hour access; connecting their computers to national and international networks; maintaining user-friendly programmes so that the databases can be interrogated easily and efficiently; offering downloading facilities enabling users to store and display retrieved information locally; providing gateway access that permits users to switch to other hosts; connecting to document delivery services by means of which the full texts of retrieved references are delivered electronically (electronic mail, fax) or by post. Hosts market their services at exhibitions and conferences, and provide systems and database manuals, newsletters, 'help desk' services and training courses

4. ONLINE SEARCH SERVICES

Online search services also known as online systems suppliers search services, or online service spinners, are responsible for mounting databases on a computer and making the arrangements necessary for such databases to be searchable from a large number of remote user workstations or terminals. Online search service systems that provide access to a large number of databases generally convert those databases into uniform format with some standardization features so that the basic commands and search techniques apply across all the databases offered by a given vendor. Naturally, the intending user needs awareness of the range of search services that are available. It might so happen that one database may be available from several search services (vendors). Access to that database may be considerably cheaper, especially once the telecommunication charges have been taken into account via one search service than the other. More over a different vendor may offer search facilities which support much more effective searching for a specific (given) topic than might be possible via another search service (vendor). Some services might offer customers other benefits such as ease of searching, processing speed and competitive pricing.

There are a number of different types of such services such as: i) The traditional Super market online search services; ii) Specialist online search services; iii) Publishers as search services; iv) Platform independent services; and v) Bibliographic utilities.

In recent times, online service suppliers are attempting to respond to the long felt need of devising common interfaces to tools such bibliographic databases and directories including directories of Websites, which indicate the location of information and the full text of the document which contains information. Some of the sophisticated online search services are trying also to offer access to other information channels, such as databases mounted by other vendors, the contents of other Websites, information collections such as libraries, and people as information channels. This new aspect of the service described as an Integrated Information Solution (IIS). Some of the examples of services which seek to generate integrated information solution are: i) K R Science Base for the WWW, ii) DIALOG Web, iii) Engineering Information Village, etc. Such US need to be targeted to meet the needs of specific groups, and the service supplier must understand, those needs, not only in terms of the type of the database to be accessed, but also in terms of specific features of interfaces and the most acceptable pricing strategies

4.1. The Online Search Process

The process of online searching of remote database in most cases involves a dialogue between the searcher and the host computer on which a range of databases are mounted. A computer terminal operated by the searcher is connected to the host computer by means of a telecommunication link. An outline of the equipment is shown in the figure.

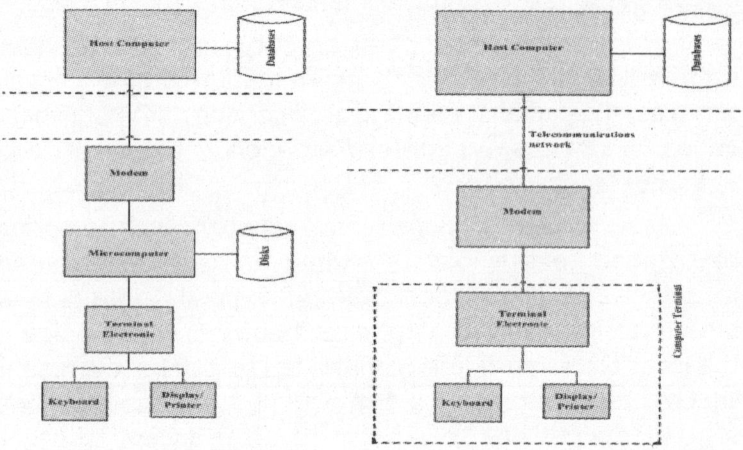

Fig. 7.1. Online Search Process

The link between the user terminal and the host computer is often via a packet switched network. The flow of data is in one direction, from the keyboard to host (requests), and, in the other from host to visual display screen (information). In this dialogue, the host computer imposes constraints on what the searcher can do and when. For example, commands must be constructed in exactly the required format and often it is necessary to wait for a reply from the host before entering the next command even though the content of the command may not be dependent on the answer to the previous command.

4.2. When to Access an Online Search Service

There are situations, when we should consider accessing an online search service. One such situation obviously is that when we come to know that a specific piece of information that we need most has been published somewhere and we are not able to have access to the source, which provides the information locally. In other words, there are a number of main sources of information that might be consulted during a search for information. The core sources to which The online seat-eh services provide access to are databases. They include both bibliographic as well others. Some sources may refer to locations where the requisite information could be found

4.3. The Online Search

The first stage; in conducting a search is to develop a clear specification of the information required by the end-user. The search may he conducted by the end-user alone or by the end-user and the Intermediary in cooperation and consultation. Sometimes, it may not be possible to specify exactly what information is sought by the end-user before performing the search. However it is possible to strive for as precise a specification as the user can achieve on the basis of present knowledge. The specification may include a preliminary attempt to express the search in the indexing language of the database to be searched, and to frame a search strategy:

The second stage will be the selection of the database or databases and selection of appropriate service vendors. After these preliminary planning stages are over, the searcher connects to the chosen search service and may view any information on the screen. Once the database or range of databases is selected, the search proceeds according to a series of parameters introduced by the user and the system responds by indicating the number of records that match the search criteria. Thereafter, the user may opt to display the details of these records. If the search is for a specific item of information or document this may be read online. Usually the user will assess the relevance of the records on the basis of abstracts, and then performs other operations such as downloading or print records or view full text. It may be mentioned that a number of issues need to be considered in managing online search service. The future developments will be in the areas of designing suitable interfaces, telecommunications, pricing and strategic alliances, between online services and organizations connected with document delivery service.

4.4. Online Service Interfaces

The first online service utilized a simple text-based interface in which content was largely text only and users made choices via a command prompt. This allowed just about any computer with a modem and terminal communications program the ability to access these text-based online services. Compuserve would later offer, with the advent of the Apple Macintosh and MS Windows-based PC's, a GUI interface program for their service. This provided a very rudimentary GUI interface. CompuServe continued to offer text-only access for those needing it. Online services like Prodigy and AOL developed their online service around a GUI and thus unlike CompuServe's early GUI-based software, these online services provided a more robust GUI interface. Early GUI-based online service interfaces offered little in the way of detailed graphics such as photographs or pictures. Largely they were limited to simple icons and buttons and text. As modem speeds increased it became more feasible to offer images and other more complicated graphics to users thus providing a nicer look to their services (John Java).

4.5. Digital Object Identifier (DOI)

Unique identifier, called Digital Object Identifier (DOI), is being used to support links to full-text or to bibliographic databases. The Digital Object Identifier (DOI) (http://www.doi.org/) is a system for interoperability identifying and exchanging intellectual property in the digital environment. It provides framework for linking customers with content suppliers, facilitating electronic commerce and enabling automated copyright management for all types of media. The DOI was developed to ensure precise identification of content and thereby enable precise management of rights. More than 200 publishers have adopted the technology behind DOI. One of the initiatives to support and promote concept of DOI is CrossRef.org. The CrossRef.org (http://www.crossref.org/) is a collaborative reference linking service using DOI and associated metadata for linking citations. Crossref has more than 3200 publishers and societies that participate accounting for over 23,000 journals with more than 44 million content items, including journal articles, conference proceedings, books, book chapters, reference entries, technical reports, standards, and data sets in the database. It functions as a sort of digital switchboard. While the site does not hold full text content, but rather effects linkages through Digital Object Identifiers (DOI), which are tagged to article metadata supplied by the participating publishers. A researcher clicking on a link will be connected to a page on the publisher's Web site showing a full bibliographical citation of the article, and, in most cases, the abstract as well. The reader can then access the full-text article through the appropriate mechanism. While subscribers will generally go straight to the text, others will receive information on access via subscription, document delivery, or pay-per-view.

The DOI registry contains the information about the provider of the article and it links the users directly to the URL of the article even if the publisher of the content changes. However, with libraries subscribing to resources from primary publishers and aggregators, articles are available to the library users from multiple sources, i.e., directly from the primary publisher, through aggregators and through library holding in print form library. The availability of copies of articles from multiple sources has led to the problem of appropriate copy in the library subscribing to multiple databases. The OpenURL technology evolved as a solution to answer the problem of appropriate copy.

5. ONLINE SERVICES IN LIBRARIES

Online services in library are now challenging for modern library professionals. We have to remain with the latest technology and its use by competitors. These call centers and their work environment is totally different form

Library. All time availability and money-based service are two main factors for them on which they are giving more attention. To competitors with them and to exist in the environment we should be professional. We have to provide what others fare providing with best quality. The quality of Information depends on two things one is relevance and the second is timeliness. I think online services are efficient achieve those two things because if electronic information is there we can see its relevance the post it within fraction of second. So if we want achieve quality services then we should think about online services. We can say by experience that all teachers and students of academic library always demanding readily electronic information.

The process of delivering library service is given under. We have things interconnected with each other Librarian, Computer networks, and Users of document. The real impact of online service is that how this things are connected each other at right time with correct relevance.

There are two online services in particular. One is Prodigy and the other is AOL. The prodigy first emerged on the underground rave scene in the early 1990s, and has since then achieved big popularity and worldwide renown, with their most popular songs. AOL is the world's leading interactive services provider. AOL's network of Web properties attracts 111 million unique visitors a month to some of the best known brands on the Internet, including AOL.com, Map Quest, AIM, Moviefone, ICQ and Netscape. There are basically four aspects which we can do: (1) Communication, (2) Document or file transfer, (3) Interactive browsing, and (4) Bulletin boards. Corresponding to these activities there are four basic tools.

5.1. Types of Online Services in Libraries

There is wide variety of online services in different libraries. We can take an example of academic libraries at several locations. In other words, it is collection of all bibliographic details of library holdings. Now it is available online with all types of libraries in the world.

5.2. Library Catalogue

It is a register of all bibliographic items found in a library or group of libraries, such as a network of libraries at several locations. In other words, it is collection of all bibliographic details of library holdings. Now it is available online with all types of libraries in the world.

5.3. WebOPACs

Online Public Access Catalog (OPAC) is an electronic library catalog, which contains complete bibliographic information of all items in the library. It brings information at the fingertips of members, whether the member is in the library or at a remote location. Information is given about where material is located in the library, whether it is available for loan, when an item is due back if on loan, and how long it may be borrowed. For Example - OCLC is a nonprofit, membership, computer library service and research organization, Built for retrieval of Information and reducing information costs. Total 69,000 libraries in 112 countries and territories around the world are using OCLC services for locating, acquiring, cataloguing, and lending and preserving all types of library materials.

5.4. Library Thing

Library Thing is an online service to help people catalog their books easily. The User can access catalog from anywhere. Library Thing also connects people with the same books, comes up with suggestions for what to read next. Tim Spalding, a web developer and web publisher based in Portland, Maine, created Library Thing. It is a full-powered cataloging application, searching the Library of Congress, all five national Amazon sites, and more than 80 world libraries. It uses Amazon and libraries that provide open access to their collection with the Z39.50 protocol. The protocol is used by a variety of desktop programs, notably bibliographic software like Endnote. Library Thing appears to be the first mainstream of use of Lib 2.0.

5.5. Automatic Book Circulation System

Yokohama national University Library of Japan has this system. It is self-service. Borrower can issue his book with help of following machine. The borrower can borrow books using the Automatic Book Circulation provided that they have a barcode label on the cover.

5.6. Use of RFID Technology

The concept of RFID (Radio Frequency Identifications) technology was developed in 1948 RFID is used in libraries for Self-issue, Self-Return, Combined Issue/Return, Fine/ charge payment, Automatic Sorting, Security, Stock management and Accessioning of Library reading material.

5.7. Renewing library material online

Library users can renew library resource online using their burrower number. Michigan State University library have this facility. The following illustration depicts about the source and layout of the online renewal service.

5.8. View your circulation record

Chinese University if Hong Kong- University library have this facility that user can view the history of the items checked out from library through the Library Online Catalogue. By logging in the View his Circulation Record at http://library.cuhk,edu.hk/ with name, Library Card Number and Library Password, and clicking on the hyperlink "My Reading History", he can view the items that he checked in the past. You may delete the undesired item(s) appearing in the list. If you want to disable the collection of your check out history, you may click on the hyperlink "Disable reading History (Optout)". To enable the collection of checked out history, simply click on the hyperlink "Retain

Reading History"

5.9. Interlibrary Loan Materials

Inter Library Loan facilitates to borrow the books from other Library through resource sharing method. IL Laid is the software used to manage all interlibrary loan requests. It allows the borrowers to monitor the status of requests/ renewal and establish/modify preferences for receiving electronic documents with the help of personal account of IL Laid.

5.10. Faculty Services

Providing services to its users and to get the cent percent satisfaction from its users is the main objective of any academic library. Library has to give user oriented services to its users so that he will get his information without wasting his time. Then only he will satisfy with what he got form library. Students and teachers are main users of academic Library. Keeping target to them any academic library can render some kind of services of its Faculty.

5.11. Auto Alert Service

Auto Alert Services are automated email notices sent by library to alert its users about newly available publications in the field of interest. It helps to inform and keep updated to its regular user. This service is not new but the structure is somehow changed. Previously it was done manually and now by computer. We can give this service with the help of software. I et us see how it works Firstly we have to collect user information with their subject interest. Secondly put all data in the software. The software is attached with catalogue. The work of this software is to match the relevant keywords with both Catalogue entries and subject interest of users. After getting bibliographic details of document Auto generated E-mail will be send to the respective user.

5.12. Auto Overdue Reminder Service

Efficient Library management software is finding such books, which are delayed by the users add also sending them auto-reminder for the same. As soon as the computer system will on, it will start to send reminders to the persons who have delayed books with them.

5.13. Online Newspapers Reading

Every teacher and student in educational organization is in search of today's updates, for News and events surrounding them. They will reserve the time and come in the library to see today's newspapers. It is not necessary to come in the library when he is having online newspapers reading service. There are some websites for the same.

http://www.ipl.org/div.news/,

http://www.onlinenewspapers.com/india.htm

5.14. Various Full-text Databases

A full-text database is a collection of documents or other information in the form of a database in which the complete text of each referenced document is available for online viewing, printing, or downloading. In addition to text documents, images are often included, such as graphs, maps, photos, and diagrams. A full-text database is searchable by keyword, phrase, or both. Academic library also can subscribe some databases for the use of its students and faculty. EBSCO is remarkable example of Full-text Database and has served the library industry for more than 60 years. By placing customers at the core of business, it has tapped the resourcefulness in developing the highly quality products and service. Now INFLIBNET is having number of databases.

5.15. Online Periodical Reading Service

The academic library can make available some online periodicals. There are some agencies that are giving magazines with free online access and some are required subscriptions for accessing their databases. EZineMart.com is offering an online magazine store that is allowing users to access some leading magazines in digital format. EZineMart.com also sells subscription of the print editions and the paid magazines also. Widely variety of scholarly journals as well as popular magazines, heavily used periodicals and many newspapers are also available in the website: http://ezinemart.com/

5.16. The effectiveness of Online services in Library

The impact of online services of academic library on users and their needs is other aspect on which we can give sort of stress because it is equally important as its execution. We have to see how it is useful to the users.

5.17. To Improve and Expand Opportunities for Communication

The online services of academic library should improve and expand opportunities for communication between user and library staff. It will help to build up good relations and respects among them. One thing is clear that now day's users arc not more rely upon library staff because their need for information is survived by some other aspects such as textbooks, ready-made subject notes and guides.

5.18. Online Library Services Support User Involvement in Library Development

User focus is a key component in online library services. Here we are discussing different approach for user's involvement in Library development. The application of information technology in bringing end user satisfaction has widely been accepted as an image of Modern Library. User expectations, user experience, user skills, user involvement in Library development has been discussed in details as follows.

5.19. Wider User Satisfaction in Less Time

As per observations by experts user of academic library has its very narrow approach about coming to college and using library. He is having very limited time which he can spend in the library. So when it's compulsory to visit library at that time only he will come in the library for movement. In that particular span of time if he will get his relevant information then only he will become satisfy. Online service facility will serve his need very effectively. He can browse any information from his home too. So defiantly his level of satisfaction will become wider and wider.

6. BARRIER OF ONLINE SERVICES IN ACADEMIC LIBRARIES

The academic Library can provide such service but the output is depending on some boundaries. They will put limitations on its positive end result. These aspects are discussed as follow.

6.1. Lack of Awareness

Use of on line services is limited due to access, expense, and skill requirements. Although usage is growing, on-line services and computers reach only a fraction of the total population. Some users are always doubtful of machines, and some resist using means of communication they consider cold and impersonal. Adjustment to technological change is slow, and some social and economic barriers will persist. Just as they are some students don't having computer knowledge and on-line services. So there is the need of emphasis about the awareness of new technology.

6.2. Limited Access

Participants in on-line services do not represent the entire community. In particular, College non-teaching staff/ Peon, disabled students, the old professors, often have limited access to these resources. As there is increase in demand for using the computers use and on-line services become more common and more available in public places, such limitations may become less pronounced.

6.2. Lack of Reliability

On-line services must be used in conjunction with other techniques that allow users to get information quickly. They need skilled library staff to make a commitment of authentic information and to use a computer to obtain in the same. It is observed that users cannot be reached to its E-information as quickly as with a printed pamphlet, fact sheet, report, or other materials delivered to the door.

6.3. Face-to-Face Interaction

On-line services cannot replace meetings, which allow members to act together with one another and focus on key points of discussion. Even with the interaction, on-line services provide, they lack the dynamic face-to-face interplay and generates ideas during a meeting or focus group.

6.4. Information overload

Overloading of Information is a possible problem. As on-line services make communication easy and many users to join, the pure amount of information is available and becomes overwhelming. Also libraries are unlikely receiving one-sided comments unless it helps to user with focus on specific service.

7. UTILITIES OF ONLINE SERVICE

Revolution in information and communication technology has made far-reaching impact in past two decades within the library functions, information systems and services. The concept of the virtual or digital library has been evolving since the inception of the Internet. It means an electronic access system that provides users with the means the discovering and retrieving information online.

The information may be retrieved from within the hosting system or through links to other systems. The intent is to offer the same type of resources and services that are available in the traditional model library in online form to serve the library community. This has widened the scope of the outlook of library services and accentuated the following factors:

- Increased productivity in terms of both work as well as service
- Extension of library services beyond the library peripherals
- Participation into outside networking systems for the resource sharing.
- Economy in expenditure
- Proper and optimum utility of library materials
- Proper and optimum utility of library materials

The disadvantages can also be managed with comprehensive planning and sound managerial tactics.

8. MODELS: ONLINE LIBRARY SERVICES

Library 2.0, Business 2.0, and Web 2.0 are some of the defined model for a modernized form of library service that reflects a transition within the library world in the way that services are delivered to users. The focus is on user centered change and participation in the creation of content and community. This includes online services like the use of OPACs systems and all increased flow of information for the user back to the library. Here library services were constantly updated and reevaluated to best serve library users. Online sources and services free online journals-books, encyclopedias, conference proceeding, newspaper, dictionaries, catalogues etc. Newspaper clipping service includes selection, scanning a saving, online searching and saving and finally access and retrieval. Digitization of special collection like photos, maps, dissertations, thesis, films and others. Examination cell can have exam documents, model exam cell and question papers, group study cell etc. Digital reference service. They can have different modes of services as telephone enquiry service, online enquiry, service, online enquiry, email, chat based and virtual reference service using different formats such as CD/DVD/Photos etc.

9. ONLINE LIBRARIES SERVICES IN INDIA AND ABROAD

When we look at the libraries of western countries or developed countries, they offer the majority of services. Right from public libraries, Academic libraries, Special libraries, National libraries, and Information centers are involved in networking, Intranet facility, sharing information resources and so on. For e.g. **OCLC WorldShare** provides a Web-based platform for collective innovation with shared services, integrated applications and a streamlined approach to managing library workflows. Together with WorldCat, WorldShare helps the world's libraries connect in new ways to operate, innovate and collaborate at Webscale. **LibWeb** is a distributed library network of Russia.It is a subject-oriented library network ensuring access to and to exchange of bibliographic, technological and other information. An overwhelming majority of LibWeb resources would be available via Internet for scientific, cultural and educational institutions and organizations as well as for their (staff) members free of charge.

Lib-web-cats (library **web** sites and **catalogs**) are a directory of libraries worldwide. The majority of the libraries of North America and the number of libraries in other parts of globe have links to the library's website and online catalog. The example is Online Public Library is a public library's website and online catalog. The Online Public library is a public library for the World Wide Web. The Online public library is hosted by the school at Drexel, College of Information with major support from the college of Information at Florida State University. Another example is Questia is an online scholarly library that augments and complements any academic library collection. Questia provides students with convenient access to books and articles in the humanities and social sciences via the Internet, and to facilitates topics, do research an write provides an individual with unlimited access to the materials in the collection and to their unique research tools. These shows that majority of the libraries in western countries are involved in sharing and retrieving all kinds of information via net.

The importance of online library services in India was perceived by National Information System for Science and Technology (NISSAT) way back in 1985 which load to establishment of several National Access Centers to International Database Services (NACIDS).The user information products and information carriers constitute the three important components of any online service. Some of the online services available in India are medical information service of NIC,National Union Catalogues of Scientific Serials (NUCSSI) of NISCAIR, current contents Indian Journals in Science and Technology, and databases in certain specialized subjects are as such as Polymer Science, Indian Patents, and Indian Standards etc. are available online.

On the same ground, most of the online computer system networks have been developed. The major networks in India are: INFLIBNET, NICNET, INDONET, DELNET, etc. Others important libraries and information centres are providing online services in India such as: Delhi University, IITs, IIMs, IGNOU, NISCAIR and many other libraries and information centers are involved in online services like union catalog, resource sharing services/consortia, open access to digital libraries etc. Delhi University library system offers various online services like WebOPACs, UGC-Infonet Digital Library Consortium, etc. The digital Library of India is digitizing all the significant literary, artistic and scientific works of mankind and making them freely available, in every corner of the world. The online services of IGNOU are sharing subscribed online databases including e-books, e-journals, indexes, bibliographies for intranet users, free trial based online resources in public domain, open access digital libraries etc.

DELNET has been actively engaged with the compilation of various Union Catalogues of the resources available in member-libraries. It has already created the Union Catalogue of Books, Union List of Current Periodicals, Union Catalogue of Periodicals, CD-ROM Database, Database of Indian Specialists, Database of Periodical Articles, Union List of Video Recordings, Urdu Manuscripts' Database, Database of Theses and Dissertations, sample databases of language publications using GIST technology and several other databases. The data is being updated in each of these databases and is growing rapidly. All the DELNET databases have been resident on DELSIS, an in-house software developed on BASISPlus, an RDBMS, the product of Information Dimensions Inc. of USA which has been provided to DELNET courtesy National Informatics Centre, New Delhi.

In India, the following networks offering online services on the Internet are:

(a) Education and Research Network (ERNET): It was initiated in 1986 by the Department of Electronics (DoE), with funding support from the Government of India and United Nations Development Program (UNDP), involving eight premier institutions as participating agencies NCST (National Centre for Software Technology) Bombay, IISc (Indian Institute of Science) Bangalore, five IITs (Indian Institutes of Technology) at Delhi, Bombay, Kanpur, Kharagpur and Madras, and the DoE, New Delhi. ERNET began as a multi-protocol network with both the TCP/IP and the OSI-IP protocol stacks running over the leased-line portion of the backbone. Since 1995, however, almost all traffic is carried over TCP/IP. It has made a significant contribution to the emergence of networking in the country. It practically brought the Internet to India and has built up national capabilities in the area of net-working, especially in protocol software engineering. It has not only succeeded in building a large network that provides various facilities to the intellectual segment of Indian society—the research and education community, it has over the years become a trendsetter in the field of networking (Wikipedia, 2012).

(b) Software Technology Network (SOFTNET): It started offering Internet services apart from point to point links since 1993.

(c) National Informatics Centre Network (NICNET): It offers internet services since 1994. It is a viable gateway to internet in the country. With more than 700 micro earth station nodes all over the country, it has the widest reach in the country.

(d) Videsh Sanchar Nigam Limited (VSNL): Since August 1995 for commercials use the Internet connections are provided by Videsh Sanchar Nigam Limited (VSNL). It offers shell' or terminal dial up and TCP/IP' type of connections. VSNL's Online sources and services access node was commissioned at Mumbai connecting to interned at USA via satellite and to the Internet node in Europe via submarine cable providing diversity and highly reliable network connectivity.

10. CHALLENGE TO LIBRARIES

Today online services are being used in all walks of the life such as business, journalism, defense, education, medical science and technology, etc. Therefore the libraries are not an exception as they impart informal education. Without library, research/teaching could not be possible complete or to fulfill the objectives. It is pertinent to have the facility of internet because of the present day challenge as the survival of libraries without it, is not possible. The internet is providing not only quick access to information but also made available all the time whenever we need.

With the advent of information technology the dream of Dr. Ranagnathan has come true which is inherited in his fourth law "Save the time of the reader". But most of the libraries still do not have much resource to switch over to computerization as it is required sufficient funds to start with and to have internet connection thereafter.

11. IMPORTANCE OF ONLINE SERVICES IN LIBRARIES

All academic libraries are reshaping their services and services strategies. New storage Medias and new channels for transmitting information are changing total picture of process and the result in nationalize distance-learning concept. Everything is available on your desktop so non need to go or to wait for any kind of help or assistance. We speak about electronic references, full text data access, Web resources that are integral part of all education in the digital environment. Past examination question papers, Course handouts, Auto alert service and online articles delivery service, online research assistance in Research Centre. All types such information is an integral part of education system. Especially students and faculty are demanding it very much without wasting their time. Therefore solution for this is online services. Every academic library has to involve fully in the process of delivering education with quality services.

12. BENEFITS OF ONLINE RESOURCES AND SERVICES

There are following benefits of online resources and services:

- Provide information on world events, technical, business and professional matters, etc.
- Provide access to reference materials, different databases and library catalogues world wide of the interested areas.
- Retrieve journal articles, books, computer programs and graphic images from different services and to

download them on to the personal system.

- Provide latest information which may still be months away to appear in the print form.
- Seeking and finding information can be almost instantaneous.
- Provide electronic copy of different documents available on the Online sources and services very quickly.
- Information can be searched, clipped and saved online.
- Cost of accessing and retrieving information is almost negligible.
- OPACs on Internet allow registered users to place reservation on items or use other services, such as checking how many items they have on loan and renewing them.
- Provide huge R&D information services.
- Extracted information can be downloaded and incorporated into a document without the need for receiving the data.
- Reduction in the number of costly subscriptions of periodicals and journals.
- Reduction in the space required to store paper based information.
- The greatest advantages of the online are that a group of libraries can logically can logically set up net-works of their own using the online sources and services backbone.

13. LIMITATIONS OF ONLINE RESOURCES AND SERVICES

There are following limitations of online resources and services:

- Access time depends on network performance.
- Connection failure may cause serious problems.
- Noise in telecommunication lines.

- Lack of expertise.
- Lack of single protocol, uniformity and proper indexing.
- Slow response time.
- Poor quality of data, a lot of useful information available without proper organization and structure.
- Getting information through Internet in India is quite difficult due to the lack of dedicated phone lines for internet access.
- The telecommunication infrastructure in India is such that accessing Internet is slow.

14. CONCLUSION

Now we can say that modern academic libraries are relying more on online services. It is good sign for digital revolution in the field of library and information science. The competitors like private information centers and cell centers are fully depending on electronic information. So they are very fast and getting lot of business. Now days some traditional library works are not relevant and we have to refine them. Always there is complaint from academic library staff that users are not coming to the library and not using library recourses very frequently. This is big problem created by library professionals. It may not be acceptable but doesn't matter. We are sitting in the library and doing traditional library jobs only but we are not becoming active and running behind the users. We do not understand their actual information needs. So I think we professionals are making mistake. Whatever things dare with the library it should be in tremendous use and for this we have to ready to accept new techniques such as web 2.0 in general and library 2.0 for library. All library professionals have to try their best for meeting loud demand of digital information. They have to cultivate rare users to its habitual users. Right attitude about work and strong will power is more than enough to provide best services and achieve maximum users' satisfaction.

Hence new information and communication technologies as well as new educational model require librarians to re-evaluate the way, they develop and manage and deliver resources and services. In the not too distant future integrated online library systems will have new and even more powerful features ranging from intelligent interfaces of data mining capabilities.

REFERENCE

1. DOI. (2012). Digital object identifier (DOI) Retrieved 11 May, 2012, from http://www.doi.org/index.html
2. East, H. (2003). Online services. In Feather, J. & Sturges, P. (Ed.), *International Encyclopedia of Information and Library Science* (2 ed.). New York: Routledge, pp.466.
3. Lib-web-cats (2012). *A directory of libraries throughout the world* Retrieved 10 May, 2012, from www.librarytechnology.org/libwebcats
4. OCLC. (2012). WorldCat at a glance Retrieved 10 May, 2012, from http://www.oclc.org/worldcat/about/default.htm
5. Prytherch, R. J. (Ed.) (2005) Harrod's librarians' glossary and reference book. Hampshire, England: Ashgate Publishing Limited.
6. RFBR (1997). LibWeb Retrieved 09 May, 2012, from http://www.gpntb.ru/win/libweb/about/direct_e.htm
7. Wikipedia. (2012). Education and Research Network (ERNET), India, Retrieved 10 May, 2012, from http://en.wikipedia.org/wiki/ERNET

8
Electronic Resource Management in Digital Era

1. INTRODUCTION

In the fast-emerging and ever-growing information explosion it is very difficult to retrieve particular information without try to improve the services of libraries. The impact of technologies such as CD-ROMs, multimedia, computer networks, Internet, etc. have led to a paperless society. With the availability of computers, capable of computing at very high speed and having large disc storage space, it is possible to digitize and store information in the form of high quality graphics, color images, voice signal and video clips at a relatively affordable cost.

The role of mass media like newspapers and radio communications in bridging information awareness to the people has been praiseworthy. However this was limited to print media or hard copy format. As change is eternal, new awareness methods to match the knowledge explosion came into existence in the form of electronic media to disseminate the information. Electronic revolution has transformed the society of people into information savvy. To facilitate electronic media to work knowledge resources have necessarily to be converted form print media to machine-readable data thus paving the way for emergence of electronic resources. Electronic resources are the replicas of print form in digitized forms.

2. BACKGROUND

The pursuit of electronic resources by libraries was driven by the nucleus value of library science. It is possible to recognize in Dr. S. R. Ranganathan's five laws of library science the motivation that drove libraries to incorporate electronic resources into services and collections. Paraphrased to better suit electronic resources, the laws read: resources are for use, every person his or her resource, every resource its user, save the time of the user, and the library is a growing organism (Ranganathan, 1957).

Each technological development in library electronic resources during the 21st century was intended to make access to resources more direct, convenient, and timely for the user. The implementation of electronic resources made the library a growing organism as libraries adopted processes and reorganized staff repeatedly to accommodate the changes inherent in the use of constantly changing technology. The library profession recognized the potential of computers to make library resources more accessible early in the development of computer technology. Librarians were often enthusiastic and sometimes early adopters of technology. Since the advent of DIALOG in the 1960's, the proliferation of computer-based bibliographical resources has dramatically changed the way library collections are processed and accessed. In the mid-1060's, the use of electronic resources in libraries began with the development of the Machine Readable Cataloguing (MARC) format, a full 30 years before the introduction of the WWW and its subsequent ubiquity. Bibliographic databases become available at approximately the same time.

Libraries provided access to data sets such as census and survey data as early as the 1970's. During the microcomputer revolution of the 1980's libraries acquired software and data on diskettes and offered databases on CD-ROM. Databases on CD-ROMs began to contain full text. Search interfaces became more straightforward and simpler to use. Online catalogues became more common and libraries began to offer them through the pre-WWW Internet.

Tim Berners-Lee created the WWW in 1990. The subsequent development of the Mosaic browser in 1992 led to widespread use of the Web beginning in 1993. The graphical interface and the later development of Web search engines google, yahoo! made resources on the Internet more accessible to average users.

Web-based electronic resources were widely available beginning in the mid-1990's. Libraries offered Web-based catalogues, bibliographic and full-text databases, electronic journals and eventually electronic books through the Web. Users no longer had to go the library to do a significant amount of their research. International Encyclopedia of Information and Library Science define the emergence of the World Wide Web has enabled a revolution in electronic information resources. This environment differs from the earlier situation in that (Hartley, 2003):

1. The available information is not restricted to text but includes large numbers of images, audio and multimedia items so that it is more appropriate to think of them as information objects rather than documents.
2. The information available is an amorphous mass to which anyone can add if they have even a limited knowledge of HTML and thus the available information is no longer subject to quality-control mechanisms prior to publication.
3. The information is not structured to facilitate retrieval, but through the hypertext links it is structured to facilitate browsing and easy moving between information objects. Links can all too readily be broken.

4. The Web browser environment has continued the trend towards user-friendly interfaces that was initiated by the development of CD-ROM and Windows.

3. ELECTRONIC RESOURCE MANAGEMENT (ERM)

The development of ERM became necessary in the early 2000s as it became clear that traditional library catalogs and integrated library systems were not designed to handle metadata for resources as variable as many online products (Wikipedia, 2012). The idea of developing electronic resource management systems emerged in 2001-2002, growing out of research by *Tim Jewell* at the *University of Washington*. The Digital Library Federation and NISO began work in May 2002 to develop standards for ERM initiative. These standards were published in the 2004 as *Electronic Resource Management: Report of the DLF ERM Initiative*. The initiative's aim was to provide the community with a set of specifications that would encourage the development of electronic-resource management systems based on standards and best practices. Since the publication of the report, several vendors of integrated library systems have released ERM products.

Electronic Resource Management (ERM) is an area of technical services responsible for the evaluation, selection, pricing, securing, maintenance and provision of electronic resources such as e-journals, e-books and databases. ERM has emerged as a distinct activity within acquisitions units and a dedicated specialization for librarians (Bergman, 2005). In present situation the role of librarians who deal with electronic resources very challenging. The huge growth of electronic collections, the increasingly central role that these collections play in libraries, the large budgets that are involved in their acquisition, the endless variation in the packages offered by the hundreds of players in the market, the frequent changes in business models, and, above all, the lack of automated tools to deal with the complexity of e-resource management. Much of a librarian's success at carrying out necessary tasks is based on personal experience. The knowledge and experience gained from dealing with e-resources is often vested in few people, sometimes only one, libraries are left at risk. Furthermore, the provision of meaningful metrics, such as detailed cost analyses and statistics on performance and usage, remains problematic, but without such metrics, managers cannot make fully informed decisions. As the spending on e-collections increases, so does the need for a better solution: "a system that supports management of the information and workflows necessary to efficiently select, evaluate, acquire, maintain, and provide informed access to electronic resources in accordance with their business and license terms" (Anderson *et al.*, 2004).

In the presence of comprehensive commercial solutions, some institutions themselves developed systems that deal with various aspects of e-resource management. Now, a number of vendors are working on providing complete solutions that will help librarians not only maintain collections but also develop them further. The offering of some vendors consists of an ERM system that forms an integral part of their integrated library system. The integration with systems that already support various aspects of the e-resource life cycle is likely to be the key to success for e-resource management solutions.

4. NEED OF ELECTRONIC RESOURCES

Electronic publishing has led to new era of communications and information sharing. It creates Opportunities for users as well as authors and publishers. Many of the electronic books or electronic publishers ' web site freely permit and encourage readers to provide feedback on works, often directly to the author rather than to the publisher. Nevertheless users may establish their own accounts, charge services to credit cards or pay by prearranged method, and have requested material delivered directly to them by fax, e-mail, etc. Today, libraries of all kinds have been spending larger and larger shares of their budgets to adopt or gain access to electronic resources from publishers and vendors. This is due the fact that Electronic resources have enabled libraries to improve services in a variety of ways. First, most e- resources come equipped with powerful search-and-retrieval tools that allow users to perform literature searches more effectively and efficiently. Users can access the information with multimedia (i.e. sound, video, animation, graphical form and so on.).

5. DEFINITIONS: ERM

An e-resource is defined as a resource which requires computer access or any electronic product that delivers a collection of data, be it text referring to full text bases, electronic journals, image collections, other multimedia products and numerical, graphical or time based, as a commercially available title that has been published with an aim to being marketed. These may be delivered on CD ROM, on tape, via Internet and so on (Bajpai, Mal & Bajpai, 2010).

ERM is the practices and software systems used by libraries to keep track of important information regarding electronic resources, especially internet-based resources such as e-books, e-journals, e-newspapers, databases, bibliographic databases etc. An E-Resource is an electronic information resource that you can access on the web, on or off campus. You can get the information you want, when you need it, 24 hours a day, 7 days a week.

Simply we define to Electronic resources than we define like information resources in electronic form that's call Electronic resources (electronic resources). Many definitions are available on-line some definition like "Term used to describe all of the information products that a library provides through a computer network. This includes electronic books and journals, bibliographic databases, and library website pages" and Online tools that index, abstract, or provide electronic access to articles, books, dissertations and other types of content. Many of these databases offer limited full text.

6. TYPES OF ELECTRONIC RESOURCES

E-journals, e-books, e-databases, CDs & DVDs, e-theses and dissertations, e-reference sources, e-zines, e-newspapers, etc. are come under Electronic resources (Singh, 2010).

1. E-Journals: E-journals (Electronic journals) publishing on the web is a flourishing field, providing users with online access to various journals. The advent of electronic full text journals affords the opportunity to take a fresh approach, recognizing that any risk to publishers in new electronic age is likely to fall on small and medium size libraries, which are operating on restricted budgets. Many e-journals are available on-line. Some publishers provide free on-line access to journals published by them against print subscription of library. One of the most important benefit is that multiple users at one location can access the same article at the same time. However, many publishers require libraries to subscribe to their print version in order to access the electronic version. Selection of E-journals guidelines includes the following:

- *Content* : Comparison with the print versions.
- *Added Value* : Wider access, search ability, potentially greater currency.
- *Functionality* : Usability, searching limit functions, linking.
- *Technical Considerations* : Hardware and software requirements.
- *Licensing arrangements* : License restrictions, ongoing access rights, costs.
- *Service Impact* : Documentation, publicity, staff training needs.

2. E-newspapers : It is the online accompaniments of established newspapers where news articles and the latest updates are published on the web.i.e. http://www.newslink.org

3. E-magazines : E-magazine is equivalent to e-newspapers but published by established print magazine publishers. Many magazine titles such as The Economist, Times, National Geographic and so on, have also established online websites.i.e. http://www.world-newspapers.com/

4. E-databases : E-databases may consist of books, periodicals, reports & theses, etc can be converted to electronic form that allows access through network. More and more online database in bibliographic as well full text sources are available and also added up frequently with the growing demand of users. Some databases are web enabled and some are networked solution. Web enabled databases are easily accessible from the user desktops through the web browser while the networked solutions may require special installation at client side.

5. E-Thesis and Dissertation : It is an electronic document that explains the intellectual works or research of a researcher.

6. CD-ROM : It has provided new dimension for information for information storage and retrieval. Now-a-days most of the work on e-journals has concentrated on distribution via the Internet and CD-ROM as well.

7. E-reference Sources : It is an electronic version of references sources, such as Encyclopedias, Dictionaries, Biographies, etc. i.e. *http://www.britannica.com*,

8. Research Guides by Subject : Subject guides are web resources designed by University of Chicago Librarians, which provide an overview of resources in a subject area. They include staff contacts, print collections, electronic resources, as well as links to other relevant Web sites. Subject guides are a good place to start when you are beginning research on a specific topic. You can locate subject guides from our Database Finder page or go to our Web site and select Research Guides by Subject.

9. Indexes : An index is a reference source which provides bibliographic information about journal articles, as well as other types of materials. While indexes have long existed in print, online indexes have expanded the type of work done by researches. More options than looking for materials by subject, author or title. Online indexes allow you to look beyond subject, author, or title. They allow you to look for keywords or phrases throughout the bibliographic information—including the abstract. Sometimes people refer to indexes as "Article Databases," since they are mainly used to search for articles in journals. Many also include the full-text of an actual article online. However, it is important to realize that many indexes cover other research materials such as conference papers, book chapters, dissertations, research studies, etc. You can locate indexes for your subject area through the Database Finder page or go to our Web site or by selecting Research Guides by Subject.

10. E-Books : An E-book or an electronic book is an electronic or digital equivalent of a print book. E-book is either read on personal computer, or on dedicated hardware device known as E-book device or E-book reader. Since 1970s, the development of electronic versions of printed books (e-books) has become as a part of the whole electronic publishing phenomenon. E-publishing of books is a major development that is quickly causing changes in the industry. E-book technology is faster and can be implemented without the need for expensive print jobs. Traditional concept of a book includes novels, dictionaries, textbooks, anthologies, instruction manuals, proceedings of meetings and directories whereas the term "electronic books" has been applied to some type of CD-ROM systems, palm-top CD players, on-demand text, electronic document systems of various kinds and nearly any kind of computer-based text. E-books are changing the fundamentals of reading. They may become a significant, enduring part of culture, society and the life of the mind.

11. Library Catalogue : Most libraries now provide access to their catalogue from their web sites. Many others provide information about their holdings into larger databases such as World Cat or the RLG Union Catalogue. The Library provides links to these catalogues under the "Catalogue " section on its web site.

12. Statistical Sources : The Library has access to a variety of subscription databases, which provide economic data or statistics. You can locate these resources through the Library's Database Finder, the Library Catalogue, or through many of the Library's Research Guides by Subject. Be aware that there are many statistical sources available in print, which cannot be found online.

13. Sound Recordings : There are only a few Library databases, which provide access to sound recordings. If you are looking for music online, start at the Music Subject Guide for the resources.

14. Image Databases (Art, Maps, Medical, etc.) : Some databases include graphics or images, such as photos, paintings or maps. You can use the Database Finder page to locate these. The Art Subject Guide also provides extensive information about locating images.

7. FEATURES OF ERM SYSTEMS

There are various features of some ERM systems include:

1. Supporting acquisition and management of licensed e-resources
2. May be integrated into other library system modules or may be a standalone system
3. May have a public interface, either separate or integrated into the OPAC
4. Providing descriptions of resources at the package

(database) level and relate package contents (e.g. e-journals) to the package record

5. Encoding and perhaps publicly displaying licensed rights such as e-reserves, course packs, and interlibrary loan
6. Tracking electronic resources from point of order through licensing and final access
7. Providing information about the data providers, consortia arrangements, access platform
8. Providing contact information for all content providers
9. Logging problems with resources and providers
10. Providing customizable e-mail alerting systems (e.g. notices to managers when actions are expected or required)
11. Linking license documents to resource records
12. Supports retrieval of SUSHI usage statistics

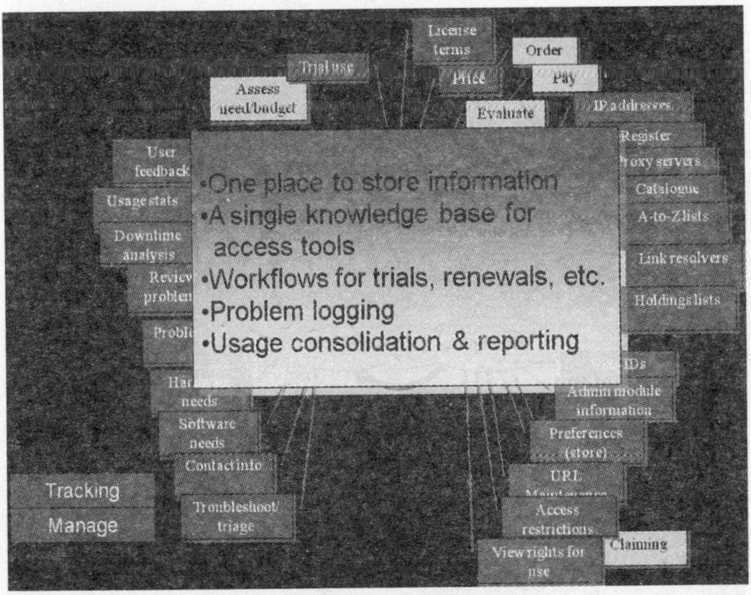

Fig. 8.1. Features of ERM Systems

8. DIGITAL LIBRARY FEDERATION (DLF) ERM INITIATIVES

Although the need for dedicated ERM systems was recognized as early as 1994, library software providers were slow to heed the call. Their lack of responsiveness can be attributed in part to poor communication channels between libraries and vendors, lack of consensus on required system features, and inability of librarians to properly convey their technological needs (Kennedy, 2004). As will be reviewed, many libraries therefore took up the challenge themselves, embarking on a range of in-house and consortia ERM systems development projects. These proprietary projects varied in success, demanded the continual attention of technical personnel, and could not be shared with other institutions due to a lack of standardized vocabulary. Yet they also pointed the way towards effective solutions by identifying the need for standards and clarifying system requirements.

The Digital Library Federation, a consortium of research libraries and related organizations, began exploring the mounting ERM issue in 2000. The study was spearheaded by Tim Jewell, Head of Collection Development Services for the University of Washington, and initial findings were published in a 2001 report. The study confirmed the importance of standards for guiding the long-term progress of ERM systems, and a formal working group was soon formed to define those standards. Both George and Seaman (2003) and Chang (2003) provide comprehensive overviews of the Digital Library Federation and its ERM Initiative during the time the project was underway.

In August, 2004, the Digital Library Federation published its final report, entitled the "Electronic Resource Management: Report of the DLF ERM Initiative" (hereafter, "DLF ERMI").After reviewing the features of existing ERM systems, the study identified seven key areas of ERMS functionality:

1. Descriptive bibliographic data
2. Licensing details

3. Financial information
4. Order status information
5. Administrative/technical activities
6. Support information
7. Usage statistics

These functions were defined in a series of deliverables attached to the DLF report, including:

1. A data dictionary identifying and standardizing terms and data fields.
2. An entity-relationship model mapping the relationships between data fields.
3. A specification of approximately 50 functional requirements for ERM systems.
4. A workflow diagram emphasizing the difference between print and e-resource work processes.
5. A formal recommendation for the development of a new metadata schema to support ERM data exchange, based upon the report's data dictionary.

Additional discussions of DLF ERMI goals and deliverables may be found in Grover and Fons (2004), Chang (2003), and Sadeh and Ellingson (2005), with perhaps the most detailed review made by ERMI's lead investigator, Tim Jewell (2005). The argument for dedicated metadata standards in e-resource management is set forth persuasively in Farb and Riggio (2004).

9. THE LIFE CYCLE OF E-RESOURCES

Librarians say that the lives of e-resources are as complicated and challenging as those of human beings: e-resources are born, and at times they also die or are reincarnated under a different name or in a different shape; they form families, and the families may unite with other families, quarrel, or split up; treaties between families are signed and can be later discarded; and so on. Keeping in mind that change is always a possibility, we will now look at the life cycle of an e-resource.

The typical life cycle of an e-resource that is available for a fee would include the following stages:

1. Discovery : The awareness of a new e-resource originates from a faculty member's request, a recommendation from a subject librarian, an advertisement, a message in a forum, or any other source. The librarian then locates information about the e-resource information that might include, for example, the bibliographic details of an e-journal, the coverage period available, the packages that include this e-journal, and the interface or interfaces through which such packages are offered. The way in which a librarian finds the necessary information is related to the role of the ERM system as a collection management tool, as explained later.

2. Trial : In many cases, a librarian will want to try out an e-resource before deciding whether to purchase a license for it. A trial enables the librarian to offer the e-resource to some or all users - who may include patrons and librarians alike - and then base a decision on their feedback. During the trial process, the librarian activates the e-resource in the desired areas of the library environment, notifies the relevant audience, and obtains feedback. Librarians pay considerable attention to specific issues when testing an e-resource. One example is the technical infrastructure required by the user interface. The librarian needs to document issues related to web browser and plug-in compatibility, which may have an impact on how browser configurations are rolled out to library and faculty computers or even whether the institution can support the interface at all. Furthermore, the testers need to evaluate the usability of the interface, because the library may well have a choice of interfaces from different providers of a package of resources or subsets thereof. When the trial is complete, the librarian should be able to justify the choice of interface to the institution as a whole as well as to its various departments.

3. Selection : Once the trial is over, the librarian decides whether to acquire the e-resource. A decision not to purchase the e-resource results in its deactivation in the library environment (if it were activated previously as part of the trial process).

4. Acquisition : If the librarian decides to go forward and subscribe to the resource, he/she carries out an acquisition process that somewhat resembles the process for print resources; however, an additional level of detail is required, such as information about the license and the availability of the resource to various populations of users. Also, when a library is acquiring e-journals as part of a package from an e-resource aggregator, such as *EBSCO*, the librarian needs to know which journals are covered by the package and for what period of time; ideally, the librarian would have the option to pay one lump sum for the entire package or to pay separately for each title. Moreover, the print and electronic formats may be linked in such a way that cancellation of the print format would invalidate the license agreement for the electronic format.

Another issue is how to handle the distribution of a payment between the licensor of the package and one or more interface providers. In the UK, for example, a library can obtain INSPEC from the IEE and access it through an interface from a UK data center such as EDINA or MIMAS - a service for high a fee is levied.

5. Access : Access, of course, is a major issue when dealing with e-resources. Once a library has acquired an e-resource, the librarians want to ensure that it is well used. First, they need to make certain that users can access it easily - for example, from an A-Z list; from the OPAC, if relevant; from a meta-search tool; or via a link server. Issues such as access by specific user groups or by remote users (for instance, proxy setup) also need to be solved. After the initial configuration of access, which might have been taken care of, at least partially, at the trial stage, librarians must deal with routine maintenance, problems such as the temporary unavailability of the resource, and changes in the provider's address or the manner of access.

6. Decision to renew or cancel : An e-resource subscription is typically valid for a defined time period. When the period ends, the librarian must either renew the subscription or cancel it. Unlike the decision at the selection phase, this decision is based on the information accumulated in the management system, such as the actual usage of the resource while it was available, the reliability of the interface, and the responsiveness of the provider. Whatever the outcome of the decision - renewal or cancellation - the system needs to support it. Furthermore, even after a subscription has been cancelled, the library might have perpetual access or archiving rights to the data, another area that librarians must deal with on an ongoing basis.

The description provided here is a simplified version of real life. Many e-resources today are purchased through consortia, which wield considerable purchasing power. In a consortial environment, the procedures involved in acquisition, access, and decision making are much more complex. An ERM system needs to address the heterogeneous needs of these consortia, particularly the differing levels of information sharing and the diverse management requirements centralized versus localized or a combination of the two.

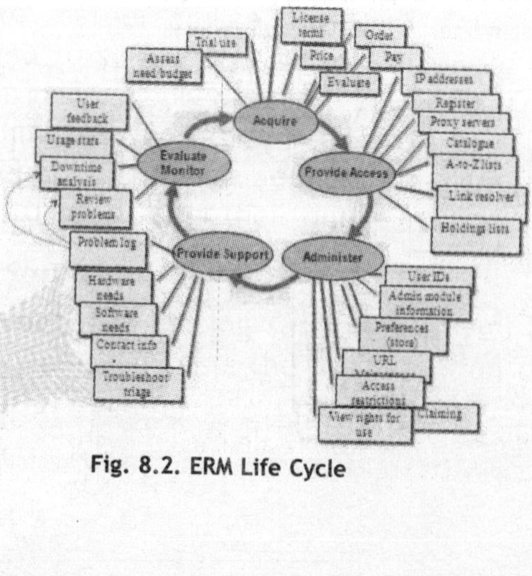

Fig. 8.2. ERM Life Cycle

10. STANDARDS OF ERM SYSTEMS

ERM systems need to integrate into an existing library and the institutional environment. The use of standards is, therefore, of major importance for enabling such integration to succeed. Let us examine a few illustrations of the importance of standards as related to integration and observe how an ERM system would take advantage of such standards.

One of the most important standards for application integration is the Simple Object Access Protocol (SOAP), an XML-based protocol that facilitates the exchange of information between applications and the calling of procedures remotely from one application to another over HTTP. SOAP is a core standard for the web services architecture [9] for integrating applications built on heterogeneous platforms. ERM vendors should provide appropriate interfaces in the form of web services to facilitate the integration of their ERM system with other applications.

The exchange of metadata between subscription agents and an ERM system is another area in which standards may help considerably. For example, the ONIX for Serials [10] standard, now under development by EDItEUR [11] and NISO, will facilitate the exchange of serials subscriptions and holdings, and possibly also the process of automatic electronic check-in.

Another aspect that relates to integration and standards is the recording of e-resource usage, particularly when the user moves away from locally administered web pages to those of information providers. More often than not, libraries rely on statistics provided by the vendor, statistics that come in many formats. Recently, moves have been made to standardize usage statistics from vendors; of particular note in this area is Project COUNTER. The COUNTER specifications define not only terminology - for example, "session", "search", and "full-text article" - but also a standard reporting format (COUNTER, 2004). When COUNTER-compliant vendors provide data in XML according to the proposed schema, an ERM system will be able to upload COUNTER statistics into the ERM database and thus enable librarians to analyze usage statistics with other data pertaining to an e-resource.

Hence, the developers of ERM systems must take into account current and emerging standards if they are to integrate their system with a portfolio of library applications. Both public-sector and corporate organizations have long been demanding that library applications be seen as just one component in the delivery of services to users. The key to interoperability is the development of systems that conform to standards and that publish APIs. With the emergence of Web services as a set of standards for application integration, the task of integrating library applications with other institutional systems will become easier.

11. CHALLENGES FACED WITH ERM SYSTEMS

The important challenge is to clarify what we mean exactly by "e-resource". An individual electronic journal such as *D-Lib Magazine, Nature* etc. is an e-resource, as in electronic book or an abstracting and indexing database such as MEDLINE, but an e-resource can also be a package of e-journals or a database of abstracts and indexes that includes the full text of some or all article referenced by indexes. Furthermore, libraries face a number of challenges as they seek to continue offering the high level of services that users have come to expect. Some of the challenges facing with e-resource management are discuss below:

1. Preservation : Though the Electronic resources are enabling information to be created, manipulated, disseminated and located with increasing ease, preserving access to this information posses a great challenge. Unless, preservation of digital information is actively taken, the information will become inaccessible due to changing technology platform and media instability.

2. Lack of Professional Skills : Due to lack of management and technical skills, the library professionals are not able to handle the Electronic resources. The professional staffs are required to constantly update their own knowledge and skill base so as to work in today's rapidly changing digital environment.

3. Inadequate Library Fund : Most of the libraries have inadequate fund for acquiring Electronic resources and so the users do not get their needy information at the right time. Libraries are at a disadvantage when acting alone in this environment and there is need for cooperative purchasing through library consortia.

4. Technical Infrastructure : In a digital information service system, infrastructure such as software, hardware, internet facilities and other physical equipment are required to provide easier, faster and comprehensive access to information. Therefore, libraries in the digital age need to enhance and upgrade current technical architecture to accommodate Electronic resources.

5. Lack of Cooperation of Staff Members : The support and cooperation of staff members, programmers and technical staff are very essential to provide effective service in a digital environment. As such, the library staff should not only be technically competent but should also user-friendly-approach.

12. ORGANIZATION OF ELECTRONIC RESOURCES

In any Library Information System (either traditional or modern library system), organization of resources is also one of the important and crucial works to function smoothly the library services. As such, the system manager should have good professional skills to organize the available resources effectively. In a modern digital library information system, the professional should have skills like computing, database management, networking, and other management skills relating to IT environment. Therefore, the system manager should keep in mind the following points while organizing the Electronic resources:

(a) To include those resources either in OPAC or to make different list for browsing;

(b) To organized accessing under a separate authority;

(c) To provide access either by alphabetical or under specific subject headings;

(d) To organize the Electronic resources within the context of other resources and websites;

(e) To check the method of access to Electronic resources, abstracting or full.

Since most of the user's search the resources under subject heading predominantly, organization of Electronic resources should be in such a way that the users could be able to retrieve different sets of information or records.

13. SELECTION OF ELECTRONIC RESOURCE MANAGEMENT

An ERM system can facilitates this process by providing a global picture of the e-resources world. Selection is not a new term to librarian and staff as they have been doing it since long back the libraries started acquiring printed material. However libraries are now focusing to adopt Electronic resources information technology approaching towards the Electronic resources rather than printed materials as technology developed. In fact, the emergence of Internet, particularly, the www (World Wide Web) has a triggered proliferation of web based full text online resources as a new media of information delivery. As the web has grown, not just in popularity and use, but also in content, librarians are trying to meet the needs of the user and identify new resources, such as online databases, web based resources, collections in digital library, e-books, e-journals etc.

The selection process should be done in relevant with the demands of the users, committee, focus group, user's recommendation etc. Apart from this, it should take into consideration the following steps:

1. to identify library needs;
2. to identify content and scope of the Electronic resources;
3. to evaluate quality of that particular resource and search capabilities;
4. to estimate the cost;
5. to check either subscription based or web based when acquiring;
6. to evaluate the systems and technical support;
7. to review licensing agreements;
8. to evaluate application software and installation, updated sporadically or in regular schedule; and,
9. to check the facilities for educational support and training.

Electronic resource selection for library and consortia purchase requires considerable care, effort and judicious involvement of the members. Some of the criteria for selection of Electronic resources such as well-established multi-disciplinary resources with broad coverage should be preferred over highly specialized sources targeted for specialists, though the requirement would primarily be based on the target users. The electronic resources already on subscription in the beneficiary institutions should be preferred over those which are not being used in any of the beneficiary institutions. Resources that are 'electronic-only' should be preferred over those that are print-based unless completely unavoidable. Resources that are very important but highly cost-intensive should be preferred over those which are less important or less-used but low cost. Resources where electronic versions are made available free on subscription to their print versions should be avoided as far as possible; and selections should be made on their usage / suitability to their respective institutions. This is important for a balanced resource coverage and satisfaction of the user's needs of the participating institutions.

14. USE OF ERM SYSTEMS IN LIBRARIES

The integration and focus on process simplification improves the effectiveness of the ERM system and allows the promise of the ERM to be fulfilled, various tools required for managing e-resources and end users' access to them. For instance, users can access an e-journal via an A-Z list, library portal, library OPACs, or link server. The Verde ERM system has been constructed to integrate with such tools.

Verde provides a single point of administration for e-resources and a comprehensive solution for managing the complex and multidimensional relationships that characterize such resources. Verde supports the service requirements of e-resources through complementing, rather than duplicating, existing systems organized by libraries. Verde interacts with other systems to deal with the various stages of an e-resources life cycle. For example, setting up an e-resource at the trial stage may require the activation of the e-resource in a link server and also in an A-Z list or library portal. Once acquired, the new e-resource might also be presented in the OPAC for general availability. Cancellation, on the other hand, typically results in deactivation of the e-resource in all the components of the library system (unless perpetual access or archiving rights to the data are retained).

Verde is compatible with federated/meta-search tools in search tool, such as MetaLib, can be maintained and managed in Verde. Verde offers a web-service (SOAP) layer, enabling the ERM system to interact not only with Ex Libris products but also thirds-party products.

There are several reasons to use the electronic resources in libraries. These can be summarized as follows:

(i) Increase the technological development.

(ii) Easy to access and search.

(iii) Ever increasing price rate of the print journals.

(iv) Irregular publication and the long time gap between publication of a journal and its availability in the market.

(v) Problems related to conversion rate of foreign currencies.

(vi) Lower price per user or free.

(vii) Low searching time.

(viii) Availability of vast amount of the electronic resources.

15. POSITIVE IMPACT OF ERM IN LIBRARIES

There are several positive impacts of electronic resources in libraries as follows:

(i) Available as soon as the print version is published.

(ii) E-publishing may be 70-90% less costly than paper.

(iii) Access for 24×7.

(iv) Subjects can be searched across a range of titles.

(v) Many users can use electronic resources simultaneously.

(vi) It provides timely access to documents.

(vii) Economy in maintenance.

(viii) It is interactive; they can foster an online exchange of ideas by e-mail.

(ix) Interactive between authors and readers and readers and allow readers to comment on articles that appears in a journal.

(x) Space saving in libraries.

(xi) Monitoring is much easier to find out the use of electronic media.

(xii) It can be easily manage by adding bookmarks and personal notes to the sites.

(xiii) Compatibility with the search engine.

(xiv) It can solve the problems of missing issues of journals.

(xv) It can easily merge with altering service.

16. NEGATIVE IMPACT OF ERM IN LIBRARIES

There are several negative impacts of electronic resources in libraries as follows:

(a) Hardware and software compatibility issues between publishers and users.

(b) Initial high infrastructure and installation cost is required.

(c) Need special equipment to access.

(d) High speed of communication is required.

(e) Excessive printing of documents.

(f) Difficulty inherent in relating to a large amount of data on a screen.

(g) Efficient manpower is required.

(h) Causes more concern about copyright.

(i) Many readers prefer paper and print to a computer screen.

(j) Sometimes unavailable to international users due to legal issues.

With the rapid advancement in information communication technology, modern libraries and Information centers have been blessed with electronic materials and therefore libraries are gradually shifting towards the electronic libraries with electronic resources. Thus the Electronic resources have significant roles to play in teaching and learning process and hence it is the high time for the teachers to get an awareness of these resources for their future academic growth. It is observed that the availability of Electronic resources on the campus is almost sufficient for all the existing disciplines but the infrastructure to use these resources is not adequate and can hinder the ability to meet the requirements of users. It is concluded that the faculty members are using electronic resources, which are subscribed by the SMIT, effectively. Internet access speed can be increased for speedy retrieval of information.

It is perceived that patrons will be in favour of electronic resources and demand for a simplest most direct path to information irrespective of the methods that are being adopted. Portability, sharing and convenience are increasing important for end users. Libraries need to manage electronic resources effectively to the optimum utilization by overcoming the issues and challenges. Growth of electronic resources even though slower than what is expected will force the libraries to switch over to more and more electronic resources in future. However, with the innovative approaches to solve these issues and with a high degree of emphasis on standardization, the task of managing electronic resources will become less complex in the future. Electronic resources and services have been ever increasing day by day in the present day contemporary information environment, to overcome the problems of diminishing budgets, increasing information needs of the academicians and the researches, publishing of newly generated knowledge in varied forms and formats, problems faced by libraries in providing varied services, collecting of all documents published both at national and international levels.

17. THE MOST POPULAR PUBLISHERS OF ELECTRONIC RESOURCES

Table 8.1

E-Resources	***Websites***
All Ebscohost Resources	http://search.ebscohost.com/
American Chemical Society (ACS)	http://pubs.acs.org/
American Institute of Physics Journal (AIP)	http://journals.aip.org/
American Physical Society (APS)	http://www.aps.org/

ASME	http://asmedl.org/journals/doc/ASMEDL-home/jrnls/
Cambridge University Press (CUP)	www.cambridge.org/
Decker	http://www.deckerpublishing.com/
Emerald	http://www.emeraldinsight.com/
ICE Virtual Library	http://www.icevirtuallibrary.com/
IEEE/IEE Electronic Library (IEL)	http://ieeexplore.ieee.org/Xplore/dynhome.jsp
IGI Global	http://www.igi-global.com
ISI Web of Knowledge	www.webofknowledge.com
J-Store	http://www.jstor.org/
Nature	http://www.nature.com/
Ovid	http://ovidsp.ovid.com/
Oxford University Press (OUP)	www.oup.com
Project Muse	http://muse.jhu.edu/
Royal Society of Chemistry	http://www.rsc.org/
SAGE Online Journal	http://online.sagepub.com/
Science Direct	http://www.sciencedirect.com/
Sci-Finder Scholar	Sci-Finder Scholar
SCOPUS	http://www.scopus.com/home.url
Springer Link	http://www.springerlink.com/
Taylor & Francis	http://www.taylorandfrancis.com/
Thieme-e-journals	https://www.thieme-connect.com/ejournals
Ulrichs Web	http://ulrichsweb.serialssolutions.com/login
Wiley-Blackwell	http://eu.wiley.com/WileyCDA/Brand/id-35.html

18. CONCLUSION

It is perceived that patrons will be in favor of electronic resources management and demand for a simplest most direct path to information irrespective of the methods that are being adopted. Portability, sharing and convenience are increasing important for end users. Libraries need to manage electronic resources effectively to the optimum utilization by overcoming the issues and challenges. Growth of electronic resources even though slower than what is expected will force the libraries to switch over to more and more electronic resources in future. However, with the innovative approaches to solve these issues and with a high degree of emphasis on standardization, the task of managing electronic resources will become less complex in the future.

REFERENCE

1. Anderson, I., et al. (2004). Report of the DLF Electronic Resource Management Initiative *Functional requirements for electronic resource management*. Digital Library Federation: Washington, DC,
2. Bergman, B.J. (2005). Looking at electronic resources librarians. Is there gender equity within this emerging specialty? *New Library World*, 106(1210/1211), 116-127.
3. Chang, S. (2003). The DLF electronic resource management initiative. *OCLC Systems & Services*, 19(2), 45-47.
4. Farb, S.E., and Riggio, A. (2004). Medium or message? A new look at standards, structures, and schemata for managing electronic resources. *Library Hi Tech*, 22(2), 144-152.
5. Grover, D., and Fons, T. (2004). The Innovative electronic resource management system: a development partnership. *Serials Review*, 30(2), 110-116.
6. Hartley, R. J. (2003). Electronic information resources. In Feather, J. & Sturges, P. (Ed.), *International Encyclopedia of Information and Library Science* (2 ed.). New York: Routledge, pp. 173.
7. Jewell, T.D. (2005). Electronic resource management: the quest for systems and standards. *The Serials Librarian, 48*(1/2), 137-163.
8. Kennedy, M.R. (2004). Dreams of perfect programs: managing the acquisition of electronic resources. *Library Collections, Acquisitions, & Technical Services, 28*(4), 449-458.
9. Ranganathan, S. R. (1957). *The Five Laws of Library Science*. London: G. Blunt and Sons.
10. Sadeh, T., and Ellingsen, M. (2005). Electronic resource management systems: the need and the realization. *New Library World*, 106(5), 208-218.
11. www.w3.org/TR/soap12-part1/
12. www.w3.org/2002/ws/Activity.html
13. www.editeur.org/onixserials.html

9

Digital Preservation System and Strategies

0. INTRODUCTION

Preservation is the umbrella terms now apply to a wide variety of collection management responsibilities intended to preserve collections of print and non-print materials for future generations. The preservation of library materials involves two aspects. First is the preservation of the widely used material from wear and tear and second one is the preservation of the archival materials of the library which has become fragile due to aging. Both the issues are important since it is often very difficult to replace the material once deteriorated. Marking the first one available in digital form will eliminate need of acquiring the multiple copies and also the chances of further deterioration. Another one i.e. the archival material may be preserved in original form after getting digitized as the original copy can be easily kept away from the users since they may use the digital copy.

1. WHAT IS DIGITAL PRESERVATION?

The Term "digital preservation" refers to both preservation of materials that are created originally in digital form and never exist in print or analogue form and the use of imaging and recording technologies to create digital surrogates of analogue materials for access and preservation purpose. Digital preservation is a long-term, error-free storage of digital information, with means for retrieval and interpretation, for the entire time span the information is required for.

According to *Harrod's Librarians Glossary and Reference Book* "digital preservation is the methods of keeping digital materials 'alive' so that they remain usable as technological advances render original hardware and software specifications obsolete".

P.K. Mahapartra and B. Chakrabarti also define "digital preservation at least in a library context as the process of keeping collections and the information they contain available for use as long as they are needed".

Digital preservation is the set of processes, activities and management of digital information over time to ensure its long term accessibility (Wikipedia, 2012).

Thus, digital preservation is preserving the digital medium that holds the digital information by storing it in the correct environment and various agreed storage and handling procedures, copying the digital information into newer, fresher media before the old media deteriorates. It includes deciding what to digitize, format for texts and images quality of images and costs.

2. OBJECTIVE OF DIGITAL PRESERVATION

1. Protect Originals : Most common application of digital technologies in an archive or library is digital copies that can be used for ready reference in lieu of causal browsing through the original sources. Preservation goals are met because physical access to the original documents is limited.

2. Represent Originals : Digital system could be built that represents the information content of the original sources in such detail that the system can be used to fulfill most, if not all, of the research and learning potential of the original documents. High-resolution systems of this intermediate level of quality open new avenues of research and use and could have a transformative effect on the service missions of those who create the products.

3. Transcend originals : Very small but increasing number of applications, digital imaging holds the promise of generating a product that can be used for purposes that are impossible to achieve with the original sources. This category also includes digital imaging products that incorporate searchable full text (marked up or raw). Additionally, digital products that draw together, organize, and enhance access to widely dispersed research materials may have transcendental impact on the people who use them.

3. PRESERVATION REQUIREMENT

1. Integrity of Object : A book is a book, or it exits in a set, but what are the boundaries of documents in a hypertext environment? The boundaries of digital objects are less clear, especially if they are compound objects created by assembling different media or by linking to resources from around a network.

2. Physical Preservation : The physical presence in this case refers to the computer file, the series of "1"s and "0"s that are the basis of a digital object.

3. Content Preservation : The contents of digital libraries include data, metadata, photos, text, pages, color separations, charts graphs, statistical data, diagram, illustration, audio and video clips. This aspect refers to maintaining the ability to access the content at its lowest level, such as ASCII text, without the embellishments, of font variations and layout features.

4. Presentation Format : Content is typically rendered in some presentation, format or layout that includes different font faces and sizes, the use of white space, columns, marginalia, headers, footers, pagination, and so on. In many types of digital documents (e.g., SGML XML, and some forms of PDF), the layout specifications are separate from the content. To retain the original look of a document, these layout specifications must also be preserved, especially when they contribute significantly to the understanding and interpretation of the content.

5. Functionality : Digital objects have a functionality that goes far beyond traditional paper documents. They can contain multimedia components (i.e., text, graphics, audio, and video), exist in hypertext format.

6. Authenticity : An individual accessing the object must be able to verify that it is the one she/he wants, and that the transformations to keep it accessible have preserved its original form. Thus, activities to guard authenticity include securing digital objects against unauthorized changes and monitoring digital objects through multiple "copying" cycles to ensure to that each copy is an acceptable rendition of the original, establishing authoritative depositories would also help achieve this goal.

7. Location and Reference : Digital objects can be readily altered, copied or moved. An individual must be able to match a citation to a digital object, and to distinguish it from other versions or editions.

8. Provenance : Provenance is an archival concept that asserts the origin and chain or custody of an object and contributes to defining it as a whole. Imprint statements and bookplates, for example, partly fill this rile for formally published items. Establishing an object's origin and history confirm that the work is authentic and its content are intact.

9. Preserve context : Digital objects are partly defined by their hardware and software dependencies, their mode of distribution and linkages to other digital objects. Preserving digital objects may mean weaning them from some technical dependencies, changing the mode of distribution, and deactivating links. In these circumstances, preserving context is a particular challenge.

4. DIGITAL PRESERVATION STRATEGIES

In 2006, the Online Computer Library Center developed a four-point strategy for the long-term preservation of digital objects that consisted of:

1. Assessing the risks for loss of content posed by technology variables such as commonly used proprietary file formats and software applications.
2. Evaluating the digital content objects to determine what type and degree of format conversion or other preservation actions should be applied.
3. Determining the appropriate metadata needed for each object type and how it is associated with the objects.
4. Providing access to the content.

There are several additional strategies that individuals and organizations may use to actively combat the loss of digital information.

(i) Technology Preservation : Technology preservation is not a practical approach in for data preservation as it is financially unfeasible to go for regular cycle of media refreshing i.e. maintenance of the hardware and software platforms that support a digital resource.

(ii) Refreshing : Refreshing involves periodically moving a file from one physical storage medium to another to avoid physical decay or the obsolescence of that medium. Because physical storage devices decay, and because technology changes make older storage device inaccessible to new computers, refreshing is necessary in order to achieve longevity.

(iii) Migration and Reformatting : Migration is an approach that involves periodically moving files from one file encoding format to another that is usable in a more modern computing environment. Migration seeks to limit the problem of files encoded in a wide variety to file format that have existed over time by gradually brining all formats into a limited number of contemporary formats. Migration involves change in the configuration of the underlying data, without change in its intellectual content. Migration is expensive initially, but could prove cost-effective over the long term, making migration easier and faster.

(iv) Emulation : Emulation is the process of re-creation of the H/W and S/W environment required to access a resource. Its approach is more focused on the application S/W rather than on the files containing information. It would be theoretically possible to emulate either the hardware (H/W) or software (S/W). S/W could be re-engineered in the future if sufficient metadata about it could be stored, or the S/W and operating systems that created the digital object could be stored with it, and the H/W platform to run them could be emulated in future.

Jeff Rothenberg is the principle proponent of the emulation method - in which one saves not just the data but also the program that was used to create/manipulate the information in the first place. Rothenberg suggests that the only way to decode the bit stream would be to run the old program, which would require the use of an emulator. Several different methods for defining how an emulator can be specified have been suggested, but the feasibility of these methods has not yet been fully demonstrated.

(v) Data Archaeology : Data archaeology involves recovery of data later on, using better techniques available in future depending upon the value of data. This becomes necessary rescue a digital resource that has not been migrated but contains vital information, or to which some unforeseen disaster has occurred. In this model, data would be refreshed regularly, but no migration would be performed, and no programs would be preserved to be emulated at a later storage. Data archaeology is last resort for valuable data and programs.

(vi) Output to Analogue Media : Output to analogue media basically incorporates microfilming before the digital imaging is done. This provides a preservation copy in a analogue format and circumvents some of the concerns over the longevity of the digital files. It is a fact that microfilm cannot capture all of the features of original digital object, but it could satisfy the access needs of the majority of users and would thus help to preserve the original. The method employed in this process is termed as "Computer Output to Microfilm" or "COM".

(vii) Replication : Creating duplicate copies of data on one or more systems is called replication. Data that exists as a single copy in only one location is highly vulnerable to software or hardware failure, intentional or accidental alteration, and environmental catastrophes like fire, flooding, etc. Digital data is more likely to survive if it is replicated in several locations. Replicated data may introduce difficulties in refreshing, migration, versioning, and access control since the data is located in multiple places.

(viii) Metadata attachment : Metadata is data on a digital file that includes information on creation, access rights, restrictions, preservation history, and rights management. Metadata attached to digital files may be affected by file format obsolescence. ASCII is considered to be the most durable format for metadata because it is widespread, backwards compatible when used with Unicode, and utilizes human-readable characters, not numeric codes. It retains information, but not the structure information it is presented in. For higher functionality, SGML or XML should be used. Both markup languages are stored in ASCII format, but contain tags that denote structure and format.

(ix) Trustworthy digital objects : Digital objects that can speak to their own authenticity are called trustworthy digital objects (TDOs). TDOs were proposed by Henry M. Gladney to enable digital objects to maintain a record of their change history so future users can know with certainty that the contents of the object are authentic. [16] Other preservation strategies like replication and migration are necessary for the long-term preservation of TDOs.

5. STANDARDS OF DIGITAL PRESERVATION

To standardize digital preservation practice and provide a set of recommendations for reservation program implementation, the Reference Model for an Open Archival Information System OAIS) was developed. The reference model (ISO 14721:2003) includes the following responsibilities:

(1) Negotiate for and accept appropriate information from information Producers.

(2) Obtain sufficient control of the information provided to the level needed to ensure Long-Term Preservation.

(3) Determine, either by it or in conjunction with other parties, which communities should become the Designated Community and, therefore, should be able to understand the information provided.

(4) Ensure that the information to be preserved is Independently Understandable to the Designated Community. In other words, the community should be able to understand the information without needing the assistance of the experts who produced the information.

(5) Follow documented policies and procedures which ensure that the information is preserved against all reasonable contingencies, and which enable the information to be disseminated as authenticated copies of the original, or as traceable to the original.

(6) Make the preserved information available to the Designated Community.

OAIS is concerned with all technical aspects of a digital object's life cycle: ingest into and storage in a preservation infrastructure, data management, accessibility, and distribution. The model also addresses metadata issues and recommends that five types of metadata be attached to a digital object: reference (identification) information, provenance (including preservation history), context, fixity (authenticity indicators), and representation (formatting, file structure, and what "imparts meaning to an object's bitstream").

5.1 Digital Sound Preservation Standards

The Council on Library and Information Resources (CLIR) hosted a roundtable meeting of audio experts discussed the best practices for reformatting sound from analog to digital for digital preservation in 2004. In 2006, CLIR has given 15 recommendations for improving the practice of analog audio transfer for archiving:

(1) Develop core competencies in audio preservation engineering. Participants noted with concern that the number of experts qualified to transfer older recordings is shrinking and emphasized the need to find a way to ensure that the technical knowledge of these experts can be passed on.

(2) Develop arrangements among smaller institutions that allow for cooperative buying of esoteric materials and supplies.

(3) Pursue a research agenda for magnetic-tape problems that focuses on a less destructive solution for hydrolysis than baking, relubrication of acetate tapes, and curing of cupping.

(4) Develop guidelines for the use of automated transfer of analog audio to digital preservation copies.

(5) Develop a web-based clearinghouse for sharing information on how archives can develop digital preservation transfer programs.

(6) Carry out further research into nondestructive playback of broken audio discs.

(7) Develop a flowchart for identifying the composition of various types of audio discs and tapes.

(8) Develop a reference chart of problematic media issues.

(9) Collate relevant audio engineering standards from organizations.

(10) Research safe and effective methods for cleaning analog tapes and discs.

(11) Develop a list of music experts who could be consulted for advice on transfer of specific types of musical content (e.g., determining the proper key so that correct playback speed can be established).

(12) Research the life expectancy of various audio formats.

(13) Establish regional digital audio repositories.

(14) Cooperate to develop a common vocabulary within the field of audio preservation.

(15) Investigate the transfer of technology from such fields as chemistry and materials science to various problems in audio preservation.

Updated technical guidelines on the creation and preservation of digital audio have been prepared by the International Association of Sound and Audiovisual Archives (IASA).

6. DIGITAL PRESERVATION OF E-PRINTS

Stevan Harnad's views on digital preservation of e-prints have been expressed in a number of publications and email discussion lists:

1. E-prints are "duplicates" of the conventionally published literature. In other words, they do not replace the traditional journal literature but complement it.
2. E-prints are about "immediate access". They allow rapid dissemination of the literature (in contrast to journals where there is often a long delay between acceptance of a paper and its publication). When

housed in open access repositories, e-prints are also free at the point of use (in contrast to the journal literature which is usually hidden behind a "tollgate).

3. Effort should be concentrated on filling the repositories anyone who has worked in this area known that getting the content is a major priority and a major challenge.
4. If this is the case, Harnad argues, preservation should not be a priority. In fact, it may be an unnecessary distraction.
5. Putting an emphasis on preservation may detract from or slow down efforts to fill repositories. This might be the case if repository managers delay making repositories available until there are watertight preservation policies in place, or if they put additional barriers in the way of authors before they can submit papers.
6. When there is a critical mass of content, it can be "retrofitted for more rigorous preservation." This will particularly apply if and when e-prints become the primary outlet for scholarly communication.
7. In the meantime, preservation is not an urgent priority.
8. Preservation efforts should be concentrated on the conventionally published versions of papers rather than on e-print repositories. Harnad has a striking analogy to illustrate this point: preserving e-prints it like a museum curator preserving a copy of an artifact rather than the original artifact itself.
9. Digital preservation is an important aspect of the service delivered by e-print repositories. There are number of possible reasons for preserving e-print.
10. Preserving (open) access: This is perhaps the most important reason. It would be an irony if a paper in an open-access e-print repository could be accessed

today and yet in ten years' time had been allowed to decay so that it was inaccessible. Carrying out necessary preservation work may be necessary to preserve open access to the content.

11. Where e-prints are commonly cited: Posting an e-print creates a community of users (or potential users). In some disciplines, citing e-prints may be the norm and so users would expect access to that e-print to be preserved so that citations to it would continue to be valid. Even after a paper has been formally published, researchers may expect to be able to cite the post-print in an e-print repository since access to it may be easier.
12. Where e-prints contain or sit alongside more than the conventionally published paper. In some cases, e-print may have more detail or additional data associated with them, which means that they should be preserved in their own right.
13. Where e-prints form part of a specific collection: Repository managers may want to preserve e-prints which form part of a coherent collection and where the existence of the collection itself adds value. For example, institutional repositories may wish to preserve all papers in a particular subject area, such as local or regional studies.
14. Guarantees of preservation may attract authors to submit papers: It has been suggested that making authors aware that repositories will preserve their papers maybe the carrot that will attract them to deposit their papers. As yet however, there does not seem to be any specific evidence for this.

7. GUIDELINES OF DIGITAL PRESERVATION

Some libraries have developed similar guidelines. However, a recent survey concluded that digital preservation guidelines focus on creation, receipt and capture of digital objects, and do not satisfactorily address their long-term preservation.

(a) Documenting Resources : A recurrent theme in digital preservation guidelines is documentation and description of electronic resources. The need for such deliberate description stems in part from the fact that digital objects do not carry the visible evidence of creation and use (imprints, bindings, bookplates, marginalia, or Scotch tape) of non-electronic formats. Such clues guide preservation decisions. They also help users to establish that the work is whole and intact, and to understand its provenance and the context in which it was created.

(b) Metadata : A description of a digital object is "data about data," or metadata. Such descriptive data should include the contextual information crucial to the long-term management of electronic information. Metadata elements useful in preservation might include: Identifiers; Hardware, operating system and software required to access a document; Physical details of tangible format publications such as CD-ROM, Floppy disks; Encoding standard and version; Migration history and its success; Data to assist determining authenticity; Rights management information; Versions and dates.

Conversion projects would employ additional metadata elements such as the capture device, resolution, compression, source material, and producer (of the digital document). Existing metadata schemes (e.g. MARC, Dublin Core) provide for some such information capture, but there is no consensus on which approach will work best for preservation purposes. In MARC, for example, some of the necessary data is captured in notes' fields that may not use sufficiently detailed or consistent language for subsequent search and retrieval.

(c) Unique Identifiers : On element of describing a digital object is to assign it a unique and persistent identifier. An identifier is a number, like an ISBN, which is associated with a particular instance of a digital object. Unlike an URL, it is independent of the location of that object. A unique, widely supported identifier for digital objects would help establish the authenticity of the object by confirming to a user that the resource she/he is accessing is the one cited. It could also help establish the relationship between copies or versions of digital objects, as any modification of the original would result in a modification of its identifier. Some organizations involved in digital preservation are currently using. PURLs (Persistent Uniform Resource Locators), URNs (Uniform Resource Names) or modified Digital Object Identifiers. As yet, no single digital identifier has achieved widespread, international acceptance.

(d) Linking Metadata with Content : Metadata can be stored either as an integral part of the document it describes (e.g. embedded in an HTML header) or as part of a separate file of information (e.g., MARC record). One way of linking metadata and the digital object is to package them together. To this end, the aforementioned Reference Model for an Open Archival Information System (OAIS) proposes an "information package" comprised of "content information" and "preservation descriptive information". Along similar lines, a working group of the Society of Motion Picture and Television Engineers has developed a Universal Preservation Format (UPF), a data-file mechanism that uses a container structure to incorporate metadata into digital media objects. Although primarily developed for audio-visual data, the principles underlying the UPF may have wider applicability.

(e) Establishing Infrastructure : A final way in which libraries are gaining control over the preservation of digital objects is by building preservation requirements into systems development. The Australian National Library, for example, has started a Digital Services Project to develop systems to manage its digital collections and to support cooperative, shared access.

The National Library of Canada has incorporated preservation requirements in its Digital Library Infrastructure Project. The next step is to develop the systems.

The next steps remain ill defined. To reduce the uncertainty surrounding digital preservation, we can encourage creators to use practices that will aid long-term preservation, such as creating valid documents in standard document formats and address the question of which preservation strategy will work best by testing migration and emulation and identifying associated costs and tradeoffs in each case.

8. DIGITAL PRESERVATION INITIATIVES

Some of the list of digital preservation initiatives such as:

(1) The Library of Congress operates the National Digital Information Infrastructure and Preservation Program

(2) The British Library is responsible for several programmes in the area of digital preservation. The National Archives of the United Kingdom have also pioneered various initiatives in the field of digital preservation.

(3) The Safety Deposit Box software from Tessella is being widely adopted by National Archives and has been selected by the National Archives in the UK, Netherlands, Switzerland, Finland, Estonia, Malaysia and Austria as well as FamilySearch and the Wellcome Collection. It was awarded the Queen's Awards for Enterprise in the UK.

(4) Ex Libris Rosetta is commercial software helping memory institutions to collect, manage, archive and preserve their digital collections, ensuring its data integrity and access over time. The system enables managing digital entities end to end—from submission to dissemination. A rule-based workflow engine and open architecture allow institutions using the system

to develop unique plug-in tools and applications to enhance the systems ingest, management, preservation and delivery processes.

(5) The Meta Archive Cooperative is a library-run, collaborative approach to digital preservation that embeds digital preservation infrastructure and knowledge in each of its constituent member institutions. Composed mainly of University libraries, the Cooperative functions as a network wherein each preserved file is replicated seven times, is stored in geographically distinct locations across four countries, and is carefully managed from ingest (as a SIP) to dissemination (as a DIP).

For more details list of digital preservation initiatives. Visit the following website: http://en.wikipedia.org/wiki/List_of_digital_preservation_initiatives

9. LARGE-SCALE DIGITAL PRESERVATION INITIATIVES (LSDIS)

Many research libraries and archives have begun or are about to begin Large-Scale digital preservation initiatives (LSDI's). The main players in LSDIs are cultural institutions, commercial companies such as Google and Microsoft, and non-profit groups including the Open Content Alliance (OCA), the Million Book Project (MBP), and HathiTrust. The primary motivation of these groups is to expand access to scholarly resources.

10. CONCLUSION

Preservation increasingly involves reproducing a work in any form. The preservation strategies are actively employed the information which the technologies are enabling to be created, manipulated, disseminated, located and stored with increasing case information will rapidly become inaccessible. Preserving access to information poses a significant challenge, Refreshing of the information that is stored in never media before the old media deteriorate beyond the point at which the information can be retrieve is much needed because of the migration of information from one hardware/software configuration to another or from one generating of computer technology to a later one. Once the preservation is over storage is important for archive. The archive should have digital objects according to their expected frequency of use. The speed of access will be directly linked to expected frequency of use with the level of access being provided by different storage topologies. It needs to be duplicated to ensure security for storage and it will never allow technical failure to harm or destroy any of its collection.

REFERENCES

1. Alison, B. Preservation of Digital Information: Issues and Current status *Network Notes*
2. Bradley, K. (Ed.). (2009). *Guidelines on the Production and Preservation of Digital Audio Objects* (2 ed.). Australia: International Association of Sound and Audiovisual Archives.
3. Brian., L. a. L., Dempsey (2004). Thirteen ways of Looking at.. Digital Preservation. *D-Lib Magazine, 10*(7/8).
4. Chandra, S. (2005). *Library and Information Technology*. New Delhi: Shree publisher & Distributes.
5. Consultative Committee for Space Data Systems. (2002). *Reference Model for an Open Archival Information System (OAIS)*. Washington, DC: CCSDS Secretariat.
6. Cornell University Library. (2005). Digital Preservation Management: Implementing Short-term Strategies for Long-term Problems.
7. Council on Library and Information Resources. (2006). Capturing Analog Sound for Digital Preservation: Report of a Roundtable Discussion of Best Practices for Transferring Analog Discs and Tapes.
8. Faruqui, K. K. A., Mehtab. (2005). *Library Information Systems and e-journal Archiving*. New Delhi: Authors Press.
9. Gladney, H. M. (2004). Trustworthy 100-year digital objects: Evidence after every witness is dead. *ACM Transactions on Information Systems*, 22(3), 406 - 436. doi: 10.1145/1010614.1010617
10. Group, N. F. A. (2007). *A Framework of Guidance for Building Good Digital Collections* (3 ed.). Baltimore USA: National

Information Standards Organization (NISO).

11. Hussain, A. and Krishna K. (2006). *Digital Preservation System: A New Approach.* Paper presented at the National Conference on Information Management in Digital Libraries (NCIMDiL), Indian Institute of Technology-Kharagpur.

12. Jeff Rothenberg: Ensuring the Longevity of Digital Documents. Scientific American, 272(1), January 1995.

13. Natarajan, M. (2004). Digital Preservation of Cultural Heritage Information and its implications. *Journal of Library of Information Science,* 29(1/2), 14-25.

14. National Initiative for a Networked Cultural Heritage. (2002). NINCH Guide to Good Practice in the Digital Representation and Management of Cultural Heritage Materials.

15. OCLC Online Computer Library Center, I. (2006). *OCLC Digital Archive Preservation Policy and Supporting Documentation.* Dublin, Ohio,USA,p.5

16. Prytherch, R. (Ed.) (2005) Harrod's librarians' glossary and reference book (10 ed.). England: Ashgate Publishing.

17. Sharma, R. K. (2004). *Managing Information, knowledge and power in the Cyber age.* New Delhi: Bookwells.

18. Wikipedia.(2012).Digital Preservation, from http://en.wikipedia.org/wiki/Digital_preservation

19. www.knaw.nl/ecpa/PUBL/unesco.html.

20. www.oclc.org/research/pmwg

21. *www.arl.org/pubscat/index.html*

Bibliography

Aalexa. (2021). Retrieved 12 May, 2012, from www.alexa.com

AB, M. (2006). MySQL Documentation Retrieved 5 May, 2012, from http://dev.mysql.com/doc/

Abram. (2006). Podcasts and libraries Retrieved 11 May, 2012, from http://stephenslighthouse.sirsidynix.com/

Abram. (2006). Podcasts and libraries Retrieved 14 May, 2012, from http://stephenslighthouse.sirsidynix.com/archives/2006/11/podcasts_and_li.html

Achterman, D.(2006). Beyond Wikipedia. *Teacher Librarian, 34*(2), 19-22.

Adeyoyin, S. O. (2005). Information and communication technology (ICT) literacy among the staff of Nigerian university libraries. *Library Review, 54*(4), 257 - 266.

Alison, B. Preservation of Digital Information: Issues and Current status *Network Notes*

Anderson, I., et al. (2004). Report of the DLF Electronic Resource Management Initiative *Functional requirements for electronic resource management.* Digital Library Federation: Washington, DC,

Antherjanam, S.D. & Sheeja, N. K. (2008). *Impact of ICT on Library and Information Science: Major Shifts and Practices in CUSAT Central Library.* Paper presented at the 6th International CALIBER-2008, University of

Allahabad, Allahabad. February 28-29 & March1, 2008.

Antony, J. (1997). *Libsys-a selection for library automation and networking*. Paper presented at National Seminar on Library Automation-Problems and Prospects, Roorkee, India.

Bergman, B.J. (2005). Looking at electronic resources librarians. Is there gender equity within this emerging specialty? *New Library World*, 106(1210/1211), 116-127.

Bhattacharya, P. (2004).Advances in digital library initiatives: a developing country perspective. *International Information & Library Review, 36* (3), 165-75.

Boss, R. W. RFID Technology for Libraries Retrieved 7 May, 2012, from http://www.ala.org/pla/tools/technotes/rfidtechnology

Bradley, K. (Ed.). (2009). *Guidelines on the Production and Preservation of Digital Audio Objects* (2 ed.). Australia: International Association of Sound and Audiovisual Archives.

Brian., L. a. L., Dempsey (2004). Thirteen ways of Looking at.. Digital Preservation. *D-Lib Magazine, 10*(7/8).

British Library. (2012). Podcasts Retrieved 8 May, 2012, from http://www.bl.uk/podcast

Carlson, B. (2010). March 2.0: Success of the National Equality March relied on social media tools Retrieved 11 May, 2012, from http://www.mediabullseye.com/mb/2010/04/march-2-0-success-of-the-national-equality-march-relied-on-social-media-tools.html#idc-container

Chandra, S. (2005). *Library and Information Technology*. New Delhi: Shree publisher & Distributes.

Chang, S. (2003). The DLF electronic resource management initiative. *OCLC Systems & Services*, 19(2), 45-47.

Cobb, M.). RFID projects: Implementation considerations, RFID security concerns Retrieved 15 May, 2012, from http://searchsecurity.techtarget.co.uk/tip/RFID-projects-Implementation-considerations-RFID-security-concerns

Commission, P. (2002-2007). Tenth Five Year Plan (2002-2007). New Delhi: Planning Commission, Government of India.

Comscore. Introducing Mobile Metrix 2.0 Retrieved 10 May, 2012, from http://www.comscore.com/

Consultative Committee for Space Data Systems. (2002). *Reference Model for an Open Archival Information System (OAIS)*. Washington, DC: CCSDS Secretariat.

Coombs, K. A. (2007). Building a library web site on the pillars of Web 2.0. Computers in Libraries, 27.

Cornell University Library. (2005). Digital Preservation Management: Implementing Short-term Strategies for Long-term Problems.

Correia, A.M.R. & Teixeira, J.C. (2005). Reforming scholarly publishing and knowledge communication: from the advent of the scholarly journal to the challenges of open access. *Online Information Review, 29*(4), 488-495.

Correia, A.M.R. & Teixeira, J.C. (2005). Reforming scholarly publishing and knowledge communication: from the advent of the scholarly journal to the challenges of open access. *Online Information Review*, 29(4), 349-364.

Council on Library and Information Resources. (2006). Capturing Analog Sound for Digital Preservation: Report of a Roundtable Discussion of Best Practices for Transferring Analog Discs and Tapes.

Darch, Collin *et al.* (1999). Dirt road or yellow brick superhighway? Information and communication technology in academic libraries of South Africa. *Library Hi Tech, 17*(3), 285 - 298.

Das, N. (2007). *Open Source Software and building digital*

library using GSDL software. Paper presented at the 5th Convention PLANNER -2007, Guwahati University, Guwahati.

Davison-Turley, W. (2005). Blogs and RSS: powerful information management tools. *Library Hi Tech News*, 22(10), 28-29.

Dickson, A. & Holley, R. P. (2010). Social networking in academic libraries: the possibilities and the concerns. *New Library World*, 111(11/12), 468-479.

Digital Library of India. Retrieved 9 May, 2012, from http://www.dli.ernet.in/

DLF. (1998). A working definition of digital library Retrieved 11 May, 2012, from http://old.diglib.org/about/dldefinition.htm

DOI. (2012). Digital object identifier (DOI) Retrieved 11 May, 2012, from http://www.doi.org/index.html doi: 10.1145/1010614.1010617

DSpace (2006). DSpace repository Retrieved 5 May, 2012, from http://www.dspace.org/whos-using-dspace/Repository-List.html

East, H. (2003). Online services. In Feather, J. & Sturges, P. (Ed.), *International Encyclopedia of Information and Library Science* (2 ed.). New York: Routledge, pp.466.

El-Sherbini, M. & W., A.J. (2007). New strategies for delivering library resources to users: rethinking the mechanisms in which libraries are processing and delivering bibliographic records. *The Journal of Academic Librarianship, 33*(2), 228-242.

Epps, A. S. V. (2002). Virtual reference-the way of the future? Available at: http://caliban.emeraldinsight.com/vl=8058844/cl=31/nw=1/rpsv/librarylink/technology/july02.htm#article.

ePrints@IISc. Retrieved 9 May, 2012, from http://eprints.iisc.ernet.in

ESCAP. (2000). Are ICT Policies Addressing Gender Equality?, from http//www.unescaporg/wid/04/wideresources/11wideactivities/01cctegm/backgoundpaper.Pdf.

Falk, H. (2004). The revolt against journal publishers. *The Electronic Library,* 22(2), 184-187.

Farb, S.E., and Riggio, A. (2004). Medium or message? A new look at standards, structures, and schemata for managing electronic resources. *Library Hi Tech*, 22(2), 144-152.

Farkas, M. (2007). Your stuff, their space. *American Libraries*, 38(11), 36.

Faruqui, K. K. A., Mehtab. (2005). *Library Information Systems and e-journal Archiving*. New Delhi: Authors Press.

Fedora Commons. Retrieved 9 May, 2012, from http://fedora-commons.org

Fourie, I. (2001). Current awareness services in an electronic age: The whole picture. Retrieved May 8, 2012 from http://www.aslib.co.uk/pubs/2001/09/05/1.html

German Xing Plans Invasion of LinkedIn Turf. (2007). *Marketingvox*. Retrieved from http://www.marketingvox. com/german-xing-plans-invasion-of-linkedin-turf-030727/

Gladney, H. M. (2004). Trustworthy 100-year digital objects: Evidence after every witness is dead. *ACM Transactions on Information Systems*, 22(3), 406 - 436.

Grant, S. (2002). Ebooks: Friend or Foe? Book Report, 21(1), 50 Retrieved from

Group, N. F. A. (2007). *A Framework of Guidance for Building Good Digital Collections* (3 ed.). Baltimore USA: National Information Standards Organization (NISO).

Grover, D., and Fons, T. (2004). The Innovative electronic resource management system: a development partnership. *Serials Review*, 30(2), 110-116.

Gulati, A. (2004). Use of information and communication technology in libraries and information centers: an Indian scenario. *The Electronic Library, 22*(4), 335-350.

Hargittai, E. (1999). Weaving the Western Web: Explaining difference in Internet connectivity among OECD countries. *Telecommunications Policy, 23*, 701-718.

Harinarayana, N. S. (1991). Concept of library automation. *Herald of Library Science*, 30 (3/4), 176-177.

Hartley, R. J. (2003). Electronic information resources. In Feather, J. & Sturges, P. (Ed.), *International Encyclopedia of Information and Library Science* (2 ed.). New York: Routledge, pp. 173.

Hi5 popular in Europe. (2008). *Mediashift*. Retrieved from http://www.pbs.org/mediashift/2007/06/orkut-friendster-get-second-chance-overseas166.html

Hirshon, A. (1999). Libraries, consortia and change management. *Journal of Academic Librarianship, 25*(2), 124-126.

Hooper, T. (2001). Management issues for the virtual library. *The Electronic Library, 19*(2), 71-72.

Husain, S. and A., Mehtab Alam. (2008). Library automation software packages in India: A study of the cataloguing modules of Alice for Windows, Libsys and Vitua. *Annals of Library and Information Studies, 54*, 146-151.

Hussain, A. (2007). RFID Technology for Libraries. *IASLIC Bulletin, 52*(1), 49-56.

Hussain, A. and Krishna K. (2006). *Digital Preservation System: A New Approach*. Paper presented at the National Conference on Information Management in Digital Libraries (NCIMDiL), Indian Institute of Technology-Kharagpur.

IGNCA. Retrieved 7 May, 2012, from http://www.ignca.nic.in/

IIMT-K. Retrieved 8 May, 2012, from http://www.iiitmk.ac.in/iiitmk-services/library-services

Information Technology. (1986). In J. G. Allee (Ed.), *Webster's New Encyclopedia of Dictionaries*. USA: Ottenheimer Publishers Inc.

Information Technology. (2002) *McGraw-Hill Encyclopedia of Science and Technology* (9 ed.). New York: McGraw-Hil.

Information Technology. In M. L.-C. & T. M. Carter (Ed.), *ALA Glossary of Library and Information Science* (4 ed.). New York: ALA Editions.

Jain, P. K. & B., P. (2006). Digital libraries initiatives in India. *The International Information & Library Review, 38*, 161-169.

Janamanchi B, K. E, Raghupathi, W.& Gao, W.(2009). The state and profile of Open Source Software projects in health and medical informatics. *Int J Med Inform, 78*,457-472.

Jeff Rothenberg: Ensuring the Longevity of Digital Documents. Scientific American, 272(1), January 1995.

Jewell, T.D. (2005). Electronic resource management: the quest for systems and standards. *The Serials Librarian, 48*(1/2), 137-163.

Kabachinski, J. (2005). An introduction to RFID. *Biomedical Instrumentation & Technology*, 1-4.

Kanakachary, M. (2002). *Information technology vis-a-vis the libraries*. In A. A. N. Raju, et al. (Eds.), New vistas in library and information science. Hakkani Publishers: New Delhi.

Kennedy, M.R. (2004). Dreams of perfect programs: managing the acquisition of electronic resources. *Library Collections, Acquisitions, & Technical Services, 28*(4), 449-458.

Kern, C. (2004). Radio-frequency-identification for security and media circulation in libraries. *Electronic Library*,22(4),317-24.

Khan, K. M. (2003). *Internet: An Indispensable Tool to Access Information in Libraries in the Age of Globalization.* Paper presented at the New Challenges in Information Management and E-learning in the Globalization: Issues and opportunities, Roorkee.

Kiiski, S., & M. Pohjola. (2002). Cross-Country Diffusion of the Internet. *Information Economics and Policy, 14*(2), 297-310.

Koha. LibLime Koha Retrieved 9 May, 2012, from http:// www.koha.org/

Kroski, E. (2007). The social tools of Web 2.0: opportunities for academic libraries. *Choice*, 44(12), 2011-21.

Kumar, P. S. G. (1987). *Computerization of Indian libraries.* New Delhi: B.R. Publishing Corporation.

Libdex. Retrieved from http://www.libdex.com/ weblogs.html

Library of congress. Podcasts Retrieved 8 May, 2012, from http:// www.loc.gov/podcasts/

Library Success: A Best Practices Wiki. Retrieved 13, 2012, from http://www.libsuccess.org/index.php?title= Library_ Success:_A_Best_Practices_Wiki

Lib-web-cats (2012). *A directory of libraries throughout the world* Retrieved 10 May, 2012, from www.librarytechnology.org/libwebcats

Liebeskind, J.P., *et al.* (1996). Social Networks, Learning, and Flexibility: Sourcing Scientific Knowledge in New Biotechnology Firms. *Organization Science*, 7(4), 428-443.

Lindquist, M. G. (2003). *RFID in libraries-introduction to the issues.* Paper presented at the Biomedical Instrumentation & Technology, Berlin, Germany. http://www.ifla.org

Linh, N. C. (2008). A survey of the application of Web 2.0 in Australasian university libraries. *Library Hi Tech*. 26(4), 630-653.

Macaskill, W., and Owen, D. (2006). *Web 2.0 to go*. Paper presented at the Proceedings of LIANZA Conference 2006, Wellington.

Maness, J. (2006). Library 2.0 Theory: Web 2.0 and Its Implications for Libraries. *Webology, 3*(2).Retrieved from http://www.webology.org/2006/v3n2/a25.html

Marcelle, G. (2000). Gender Justice and ICTs, from

Mathews, B. (2007). Moving beyond the reference desk: being where users need us. *The Reference Librarian,48*(2), 9-13.

McCallum, S. (2003). 40 years of technology in libraries: a brief history of IFLA section on information technology. http://archive.ifla.org/VII/s21/publications/40YearsOfSIT. pdf

Meckel, M., Stanoevska-Slabeva, K. and Martignoni, R. (2006). *Overview of business models for Web 1.0 communities*. Paper presented at the Proceedings of GeNeMe.

Moahi, K. H. (2002). Issues of just-in-time (access) v. just-in-case (ownership) for libraries in developing countries: lessons to be learnt from developed countries. *Library Review, 51*(7), 341 - 349.

Moyo, L. M. (2004). Electronic libraries and the emergence of new service paradigms. *The Electronic Library,* 22(3), 220-230.

Moyo, L.M. & Cahoy, E.S. (2003). Meeting the needs of remote library users. *Library Management*, 24(6/7), 281 - 290.

Moyo, L.M. (2002). Reference anytime anywhere: towards virtual reference services at Penn State. *The Electronic Library*, 20(1), 22-28.

Murthy, T. A. V., & Cholin, V. S. (2003). Library automation.

Paper presented at the First international CALIBER–2003, Ahmedabad, India.13-15 Feb.2003.

Natarajan, M. (2004). Digital Preservation of Cultural Heritage Information and its implications. *Journal of Library of Information Science, 29*(1/2), 14-25.

National Initiative for a Networked Cultural Heritage. (2002). NINCH Guide to Good Practice in the Digital Representation and Management of Cultural Heritage Materials.

O'Brien, J. A., & Marakas, G. M. (2009). *Management information systems* (9 ed.). Bostan, MA: McGraw-Hill/Irwin.

OCLC Online Computer Library Center, I. (2006). *OCLC Digital Archive Preservation Policy and Supporting Documentation*. Dublin, Ohio,USA,p.5

OCLC. (2012). WorldCat at a glance Retrieved 10 May, 2012, from http://www.oclc.org/worldcat/about/default.htm

Online, O. E. D. (2010). Social networking, from www.dictionary.oed.com

O'Reilly, T. (2005). What Is Web 2.0:Design Patterns and Business Models for the Next Generation of Software Retrieved 12, 2012, from http://oreilly.com/web2/archive/what-is-web-20.html

OSI. (2006). Open Source Software Definition Retrieved 5 May, 2012, from http://www.opensource.org/docs/definition.php

Panwar, S. & M., T.A.V. (2004). *Librarian's Guide to WWW*. New Delhi: Ess Ess Publications

Payne, Alexandria & Vandana Singh (2010). Open Source Software use in libraries. *Library Review, 59*(9), 708-717. doi: 10.1108/00242531011087033.

PC Magazine. RFID Retrieved 11 may, 2012, from http://www.pcmag.com/encyclopedia_term/0%2C1237%2Ct%3DRFID&i%3D50512%2C00.asp

Poulter, A. (2003). Database Management Systems (DBMS). In J. F. a. P. Sturges (Ed.), *International Encyclopedia of Information and Library Science*. London: Routedge, pp.126.

Prytherch, R. J. (Ed.) (2005) Harrod's librarins' glossary and reference book. Hampshire, England: Ashagate Pub. Comp.

Ranganathan, S. R. (1957). *The Five Laws of Library Science*. London: G. Blunt and Sons.

Rathinasabapathi, R. (2000). *Internet: A Briefing for Layman* Paper presented at the 7th National Convention for Automation of Libraries in Education and Research (CALIBER-2000), Ahmedabad.

Reitz, J. M. (Ed.) Online Dictionary for Library and Information Science. Retrieved 12,2012,from http://www.abc-clio.com/ODLIS/odlis_p.aspx

Retrievr. (2011). Retrieved 11 May, 2012, from http://labs.systemone.at/retrievr/

RFBR (1997). LibWeb Retrieved 09 May, 2012, from http://www.gpntb.ru/win/libweb/about/direct_e.htm

Rodriguez, F. & W., E. . (2000). *Are Poor Countries Losing the Information Revolution? mfoDev Working Paper*. Washington D.C.: World Bank.

Ronan, J. (2001). Chat reference: an exciting new facet of digital. Retrieved June 08, 2012 from *http://www.arl.org/newsltr/219/chat.html*.

Sadeh, T., and Ellingsen, M. (2005). Electronic resource management systems: the need and the realization. *New Library World*, 106(5), 208-218.

Sandra, P. (1998).Flexible and extensible object and repository architecture (Fedora). *Lect Notes Comput Sc.*, 15(13), 41-59.

Saraf, V. (1998). Dynamics of the information technology and its implications for library and information education in the millennium. *Bangladesh Journal of Library and Information Science*, 1(1), 5-14.

Saraf, V. (1998). Dynamics of the information technology and its implications for library and information education in the millennium. *Bangladesh Journal of Library and Information Science*, 1(1), 5-14.

Shahid, S. M. (2005). Use of RFID Technology in Libraries: a New Approach to Circulation, Tracking, Inventorying, and Security of Library Materials. *Library Philosophy and Practice 8*(1).

Sharma, R. K. (2004). *Managing Information, knowledge and power in the Cyber age*. New Delhi: Bookwells.

Shuva, N. Z. (2005). Implementing information and communication technology in public libraries of Bangladesh. *The International Information & Library Review, 37*, 159-168.

Siddiqui, M. A. (1991). Can CD-ROM replace online? *INICAE*, 10(1), 40-47.

Singh, S.P. (2004). Collection management in the electronic environment. *The Bottom Line: Managing Library Finances, 17*(2), 55-60.

Social Media Glossary. (2008). Forum Retrieved 7 may, 2012, from http://www2.capilanou.ca/help/login-page/active-cms/glossary.html

Stapleton, P. (2003). Assessing the quality and bias of Web-based sources: implications for academic writing. *Journal of English for Academic Purposes*, 2(3). 229-245.

Stokes, A. V. (1985) *Concise Encyclopaedia of Information Technology* (2 ed.). London: Gower. pp.114-115.

Stuart, D. (2010). What are libraries doing on Twitter? *Information Today, 34*, 41-45.

Sweney, M. (2007, 24 December). Elevator Pitch: Why Badoo wants to be the next word in social networking, *The*

Guardian.

Tam, L. W. H. R., A.C. (2002). Managing change: libraries and information services in the digital age. *Library Management, 23*(8/9),369 - 377.

Tansley, R. & Harnad, S. (2000). Eprints.org Software for Creating Institutional and Individual Open Archives. *D-Lib Magazine,6*(10).

Times, N. Y. (2012). RSS feeds, *New York Times*. Retrieved from http://www.nytimes.com/services/xml/rss/index.html

TOI Correspondence (1998). Information Technology Action Plan. *The Times of India.*9 July 2012, Retrieved from http://itt.nissat.tripod.com/itt9803/itap.htm

UNESCO. (2001). CDS/ISIS Retrieved 17, 2012, from www.unesco.org/isis/files/winisis/windows/doc/.../Isis_Tutorial2.ppt

UNESCO. (2012). CDS/ISIS database software, from www.unesco.org/webworld/isis/

Vasishta, S. and Dhanda, M.K. (2010). Transferring a traditional library to modern library using barcode technology: an experience of central library, PEC University of Technology, Chandigarh *DESIDOC Journal of Library & Information Technology, 30*(1), 44-48.

Veneziani, V. (2007). Windows Live Messaging Coming To Bebo Retrieved 5 May, 2012, from http://techcrunch.com/2007/08/20/windows-live-messaging-coming-to-bebo/

WEBLIS. Retrieved 10 May, 2012, from http://portal.unesco.org/ci/en

Wei, Z. (2011). Research on the application of Open Source Software in Digital Library. *Procedia Engineering, 15,* 1662-1667. doi: 10.1016/j.proeng.2011.08.310

Wei-bo, Lin; Cheng, Yi; & Chun, Li (2011). Establishing a university library institutional repository based on DSpace and DIPS. *Energy Procedia, 13, 9322-9329.*

Wersig, G. (2003). Information Technology In J. F. a. P. Sturges (Ed.), International Encyclopedia of Information and Library Science (pp. 310). London: Routledge.

White, A., & Balsamo, J. (2005). Using LAMP to make our library shine. *Computers in Libraries, 25*(5), 6.

Wikipedia. (2012). *Automation* Retrieved 15 March, 2012, from

Wikipedia. (2012). DSpace Retrieved 5 May, 2012, from http://en.wikipedia.org/wiki/DSpace

Wikipedia. (2012). Education and Research Network (ERNET), India, Retrieved 10 May, 2012, from http://en.wikipedia.org/wiki/ERNET

Wikipedia. (2012). EPrints Retrieved 5 May, 2012, from http://en.wikipedia.org/wiki/EPrints

Wikipedia. (2012). Information and communications technology. Retrieved 6 May, 2012, from http://en.wikipedia.org/wiki/Information_and_communications_technology.

Wikipedia. (2012). Mashup, from http://en.wikipedia.org/wiki/Mashup_%28web_application_hybrid%29

Wikipedia. (2012). Open Source Software Retrieved 5 May, 2012, from http://en.wikipedia.org/wiki/Open_source

Wikipedia. (2012). Social networking service Retrieved 11 May, 2012, from http://en.wikipedia.org/wiki/Social_networking_service

Wikipedia. Database Management System (DBMS) Retrieved 5 March, 2012, from http://en.wikipedia.org/wiki/Database_management_system

Wikipedia. Radio-frequency identification Retrieved 13 May, 2012, from http://en.wikipedia.org/wiki/Radio-frequency_identification

Wikipedia.(2012).Digital Preservation, from http://

en.wikipedia.org/wiki/Digital_preservation

Williams, C. hi*et al.* (1994). Multidimensional models boost viewing options. *InfoWorld, 16*(4).

Witten, I.H. and David, B.2003. *How to build a digital library.* San Francisco: Morgan Kaufmann Publishers.

Yapa, N. U. (2003). Utilization of ICT for LIS with special reference to Sri Lanka. Paper presented at the First international CALIBER—2003, Ahmedabad, India.13-15 Feb.2003.

Ye Ying, H.C. (2006). DSpace-based Lib2·0. *Journal of Academic Libraries, Beijing*, 2-5.

Zhang, A. B. and Don, G. (2008). *Creating digital collections: a practical guide*. Oxford, England: Chandos Publishing.

Zyl, A.S.V. (2009).The impact of Social Networking 2.0 on organizations. *Electronic Library*, 27(6), 906 - 918.